Randy Charles Epping

The New World Economy
A Beginner's Guide

Randy Charles Epping, based in Zurich, Switzerland, and São Paulo, Brazil, has worked in international finance for more than twenty-five years, holding management positions in European and American investment banks in London, Geneva, and Zurich. He has a master's degree in International Relations from Yale University, in addition to degrees from the University of Notre Dame and the University of Paris–La Sorbonne. He is currently the manager of IFS Project Management AG, a Switzerland-based international consulting company. He is also the president of the Central Europe Foundation, which provides assistance to students and economic organizations in Central and Eastern Europe. In addition to *The New World Economy: A Beginner's Guide,* he has written several other books on the world economy that have been translated into more than twenty languages around the world. He has also written a novel, *Trust,* a financial thriller based in Zurich and Budapest. Mr. Epping holds dual U.S. and Swiss citizenship and is fluent in six languages: English, French, German, Italian, Portuguese, and Spanish.

Also by Randy Charles Epping

NONFICTION

A Beginner's Guide to the World Economy

The 21st-Century Economy: A Beginner's Guide

FICTION

Trust

The New World Economy

A Beginner's Guide

The New World Economy
A Beginner's Guide

Demystifying Everything from
AI and Bitcoins to Unicorns
and Generation Z

Randy Charles Epping

VINTAGE BOOKS

A DIVISION OF PENGUIN RANDOM HOUSE LLC

NEW YORK

A VINTAGE BOOKS ORIGINAL, JANUARY 2020

The Cataloging-in-Publication Data is on file at
the Library of Congress.

Vintage Books Trade Paperback ISBN: 978-0-525-56320-4
eBook ISBN: 978-0-525-56321-1

Book design by Nicholas Alguire

www.vintagebooks.com

Printed in the United States of America
10   9   8   7   6   5   4   3   2   1

To Dr. Elemér Hantos, Hungarian political and economic visionary who, already in the 1920s and 1930s, saw the importance of economic cooperation as a bulwark against conflict and war.

To my editor at Vintage Books, Andrew Weber, for his tireless work in making this book relevant and interesting to his generation. And mine. And all the generations in between.

Also, many thanks to all those who helped me with ideas and suggestions along the way. Especially my sister, Shawn Engelberg, who believes, like me, that the world economy can be demystified in a way that allows everyone to take part in the great economic debate.

If economists want to be understood, let them use plain words... [and] address those words less to politicians and more to everybody else. Politicians care about what voters think, especially voters in blocks, and not a shred about what economists think. Talking to politicians about economics is therefore a waste of time. The only way to make governments behave as if they were economically literate is to confront them with electorates that are.

—*The Economist*

Contents

Preface   xv

1. Butterflies over Beijing:
   What Is the New "Fusion Economy"?   3

2. Bitcoins and Blockchains:
   Are Cryptocurrencies Real Money?   8

3. How Do Local Economic Crises
   Become Global Crises?   14

4. Supranationals: Do International
   Organizations Like the World Bank
   and the IMF Really Promote Economic Growth?   20

5. How Do We Rank Countries
   in the New Global Economy?   26

6. Can Trade Wars Destroy the World Economy?   35

7. Brexit and Border Walls:
   Does Economic Isolation Make Economic Sense?   42

8. Does Immigration Take Our Jobs Away?   47

9. How Do Populist Leaders Use
   Our Economic Illiteracy to Gain Power?   52

10. Globalization—Problem or Solution?   57

11. Inflation vs. Deflation   64

12. What Is Currency Manipulation?   70

13. The Fear of Investing: Is It Keeping Us Poor?   76

14. Comparing Investments in the New World Economy   86

15. Income Inequality: Is It Inevitable?   93

16. What Is Hot Money?   102

17. Barbarians at the Gate?
    Private Equity Investors, Venture
    Capitalists, and High-Frequency Traders   107

18. The Twenty-First-Century Company   113

19. How Is the Digital Economy Transforming the World?   119

20. What Is the Internet of Things?   126

21. Is Data the New Gold?   130

22. How Are Robots and Artificial
    Intelligence Transforming the World Economy?   136

23. What Is the Sharing Economy?   143

24. BRICS and Beyond:
    How Emerging Markets Are Becoming
    the New Powerhouses of the World Economy   148

25. What Is the Future for the European
    Union and the Other Free-Trade Areas?   153

26. Sharp Power: How Countries Use
    Economic Power to Achieve Global Clout   160

27. Sharing the Wealth:
    How Do Charities, Private Enterprise,
    and NGOs Promote Economic Development?   165

28. Corruption and Tax Evasion:
    How Does Money Laundering Work?   171

29. The Dark Web and Other Black Markets:
    How Big Is the Illegal Economy?   179

30. How Is Climate Change
    Transforming the Global Economy?   184

31. Economics vs. the Environment: Is It a Zero-Sum Game? 190

32. What Are the Alternatives to Capitalism?   196

33. Are Trade Unions Becoming
    Obsolete in the Twenty-First Century?   202

34. Health Care: Ways That Work   207

35. How Is the Behavior
    of Millennials and Other Generations
    Changing the World's Economic Landscape?   215

36. New Ways of Working and Living
    in the Twenty-First Century   223

    Glossary   231

Preface

What is the world coming to? Populist governments around the world are ripping up trade agreements, building walls, and throwing economic cooperation out the window—all in the name of protecting jobs and ensuring long-term economic growth. It all sounds good; it's supposed to. Who needs foreigners? Who needs the rest of the world to be rich and secure?

The only problem is that much of what's being done—ostensibly for economic reasons—is actually being done to further the political agendas of exploitive politicians and ends up hurting the very people they say they want to help. The working class in many of the world's developed countries has seen real wages stagnate over the last thirty years while those in the top 1 percent have seen their income levels and wealth increase astronomically. Meanwhile, populist politicians are enacting large tax cuts, theoretically to stimulate economic growth and job creation, often creating gargantuan fiscal deficits. Not surprisingly, many

corporations are choosing to use their windfall profits to buy back
shares instead of hiring more workers—mainly benefiting wealthy
shareholders. In the end, trade wars usually help a small minority
of companies who long for protected markets—and they usually
hurt everyone else, including the very workers those trade barriers are supposed to protect.

But what can we do? Many of us are bewildered by a fast-
changing global economy that seems too big and too complicated
for us to understand. So we let the politicians make our decisions
for us. Unfortunately, the politicians are not always going to do
what's best for us. They're going to do what's best for them and
their reelection chances.

Cryptocurrencies . . . immigration . . . sharp power . . . trade
wars . . . and robots taking our jobs away. A virtual explosion of
complexity has occurred within the economy over the last few
years, and we are being asked to understand it all. Words and
phrases like *pollution rights, algorithm-based artificial intelligence,* and
hot money appear regularly in the news, and many of us don't know
what they actually mean. Furthermore, the incessant stream of
fearmongering sound bites on the news and on the Internet only
leaves us confused and anxious.

But it is, in fact, possible for us to demystify virtually all of it.
Essentially, the world economy is no more complicated than the
domestic economy that we navigate daily. We don't think twice
about using the Internet or crossing the street to get a better deal
when buying an appliance. It's not so different from crossing borders to invest our money or to buy and sell goods and services.
Sound economic judgment is one of the most-needed skills in the
world today. And since most of what we're getting from politicians is manipulative rhetoric that plays to our fears and heightens
division, we're going to have to look out for our own economic
interests. The idea of this book is not only to give you a basic un-

derstanding of what is happening in the world economy but also to provide you with the tools to be able to make sense of future economic events—good or bad.

Whoever we are—college students or businesspeople, environmentalists or farmers, homemakers or union activists—if we're going to be responsible citizens and consumers, we're going to have to learn the basics of the economy we live in. For many of us, however, the study of economics has been an exercise in futility, full of obscure graphs and equations that feel hopelessly out of touch with our daily lives.

Unfortunately, most economists today are not able to explain things simply. I remember how my first economics professor at Yale, a brilliant man by all accounts, thought that any question could only be answered with a complicated graph or formula. No question could be answered with a simple yes or no. What is inflation? He would answer with "Let me draw you an equation." What is a trade war? "Let me show you a graph." I would sit there and stare at the complex array of numbers and Greek letters he was writing on the wall and wonder, *Is this the only way to teach economics?*

Today's news is peppered with economic terms, but rarely is any attempt made to help us cut through the complex jargon we are being bombarded with. The remedy? Sometimes the answer is to find a way to relate economic concepts to everyday experiences. What is a stock index? Think of checking the cost of a few items in a grocery store to see how the market's prices, as a whole, are evolving. What is a leveraged buyout? Think of a seesaw, lifting a heavy weight at one end with a small amount of force at the other allowing investors who borrow money to get more bang for their buck. What is a tariff? Think of a tax on imported goods and services. In the end, we can all understand the world economy; it just has to be explained in simple, straightforward language.

Artificial intelligence and the exploding array of web-based communication are allowing the expanding global economy to touch our lives in ways unheard of just a few years ago. By understanding the basics of the world economy, we will be able to make better decisions about our individual and collective economic futures. And with economically literate voters pushing them on, politicians will start making more rational decisions as well, leading to a more prosperous and, hopefully, more socially conscious and environmentally sound world in the years to come. We are all citizens of this interconnected world, and we're going to have to understand the economic forces shaping our daily lives.

In this book, I have incorporated many readers' comments from my previous books. (Please feel free to email me anytime at RCEpping@aya.yale.edu.) Numerous readers from around the world have cited my books as instrumental in helping them understand our new global economy—philanthropists, e-commerce professionals, executives, and students alike.

There is no reason to feel that economics should be boring or obtuse. This book uses no graphs and absolutely no equations. And statistics are always accompanied by real-world examples to give meaning to the numbers. *The New World Economy: A Beginner's Guide,* as the name implies, will clearly and succinctly cover the basic concepts that we are exposed to in our daily lives.

How to read this book? Although it may be useful to start with the global economic concepts found at the beginning of the book, each section can be read individually. This book can be read from front to back, from back to front, or sections can be read at random—whatever works best for you. The glossary at the end is useful for quick reference when you encounter unfamiliar terms in the future. The jargon of the new world economy is increasingly dominating our newspapers, magazines, websites, blogs, and TV programs—even our watercooler conversations. If we are going to be effective consumers, businesspeople, and voters, we're going to need to be fluent in the language of the new "fusion" economy.

Whoever we are and wherever we live, we need to understand the fundamentals if we are going to get involved in the world economy. And sooner or later, we all get involved.

Enjoy!

The New World Economy
A Beginner's Guide

1

Butterflies over Beijing: What Is the New "Fusion Economy"?

When the Queen of England asked a group of eminent economists why they hadn't warned her of a recent British financial meltdown, the answer from the economists was, according to one observer, "polite mumbling into their shoes." The answer should have been "Traditional economic theories be damned! How could we—or anyone—have known what was going to happen?"

With countless influences and forces converging in the new globalized world economy, it is becoming increasingly difficult to use old formulas and paradigms to predict what's going to happen in the future. Like nuclear fusion, which joins together hydrogen atoms and releases enormous amounts of energy in the process, the converging global economy releases an enormous amount of hard-to-understand energy and unpredictable events.

It used to be that we could follow a fairly simple path to arrive at a logical economic conclusion: a better product or a more efficient company meant more productivity, which meant a higher standard of living for almost everyone. But today, things aren't so simple. How can we say that unlimited economic growth in the developing countries is a good thing if it increases the pollution leading to further global warming? And how can we say that unlimited access to our friends via Snapchat or Facebook with our smartphones leads to more happiness when, in fact, among teenagers and even preteens, happiness has actually been shown to decline the more time they spend on social media, leading to increased isolation, depression, and even suicide?

The classic view of chaos theory is that many events in the world are simply impossible to predict or control. Nonlinear events like the weather, stock market fluctuations, or how our brains react to different stimuli depend on such a wide array of factors that no one—not even someone armed with the most powerful computer—is able to say what will be the future effect of current actions. The butterfly effect, as explained by Edward Lorenz, the MIT meteorology professor who first studied chaos theory, is the idea that something as insignificant as a butterfly flapping its wings over the Amazon can cause a severe thunderstorm in Beijing's Tiananmen Square.

The twenty-first-century economy has taken this concept to another level. Causes and effects are converging, fusing together in a complex web that is nearly impossible to fully understand. But where will it all end? Elections around the world have been manipulated by strategically placed ads on social media, with unscrupulous candidates hiring data-analytics firms to find the most vulnerable voters to target. However, no one, not even the candidates or politicians involved, knew exactly what effect these actions would have.

In the expanding global economy, interconnected personal networks are growing exponentially. By the late 2010s, there were already more than thirty billion devices connected in the Internet of Things, with voice-controlled Alexas and Siris strategically placed in hundreds of millions of homes across the world, hearing every word we say. How will this access and information be used in the future by altruistic NGOs and unscrupulous politicians alike? In the world of finance and investments, the unpredictability of the new fusion economy is causing havoc. With computer algorithms guiding them, powerful investment firms move billions and sometimes trillions of dollars, pounds, euros, and yen around the world on any given day. Even they, with all their digital prowess, can't explain why, at various points, markets crash unexpectedly. These flash crashes sometimes occur in the blink of an eye, moving whole markets—or the entire world economy—without any explanation. In the mid-2010s, a sudden drop in the ten-year U.S. Treasury note, considered one of the safest and stablest financial instruments in the world, caused markets around the world to drop precipitously. Traders stared at their screens in disbelief as the plunge brought the markets to the brink of collapse. The nose-dive was seven standard deviations away from the norm, an event that is expected to happen once every 1.6 billion years. No one was able to fully explain what happened or what could be done to prevent it from happening in the future.

An isolated event in one part of the world—a default in Argentina, for example, or a change in government in Italy—can have an immediate effect on markets worldwide. Global investors who are losing money in one sector often tend to sell investments in another sector, or another part of the world, to cover their losses. When stocks fall sharply in New York or London, emerging-market funds from Brazil to India can decline sharply as investors rush to sell their shares abroad in order to raise needed cash to pay their debts at home. For no fault of their own, markets—especially those in developing countries—can be punished for something over which they have no control.

It works in the opposite way for countries that have currencies that are considered safe havens in times of economic turmoil. The Japanese yen, the Swiss franc, and the U.S. dollar, for example, tend to benefit enormously when markets crash. Even though it was the U.S. economic meltdown that caused the worldwide crash leading to the Great Recession in 2007, the first reaction of most global investors was to buy American dollars.

The United States' enviable position as the owner of the world's most sought-after currency, with almost a third of foreign central banks holding the U.S. dollar as their main reserve currency, has provided many advantages over the years, not the least of which is having the ability to easily borrow abroad to finance wars and deficit spending at home. The disadvantage is that countries with reserve currencies tend to run trade account deficits, mainly because the higher value of their currencies makes their products more expensive to export. These persistent trade deficits, however, led the U.S. president in 2018 to begin a series of trade wars, hoping to keep the benefits of holding the world's reserve currency while using the threat of global trade wars to eliminate the deficits, come what may.

After the unilateral decision of the United States to erect trade barriers during the Great Depression, the world plunged into chaos when other countries retaliated with barriers of their own. Trying to avoid a similar outcome caused by another U.S.-led trade war, in 2018, the head of the International Monetary Fund saw "darker clouds looming" and called for finance ministers around the world to gather in Washington, D.C., to discuss how to avoid a global economic meltdown. She tried to convince the other countries of the world to avoid reverting to protectionism in response to the U.S. actions, reiterating the benefits of free trade, and pointing out that every country, even China, runs trade deficits with selected partners.

Counterintuitive thinking can apply to many aspects of the new fusion economy. Innovation and success in the new global economy will depend in large part on factors that seem unimportant. Many schools are being set up to teach children how to learn skills that are completely unrelated to technology and business. The Waldorf School of the Peninsula in Silicon Valley, for example, allows no screens at all, and teachers use blackboards with chalk and beanbags and pieces of fruit to teach technical as well as nontechnical skills to the students, many of whom have parents who work in the high-tech industries nearby. The idea is to give students the opportunity to slow down and think in a nonlinear way, taking advantage of the peace and quiet resulting from the absence of computers and smartphones that allow for creative thought.

Success in the new fusion economy may depend in large measure on learning that we can't control everything. In the complex, interconnected world in which we now live, success could depend less on planning everything in advance and more on letting serendipity and "chaos" help us on our way. In the end, it could be that wild-goose chases and dead ends can take us further than following a direct linear path. With economic and political events occurring around us at an increasingly dizzying pace—from erratic politicians to economic meltdowns to terrorist attacks—the ability of any one country or individual to control or significantly influence the maelstrom of forces buffeting the economic landscape will, in any event, be increasingly limited in the years to come.

2

Bitcoins and Blockchains: Are Cryptocurrencies Real Money?

When the ancient Greeks wanted to send a secret message across enemy lines, they sometimes tattooed the message on a runner's shaved scalp, then waited for the hair to grow back before sending the patient messenger out into the world. The idea was to transmit important information in a way that was securely hidden and virtually impossible to alter. The main advantage of this primitive but effective encryption technique was that those receiving the information could be absolutely certain that, as long as the runner arrived with a full head of hair, no one had seen or changed the message en route.

With modern computers, the twenty-first-century solution to securing private information is to encrypt it in a chain of code that can never be altered without permission from all the users. This blockchain encryption technology works because the entire user world will be alerted if anyone tries to change the information. This technology can be used for a wide variety of purposes, like tracking commodities such as chickens from infancy in the coop to the frying pan or securely filing your tax returns. The idea is to ensure that the information we are receiving is exact and hasn't been tampered with.

The first use of blockchain was to encrypt and secure holdings of a currency called *bitcoin*, the world's first decentralized digital currency that didn't need a central bank or central monetary authority to control its use. Bitcoin was invented by an anonymous computer pioneer with the nom de plume of Satoshi Nakamoto in 2009. The open-source software was structured to allow anyone, at any time, to see who owns what in the bitcoin world. The system allows for anonymity because the owners of bitcoin can use pseudonyms, keeping their real identities secure in encrypted form.

The purpose of bitcoin and other cryptocurrencies was to have a user-to-user payment system that avoided the costs and control of a central authority. Some observers have been reluctant to admit that cryptocurrencies are real money, but since the beginning of time, items with no intrinsic value—such as shells, beads, or pieces of paper—have served as a commonly accepted marker for wealth. Other than being able to dive into his pile of gold coins for pleasure, Scrooge McDuck had no other possible use for his amassed wealth except to spend it in the world at large.

What is money? Contrary to popular belief, money does not make the world go 'round; the global economy runs on the trade of goods and services. But without money, trade would be a very difficult undertaking. Imagine sending peaches to France and waiting to be paid with the next shipment of cheese. Or imagine wanting to keep some of your earnings as a nest egg—Roquefort wouldn't keep very well in a bank vault. How many strawberries is a piece of cheese worth, anyway?

These issues can all be resolved by using something that *represents* value. Whether it's a piece of paper or a chunk of gold or credit in your bitcoin wallet, money serves three purposes. First, it serves as a medium of exchange, allowing us to sell our goods or services at home or abroad. Second, it allows people and businesses to store value from one year to the next. And third, it serves as a unit of account, telling us how much things are worth by providing us with a point of reference that is universally understood.

Some Pacific Islanders used to use large pieces of stone in this very way. Large stones used for currency on Yap Island were quarried on Palau, some 280 miles across the sea. Since it was so difficult to bring them to Yap, there was a limited number of money stones in the economy at large. This kept the money supply from getting out of control, and as a result, the prices of Yap goods and services remained stable.

The Yap Island stones serve as a perfect metaphor for modern cryptocurrencies in that they, unlike paper money, were stored in a neutral place and couldn't be handed from one person to another during a purchase. The ownership of each stone, therefore, had to be registered in the population at large, principally by word of mouth. When someone used one of their stones to buy a new boat, the word went out that the stone at the left end of the beach now belonged to the boat seller and no longer to the buyer.

In the world of cryptocurrencies, a transaction is undertaken in a similar way. Unless they buy a rare collectible coin issued separately, owners of bitcoins never actually have a bitcoin in their hands—the proof of ownership is registered in a blockchain-coded storehouse of information.

When the owner of a bitcoin decides to purchase something, the system is updated to reflect the transfer from buyer to seller. The transaction takes place via the buyer's and seller's bitcoin wallets, but the ownership change is imbedded in the blockchain for everyone to see and verify. Once the transaction is verified, it cannot be retracted.

Like transactions in cash and gold, one of the major appeals of cryptocurrency payments is that they can be made in total anonymity, without any central bank or monetary authority getting involved. This is why many countries have moved to ban cryptocurrencies, fearing that they can easily be used to pay for illegal goods, such as drugs or stolen guns. But how is this different from allowing traditional paper currencies to be used to anonymously purchase illegal goods? A possible solution would be to create a cryptocurrency that requires users to be transparent about their identity. This could be an ideal defense against money laundering, tax evasion, and other illicit activities because every transaction would be seen and verified by users.

Many people have been reluctant to start using cryptocurrencies, saying that they would never hold a currency that has no intrinsic value. But cryptocurrencies are actually not so different from cash and coins, which people have been using for almost as long as civilization has existed. Ever since the demise of the gold standard in 1973, when the Smithsonian Agreement of fixed exchange rates collapsed, most major currencies have been allowed to float on the international markets; their values are now nothing more than what people are willing to pay for them. What is left is a system that can work only if people are confident that the issuing authority, like the European Central Bank or the Bank of Japan, will never issue too much of any given currency, leading to a decline in the currency's value.

This system of fiat currencies, in which the major countries issue money by government decree, has not always been stable. With wild swings in values—and an occasional failure, as seen in Zimbabwe or Venezuela—the current system isn't necessarily better than an alternative system using cryptocurrencies. In fact, many cryptocurrencies, such as bitcoin, have fixed limits on the future growth of the "money supply," something that no fiat currency has. The current bitcoin protocol, written in 2008 and early 2009, caps the total number of bitcoins in circulation at twenty-one million, which is intended to guarantee its long-term stability. This limit is expected to be reached in 2040.

How are cryptocurrencies created? Bitcoins, like many other

cryptocurrencies, are put into circulation by *miners*, who are required to undertake complex computer calculations in order to receive the new bitcoins. The bitcoin system uses a carrot to entice people or companies with large computers to do the work of maintaining the system, updating the ledgers, verifying the legitimacy of pending transactions, and putting them in recognizable formats called *block candidates*. These can then be looked at and accepted by the other users as meriting a bitcoin reward.

Essentially, the system could have been set up to simply give bitcoins to the public at large—or charities, for that matter. But the bitcoin protocol anticipated that the costs of maintaining the system would become increasingly large as bitcoin becomes more and more accepted as a means of payment. It was therefore decided to give the new bitcoins to those willing to do the work necessary to keep the system up and running.

Anyone can become a bitcoin miner. The first bitcoins were mined mainly by individuals, but by the late 2010s, the amount of computing power required to perform the calculations had become so large that only big consortiums and companies were mining new bitcoins. The energy used by the massive server farms completing the calculations has been estimated to be equivalent to the entire energy consumption of Ireland. And as the computers doing the mining become more efficient, the calculations are purposefully being made more complicated to control the supply of new bitcoins.

Many bitcoin miners have set up operations in cold climates, such as Iceland, or next to hydroelectric plants like those in eastern Washington State, where it costs less to cool the computers. But since China has artificially low power rates, a large part of bitcoin mining takes place there, where the energy is fueled by carbon dioxide–emitting "dirty" coal. A long-term solution to the environmental consequences of mining bitcoin will have to be found if cryptocurrencies are ever to take their place alongside the other major currencies of the world.

There are major security risks inherent in holding a large amount of wealth in cryptocurrencies that can be transferred in a moment to an anonymous user. Several cryptocurrency millionaires were kidnapped in the late 2010s with the express purpose of getting the victim to transfer large amounts of their assets. These crimes ended with millions of dollars' worth of ransom being paid directly into the kidnappers' encrypted accounts, never to be traced. In addition, in 2019, $40 million of cryptocurrency was stolen from a trading platform called Binance when several of the platform's users' "keys" were hacked, similar to the way credit card users' data is hacked from retail stores' databases.

Another hurdle to wide acceptance of bitcoin is that transactions are becoming more and more expensive and taking a longer time to be processed. With average costs for small transfers approaching the 2–3 percent sellers have to pay for most credit card transactions, bitcoin is becoming less of a viable alternative. Newly developed cryptocurrencies are addressing these problems to provide for inexpensive and expeditious transactions in the future. Facebook, for example, announced in 2019 another form of currency, dubbed "Libra," that would be based on the value of a pool of existing fiat currencies, such as euros, U.S. dollars, and British pounds. The idea was to permit users of Facebook platforms—such as WhatsApp, Instagram, and Messenger—to send the new Libra "money" to other users in a secure and easily traceable manner.

The final issue is the high volatility of cryptocurrencies. During some periods of the 2010s, bitcoin had price swings several times greater than those of gold, the S&P 500, or the U.S. dollar. Unless a cryptocurrency holder is a risk-friendly investor, it may be better—for the moment, at least—to stick to traditional investments like stocks, bonds, and real estate. In the end, one of the biggest hurdles to wide acceptance of many cryptocurrencies has been their high volatility.

3

How Do Local Economic Crises Become Global Crises?

Just as contagious diseases spread across borders to create global epidemics, economic crises in one country can have catastrophic consequences in other parts of the world. The Great Depression of the 1930s, for example, began as a financial meltdown in the United States with millions of Americans losing their jobs and countless companies and farms going bankrupt. When the Federal Reserve moved to restrict money supply after the 1929 crash, it led to an even more severe slowdown in economic activity, which increased unemployment and bankruptcies. Faced with a severe crisis in funding, U.S. banks called in loans to foreign countries, leading to a collapse in the banking system in such debtor countries as Germany and Argentina.

The U.S. government then raised tariffs and quotas on imported goods, ostensibly to protect U.S. companies and farmers. But the Smoot-Hawley Tariff Act immediately led countries around the world to raise tariffs of their own, creating a vicious cycle where the economic downturn and isolationism in one country led to a greater downturn and even more protectionism in another—and eventually worldwide depression. Unemployment reached unprecedented levels with more than 25 percent of the workforce unemployed in Germany, Great Britain, and the United States. In Germany, the economic situation was a major cause of the rise in fascism, with Hitler's National Socialist Party seizing power as the economy failed and inflation soared.

Mirroring the economic and global crises of the 1930s, the worldwide recession of the late aughts started with the collapse of the housing market in the United States. But the enormity of the financial collapse required a level of government and central bank intervention never before attempted. When banks began failing across the globe—primarily because of catastrophic investments in U.S. subprime securities funded by unstable, short-term money market borrowing—it was clear that a full-blown worldwide crisis had arrived. Stock market declines of more than 50 percent in some countries presaged a global economic meltdown.

The concerted actions of the world's central banks, including the U.S. Federal Reserve, the Bank of England, the European Central Bank, and the Bank of Japan, helped calm things down for a while. But when entire countries began to go bankrupt—like Iceland and Greece—it was clear that the fallout of the 2008 crisis would last for years to come.

The task facing the Fed as well as the other central banks of the world in 2008 was to somehow solve the immediate problem without setting precedents that would exacerbate future crises. Some say that the reaction of the Federal Reserve to the meltdown of the dot-com sector in 2000—increasing liquidity and facilitating drastically lower interest rates—set the stage for the housing bubble and the eventual meltdown of financial markets several years later. Others say the "savings glut" in the emerging economies in Asia as well as in Germany and other export-oriented countries led to the 2008 recession, during which easy access to mortgages led to overheated housing markets from Dublin to Madrid to San Francisco.

Some point to the discovery by banks and mortgage companies in the United States that they could make a lot of money by providing loans to home buyers who normally wouldn't have been given credit. These subprime borrowers were allowed to buy homes by paying a bit more than normal rates, often with floating interest rates that rise and fall with the general credit market. The market for subprime mortgages really took off when the banks and mortgage companies figured out that they could repackage these dubious mortgages and sell them as bonds to investors throughout the world economy—mainly to cash-flush banks and financial institutions. With hundreds of billions of dollars' worth of mortgage-backed securities traded annually by 2007, the market for subprime debt had become bigger than the entire market for U.S. Treasury bonds—the biggest bond market in the world at the time.

It was initially believed that by packaging thousands of geographically diverse mortgages together, the chances of all of them becoming delinquent at the same time was extremely remote. The ratings agencies, paid enormous fees by the issuing banks, were content to use computer-generated risk analyses that assumed the various housing markets in the United States were different and that the chance that all of them would experience a decline in prices at the same time was virtually impossible. But this is exactly what happened, and millions of these mortgages became worthless. The credit crisis in the United States then spread around the world as banks and investment houses from London to Tokyo refused to provide the cash that kept the global economy functioning, and governments and central banks had to scramble to find a quick solution.

Interest rates and money supply are the major tools the Fed and other central banks have traditionally used to control economic growth; the key is in how the tools are applied. Just as the speed of an engine is regulated by its fuel supply, a country's economy is regulated by its money supply, which determines interest rates. And each country's money supply is controlled by its central bank: in Britain, it's the Bank of England; in Switzerland, it's the Swiss National Bank; in the United States, it's the Federal Reserve; in the eurozone countries, it's the Frankfurt-based European Central Bank; and in Japan, it's the Bank of Japan. These quasi-public institutions are set up by governments but are then given the independence to keep an economy under control without undue interference from dabbling politicians.

Despite the tendency of the media to concentrate on the latest major economic statistic, such as GDP growth or unemployment, there is no one single indicator that tells us how fast an economy is growing or if that growth will lead to inflation down the road. In addition, there is no way to know how quickly an economy will respond to changes in monetary policy. If a country's central bank allows the economy to expand too rapidly—by keeping too much money in circulation, for example—it may cause bubbles and rampant inflation. But if it slows down the economy too much, an economic recession can result, bringing financial turmoil and severe unemployment. When economic stagnation coincides with high inflation, sometimes referred to as stagflation, a worst-case scenario is created.

Central bankers, therefore, need to be prescient and extremely careful—keeping one eye on inflation, which is usually the product of an overheating economy, and one eye on unemployment, which is almost always the product of a slowing economy. In the twenty-first century, with the amount of capital flowing around the world dwarfing many countries' money supplies, it's almost impossible to know with certainty what the effect of any one monetary decision will have on a local economy, let alone on the world. Given the extremely low inflation rates in the 2010s, some have called for alternative methods for controlling economic growth. Instead of using the central banks' authority to raise or lower interest rates, referred to as "monetary policy," another solution would be to use "fiscal policy" to alter the money supply— essentially allowing governments to circumvent central banks by printing massive amounts of money to increase the money supply, for example. The use of a government's ability to issue new currency to influence economic growth, commonly referred to as Modern Monetary Theory (MMT), is not unproblematic in that inflation can come roaring back at a moment's notice. Even if money issued by governments like the United States is perceived as risk-free—because of the government's ability to print new money that is readily accepted by the world's investors at any time—many other governments may misuse the power of MMT to pay for massive deficit spending in ways that lack the prudent guidance provided by the world's central banks.

Although the Great Depression was one of the most glaring examples of how a local crisis can become global, many other crises have occurred since the beginning of the interconnected global economy in the nineteenth century. Everything from war to climate change to political upheaval has brought financial markets to their knees at one time. However, cyclical forces, such as overproduction, speculation, or market euphoria, are the most common causes of financial crises and are often followed by stock market crashes, massive layoffs, and closed factories.

Sometimes financial crises are caused by—and sometimes solved by—forces entirely unconnected to the original problem. The decline in prices following the U.S. Civil War, for example, ended only when increased gold production in southern Africa led to a worldwide revival of economic activity. The outbreak of the Second World War in 1939 is generally credited with bringing American industry back to life, ending the Great Depression well before the United States entered the war at the end of 1941. And the recession in most of the industrial world in the 1970s was a direct result of the decision by oil-producing countries to impose an embargo, ostensibly to raise prices.

Most of the recent financial meltdowns, from the stock market crash of 1987, to the bursting of the dot-com bubble in 2000, to the market collapse following the terrorist attacks of September 11, 2001, were exacerbated by economic and sociopolitical forces well outside the control of any one country and greatly affected markets around the world.

4

Supranationals:
Do International Organizations
Like the World Bank and the IMF
Really Promote Economic Growth?

As World War II drew to a close, winning the war wasn't the only thing Allied leaders were thinking about. Hoping to avoid the mistakes made at the end of World War I—when rampant inflation, competitive devaluation of currencies, and economic isolationism led to the rise of totalitarianism—the leaders of the United States and Britain, as well as representatives of forty-two other Allied nations, met in Bretton Woods, New Hampshire, to find a better way to run the world economy and avoid future wars.

One of the major accomplishments of the Bretton Woods Conference was the plan to link virtually all the world's major currencies to the U.S. dollar in a sort of fixed-exchange system, with the dollar serving as an anchor to global economic stability. The value of the dollar, in turn, would be linked to a fixed amount of gold—one ounce for every thirty-five dollars. In this way, it was assumed, global trade would flourish since everyone knew what each currency was worth, both in terms of the U.S. dollar and in terms of a fixed amount of gold.

The decidedly non-isolationist leaders of the Western world at the time believed that the only way to lasting peace was to have an entirely new economic system based on reciprocity and fairness. Their aim was to avoid the mistakes made at the end of World War I, when the victors tried to punish the losers, especially Germany, by imposing draconian restrictions on economic reconstruction as well as onerous payments of reparations to the victors. It was decided that the Allied victors would help the defeated countries rebuild, so as to be full participants in the postwar economy. The International Bank for Reconstruction and Development was set up to accomplish this lofty goal. Later, as the institution evolved, the name was changed to the World Bank.

Since then, the World Bank and its sister institution, the International Monetary Fund (IMF)—both based in Washington, D.C.—have not only overseen the reconstruction of war-torn Europe but have also taken on the mission of fostering economic stability and growth throughout the world. The IMF has helped many countries in financial difficulty, providing short-term loans and helping them restructure their economies so they can reenter the world economy on a stronger financial footing. The economic crisis in Argentina, for example, which had simmered for most of the 2010s, led the reformist government in 2018 to ask the IMF to provide $50 billion in temporary funding to provide time for the reforms to take effect.

The World Bank takes a more long-term view, providing loans and development assistance to countries in need, mostly in the developing world. World Bank projects include construction of schools, hospitals, and major infrastructure projects, such as power plants and hydroelectric dams. The bank's aid arm, the International Development Association (IDA), is also used to kick-start the private sector in many of the world's middle-income countries, such as Turkey and China. Through the IDA, the World Bank loans billions of dollars every year to developing countries, mainly for long-term projects to fight poverty and encourage economic growth—ranging from infrastructure projects to programs that fight AIDS and other diseases.

The original plan for the World Bank and the IMF was to provide the world with a sort of "traffic cop" to direct and organize the flow of goods and services, hoping to avoid the chaos that led to the Great Depression and the ensuing political turmoil. Since the United States held more than two-thirds of the world's supply of reserve gold at the time of the Bretton Woods Conference, it seemed logical that the world should use the U.S. dollar as the major reserve currency. The U.S. dollar was seen as good as gold because anyone could walk into a bank and ask for the ounce of gold backing up every thirty-five U.S. dollars with no questions asked.

Until the 1970s, confidence reigned supreme. The Bretton Woods system allowed countries from Japan to Germany and from France to Brazil to grow and prosper. The world had never seen such a level of economic growth over such a short period of time. But when the United States began running huge deficits— printing enormous sums of money to pay for everything from Asian wars to Great Society antipoverty programs—the rest of the world began to lose confidence.

In the late 1960s, France began losing confidence in the system and started asking for the actual gold that had been backing up the U.S. dollar, and other nations followed the example. Soon, more than half of the U.S. gold reserves had been transferred abroad. It looked as if the United States would lose its role as kingpin of the new economic order. The American government decided that the only solution was to abandon the gold standard. From 1971 onward, the U.S. dollar—and virtually all currencies in the world— became *fiat currencies,* backed by nothing more than the faith of the people using them.

From that moment on, the Bretton Woods system of fixed exchange rates was transformed into a system of freely floating currencies, with their values determined by the foreign exchange markets.

The end of the Bretton Woods currency agreement, however, did not mean the end for the World Bank and the International Monetary Fund. Both institutions are active today in promoting development and economic stability throughout the world. But many critics see the institutions as tools of the rich countries, which contribute most of the money to their budgets and consequently are allotted the lion's share of votes. The IMF, in addition, is often criticized for imposing economic straitjackets on countries in economic trouble—insisting on reductions in public spending, cuts in salaries, and the privatization of state-owned businesses—as a precondition for awarding badly needed financial aid. This one-size-fits-all solution often fails to take into account local practices and needs.

Some of the larger emerging-market countries—like Brazil, South Africa, and China—have struggled in vain to alter the IMF structure. China has even taken steps to set up alternative development institutions. The Asian Infrastructure Investment Bank (AIIB) and the New Development Bank (NDB)—based in Beijing and Shanghai, respectively—have been funded with billions of dollars—$100 billion for the AIIB and $50 billion for the NDB—to provide an alternative to the World Bank and the IMF in financing infrastructure projects in Asia and elsewhere. The Chiang Mai Initiative (CMI) also was set up to provide an alternative source of funding for Asian countries facing financial stress.

The World Bank has been criticized for supporting projects in the developing world that harm the environment. The World Bank's decisions to finance the construction of a highway into Brazil's Amazon rain forest or to fund hydroelectric projects resulting in the flooding of agricultural land in India have led some to call for a moratorium on accepting World Bank funding—at least until the environmental and social ramifications of projects can be better assessed.

Another criticism is that endemic corruption in many of the countries receiving IMF and World Bank funds has resulted in a large part of the money received being funneled to a small, powerful elite. Most of this diverted cash ends up in bank accounts abroad, far away from those it was meant to help. According to Oxfam, a conglomerate of charities concentrating on promoting development in emerging markets, more than half the companies that receive funds from the World Bank's International Finance Corporation in sub-Saharan Africa use tax havens to channel their funds.

In some cases, the World Bank and the IMF have begun to refuse new loans to countries that have a history of rampant corruption, but countries with serious corruption are often the most in need of foreign aid. Another solution is to use financial intermediaries such as private equity funds to channel development aid to countries in need, but much of the money nevertheless often finds its way into the pockets of the elite and not into the hands of the countries' needy.

One of the major criticisms of IMF and World Bank assistance is that the money provided, since it is in the form of loans and not development aid, increases the debt burden of developing countries. The money needed to service their foreign debt—basically, the interest payments and repayment of capital—consumes the lion's share of their fiscal budgets, drastically reducing the amount of money available for social welfare or building schools and hospitals.

In the end, reducing poverty in the developing world should not just be a race for more and more loans to stimulate economic production and increase incomes. Other factors have to be considered. The human development index of the United Nations Human Development Program (UNHDP), for instance, measures poverty in terms of literacy, infant mortality, and life expectancy—as well as purchasing power. In addition to providing the money to build schools and hospitals, efforts must be made to ensure that they are properly staffed and managed—and that all children actually attend the schools. In Brazil, for example, life expectancy and literacy increased dramatically when each family's benefit payments were linked to their children's attendance record at school and to regular checkups at the family doctor.

While there is no magic bullet for solving world poverty, a combined effort of local governments and supranational organizations, if applied properly, can ensure that people in the developing countries are not only given the opportunity to become richer in the years to come but are also able to enjoy the many benefits of having a better education and living longer and healthier lives.

5

How Do We Rank Countries in the New Global Economy?

Political campaigns used to be based on the assumption that economic strength would be the determining factor of who gets elected in any given cycle. Historically, almost any candidate in office would be reelected if economic growth was strong. But how do we compare countries' economic performance in the topsy-turvy landscape of the twenty-first century?

In a world where electorates get their news from tailor-made cable channels, radio networks, and web sources and where statistics are no longer seen as reliable, economic health may not be so easy to define. Political leaders around the world in the late 2010s were stunned to see that economic growth didn't necessarily translate into a happy electorate. During a generalized global boom, with GDP increasing strongly in almost every advanced industrial economy, political leaders from Washington to Paris to Bonn were seeing public approval ratings reach record lows. On the other hand, many authoritarian leaders of countries with declining economies were reelected with record levels of support.

This disconnect between politics and economics can be explained by entirely new perceptions in the twenty-first century of what defines a healthy economy.

GDP—gross domestic product—is the traditional measure of the total output of goods and services per year. Basically, GDP adds up the money we as consumers and companies and government entities spend over the course of the year. When we go to the store, or fill up our gas tanks, or watch a pay-per-view video on our tablets or smartphones, we are contributing to economic growth. When a company buys a new office building, or even rents one, it also contributes to economic growth.

GNP—gross national product—picks up where GDP leaves off and includes international expenditures in its summary of economic growth. Money coming from foreign sales of Apple smartphones or Netflix movies, for example, make GNP a broader summary of a given economy. Also included are payments and income from foreign stocks or interest payments on bonds that one country's government has sold to another—an important consideration in the twenty-first-century economy, where exporting nations like China and Saudi Arabia hold trillions of dollars in U.S. Treasury bonds.

Sometimes GNP is bigger than GDP, and sometimes it's the other way around. Countries like Ireland, which has a lot of foreign-owned companies—like the Accenture headquarters in Dublin or the Intel factory in Leixlip—tend to give the country smaller GNP than GDP because the payments to foreign owners are deducted from the GDP figures. On the other hand, since British, U.S., and Swiss residents tend to own a lot of companies abroad, their GNP is usually larger than their GDP because it includes income from foreign production that is not included in the domestic summary.

How do you compare GDP among countries with different currencies? It's difficult, because the value of economic activity in each country is denominated in currencies that are constantly changing in value. One method is to simply take the value of each country's GDP at the end of the year and translate it into one common currency using official exchange rates.

Table 5.1

GDP Comparison of Major Economies

Country	Currency	GDP in local currency	GDP in U.S. dollars
United States	U.S. dollar	20,412,870,000,000	$20,412,870,000,000
China	yuan	97,748,500,000,000	$14,092,514,000,000
Japan	yen	579,675,950,000,000	$5,167,051,000,000
Germany	euro	3,668,650,000,000	$4,211,635,000,000
United Kingdom	pound	2,259,190,000,000	$2,936,286,000,000
France	euro	2,548,050,000,000	$2,925,096,000,000
India	rupee	209,530,110,000,000	$2,848,231,000,000
Italy	euro	1,901,150,000,000	$2,181,970,000,000
Brazil	real	7,882,550,000,000	$2,138,918,000,000
Canada	Can. dollar	2,356,520,000,000	$1,798,512,000,000
Russia	ruble	112,423,840,000,000	$1,719,900,000,000
South Korea	won	1,924,712,730,000,000	$1,693,246,000,000
Spain	euro	1,312,360,000,000	$1,506,439,000,000
Australia	Aus. dollar	2,118,060,000,000	$1,500,256,000,000
Mexico	peso	23,482,970,000,000	$1,212,831,000,000

Source: International Monetary Fund, 2018

Unfortunately, using official currency exchange rates gives a skewed idea of many countries' economic health. Since the cost of similar goods and services isn't the same in every country, the total value of each countries' goods and services can vary widely. In India and China, for example, where the costs of everything from cola to movie tickets is cheaper than in high-cost countries like the United States and Singapore, their GDPs end up looking much smaller than they really are.

Most economists and statisticians, therefore, try to adjust each country's GDP using a "real-world" exchange rate. This is commonly referred to as *purchasing power parity,* or PPP. It's an important calculation for anyone wanting to get a clear understanding of the real economic value of every country. To determine which economy is the biggest in the world, for example, you have to adjust nominal GDP figures using PPP; otherwise the figures are of little value.

PPP is a simple calculation. One country's currency, such as the U.S. dollar, is chosen as the base currency. The dollar value of a selected basket of goods and services is then compared to the value of the same items in another country using traditional exchange rates. In most cases, the two values won't be the same.

Obviously, the choice of items to be included in the basket used to determine PPP has to be made carefully. Since countries use a wide variety of goods and services—beef sausage pizzas are not very common in India, for example—it is often difficult to come up with a perfectly reliable PPP. *The Economist* magazine, somewhat jokingly, came up with a PPP using the costs of Big Macs around the world. Since a Big Mac is identical in every country, and sold all over the world, the Big Mac Index has now become a reliable tool to see how prices vary around the world. If it costs twice as much to buy a Big Mac in London as it does in Buenos Aires, it means that the current exchange rates can't be used to compare the size of each country's economy. The rates have to be adjusted via PPP— making Argentina's GDP twice as big, for example—so we can better compare countries and determine who really is number one.

Table 5.2

Ranking of Countries Using "Real" GDP
(Adjusted for Purchasing Power Parity) (2018)

Country	Nominal GDP in U.S. dollars	GDP adjusted for PPP
China	$14,092,514,000,000	$25,238,563,000,000
United States	$20,412,870,000,000	$20,412,870,000,000
India	$2,848,231,000,000	$10,385,432,000,000
Japan	$5,167,051,000,000	$5,619,492,000,000
Germany	$4,211,635,000,000	$4,373,951,000,000
Russia	$1,719,900,000,000	$4,168,884,000,000
Brazil	$2,138,918,000,000	$3,388,962,000,000
United Kingdom	$2,936,286,000,000	$3,028,566,000,000
France	$2,925,096,000,000	$2,960,251,000,000
Mexico	$1,212,831,000,000	$2,571,680,000,000
Italy	$2,181,970,000,000	$2,399,825,000,000
South Korea	$1,693,246,000,000	$2,138,242,000,000
Spain	$1,506,439,000,000	$1,864,105,000,000
Canada	$1,798,512,000,000	$1,847,081,000,000
Australia	$1,500,256,000,000	$1,312,534,000,000

Source: International Monetary Fund, 2018

It can also be useful to relate a country's total GDP to the number of inhabitants, giving us a more realistic view of how wealthy a country really is. GDP per capita, therefore, is often used to compare economic power among countries. Imagine a small nation like Sri Lanka or Uruguay winning as many medals in the Summer Olympics as China or Brazil. By dividing each country's total economic output by the number of people living in the country, we get a more accurate idea of who is richer. It doesn't mean much to say that India is richer than Canada just because its nominal GDP is bigger. We need to look at how that wealth is distributed, giving us a more human value to an otherwise cold economic statistic.

Table 5.3

Ranking of Countries Using GDP per Inhabitant (2018)

Country	Nominal GDP in U.S. dollars	GDP per capita
United States	$20,412,870,000,000	$62,520
Australia	$1,500,256,000,000	$56,700
Germany	$4,211,635,000,000	$48,670
Canada	$1,798,512,000,000	$46,730
France	$2,925,096,000,000	$42,930
United Kingdom	$2,936,286,000,000	$42,260
Japan	$5,167,051,000,000	$40,110
Italy	$2,181,970,000,000	$34,350
South Korea	$1,693,246,000,000	$32,050
Spain	$1,506,439,000,000	$31,060
Russia	$1,719,900,000,000	$10,950
China	$14,092,514,000,000	$9,630
Mexico	$1,212,831,000,000	$9,610
Brazil	$2,138,918,000,000	$9,130
India	$2,848,231,000,000	$2,020

Source: International Monetary Fund, 2018

No measure of economic growth and economic power, however, is able to capture the complete picture. Quality of life, for example, isn't included in traditional measures of GDP. Hence the small monetary outlay of a French family taking a five-week summer vacation at the grandmother's country house in Provence doesn't contribute nearly as much to the traditional measure of GDP as a month at a five-star resort. Meanwhile, Japanese and American families, taking much shorter vacations, end up paying more for things like sending the children to summer camp or for expensive day care. These cultural effects can have a significant effect on the country's official GDP calculation.

When Robert Kennedy noted in 1968 that "the Gross National Product does not allow for the health of our children, the quality of their education, or the joy of their play," he was reiterating what a lot of economists were already saying: neither GNP nor GDP gives us a truly complete picture of our economic health. The renowned economist Joseph Stiglitz has in the past excoriated the United States for "GDP fetishism," calling instead for broader measures to be factored into the equation like a "Green GDP," which would include such hard-to-define concepts as sustainability, pollution, and other intangibles.

Obviously, environmental polluters have opposed such measures forcefully. When the Bureau of Economic Analysis was considering including environmental destruction in its definition of GDP, states like West Virginia opposed the effort, fearful that the state's coal miners would be put at a disadvantage. Other states, such as Oregon and Vermont, moved in the opposite direction, establishing a genuine progress indicator (GPI) as an alternative view of each state's economic health. Basically, GPI includes such negative factors as crime, pollution, and unequal income distribution, as well as positive factors, such as public infrastructure and the amount of time people get to spend with their families.

The most popularly accepted measure of economic well-being is the United Nations Human Development Index (UNHDI), which rates countries according to their levels of health, education, and income. The UNHDI measures such areas as life expectancy, access to education and adult literacy, years of schooling, equitable distribution of income, GDP per person adjusted by PPP, health care, and gender equality. Needless to say, countries that pay a lot of attention to quality-of-life issues like education and health care— like Norway, Australia, and Switzerland—appear high on the list.

Table 5.4

United Nations Human Development Index Rankings
(top score: 1.00; lowest score: 0.00)

Country	UNHDI score (2018)
1. Norway	0.953
2. Switzerland	0.944
3. Australia	0.939
4. Ireland	0.938
5. Germany	0.936
6. Iceland	0.935
7. Hong Kong, China (SAR) (tie)	0.933
7. Sweden (tie)	0.933
9. Singapore	0.932
10. Netherlands	0.931
11. Denmark	0.929
12. Canada	0.926
13. United States	0.924
14. United Kingdom	0.922
15. Finland	0.920

Source: Human Development Report Office (2018)

Some countries, such as Bhutan, have tried to look less at tangible measures and more at happiness, instituting a Gross National Happiness measure in 1972. Other measures like the Happy Planet Index use life expectancy, well-being, and ecological footprint data to determine how much happiness in each person's life is produced relative to environmental input.

Although happiness and well-being are notoriously difficult to measure, tracking opinion polls, search request data, and social media activity give us valuable information that can be used to determine which country can justifiably chant "We're number one!"

6

Can Trade Wars Destroy the World Economy?

Despite the view of some populist leaders that trade wars are good, and even "easy to win," an all-out trade war usually ends up hurting almost everyone in a given economy, even those segments the politicians say they are trying to help. Farmers and workers in the American Midwest were shocked to see that China and other countries retaliated to the opening salvos of the 2018 U.S.-instigated trade war by massively increasing tariffs of their own on American wheat, soybeans, and a variety of other goods produced in the Midwest, including Harley-Davidson motorcycles.

Similarly, when the United States put up massive trade barriers after the stock market crash of 1929, it led to a serious decline in economic activity and the loss of millions of American jobs when the rest of the world responded in kind. The result was a worldwide depression.

The goal of free trade is ostensibly to provide a level playing field, permitting individuals and companies to have the opportunity to sell their goods and services in foreign lands. In theory, when every country in the world is allowed to do what it does best—letting the French excel in fashion, for example, or the Japanese in consumer electronics, or the Americans in aircraft and movies—the world economy prospers, and almost everyone is better off. In general, trade increases income, and with access to imports, companies and consumers have more of a choice about what to do with their increased income. But what happens when one country imports more than it exports, leading to job losses? Is the answer simply to close off the country to trade?

Basically, in any multiparty trade system, there will always be imbalances, deficits, or surpluses in the monetary value of goods and services traded. When one country is experiencing an economic boom with full employment, for example, it is natural to turn to foreign producers to provide the goods and services for increased local consumption. In fact, it is the only way to increase consumption if local factories are running at full capacity—as the United States was in the late 2010s. These imports, if not made up for in an equal number of exports, are "paid for" by sending something else abroad—usually paper assets, such as stocks and bonds. The purchase of U.S. dollar securities is the way most countries have compensated for the imbalances in trade with the United States. Many countries, in Asia and the Middle East especially, have used their earnings from exports to purchase trillions of dollars' worth of U.S. Treasury bonds to use as a store against future uncertainties—or to buy U.S. goods and services in the future.

Deciding to start a trade war because you run a deficit against any one country is like saying you want to punish the country that sells you what you really want. Imagine boycotting a local coffee shop because you spend a lot of money buying your favorite low-fat latte there. In the interconnected global economy, what gets spent never stays in one place. What India earns from its many call centers can be spent on South Korean televisions; and what South

Korea earns from its exports can be spent on Brazilian chickens or American tractors. In the end, it all adds up.

The economic terms used by most politicians when beating the drums for trade wars are *trade deficits* and *trade surpluses,* which focus mainly on the trade in physical goods, implying that the only thing to be concerned with is to export more washing machines and aircraft and import fewer televisions and bananas. But many countries are making more and more money exporting services like banking, entertainment, tourism, and technology platforms. And a few lucky countries, such as the United States, have the privilege of receiving massive amounts of money every year in the form of investments from abroad.

The obsession with trade deficits is misplaced because the deficit and surplus in goods and services is offset by monetary transfers. Most economists, therefore, look at the total trade in goods and services, referred to as the *current account,* which also includes such financial transfers as money sent home by citizens working abroad and interest paid on foreign debt. This current account is balanced by the country's *capital account,* which adds up all investments—mainly international purchases and sales of financial assets. These two measures, when added together, always add up to zero. One balances out the other. Which is why the total measure of trade is referred to as the *trade balance.*

Politicians who speak of "winning" or "losing" in trade don't understand that all trade in goods and services is balanced by monetary transfers moving in the opposite direction. Essentially, all the global trade in goods and services and flows of money between countries adds up to zero, but trade is not a zero-sum game, where one country's loss is necessarily another country's gain. Every trading country since the beginning of time has learned that the benefits of trade outweigh the disadvantages. While free trade does expose a country, and its workers, to foreign competition—

which can lead to layoffs and idle factories—putting up barriers to imports from abroad can destroy far more jobs as the rest of the world's economies respond with trade barriers of their own.

Essentially, there are three forms of barriers to trade: tariffs, quotas, and subsidies. Tariffs are, at heart, a form of tax. And politicians who stand for "no new taxes" need to think carefully about calling for increased tariffs on the cost of goods and services from abroad. Because in the end—like most things in the capitalist system—taxes of any form end up being paid for by the end consumer. Alternatively, by imposing a quota, a country simply limits the quantity of foreign products that can be imported. Both quotas and tariffs raise the price of foreign-made goods. Governments can also use taxpayers' money to provide a subsidy to local producers, making the price of local goods artificially lower than the price of equivalent imported goods.

Most trade barriers are imposed unilaterally by one country acting on its own to limit imports from abroad. These barriers are usually designed to "temporarily" protect local producers from foreign competition and, in theory, allow them to improve their productivity. The problem is that local producers, once given the comfort of a protected market, rarely make the sacrifices necessary to improve their products or lower their prices.

Historically, developing countries have been some of the strongest proponents of reducing trade barriers, primarily because their only hope for sustainable growth is to have access to international markets. Those that have insisted on putting up trade barriers, such as Brazil and India, usually remain in a low-productivity trap that ensures their goods are not competitive on the international markets, and they consistently run up large trade deficits. Countries with low trade barriers, such as Switzerland and Singapore, not only consistently run trade surpluses—even with strong local currencies—they also provide their citizens with the benefits of free access to low-cost products from around the globe.

A universal free-trade agreement would, of course, solve the problem of deciding which barriers to eliminate, but getting every country in the world economy to agree on anything is not an easy task, especially at a time when politicians are taking an increasingly isolationist stance. The Doha Round of free-trade talks languished during the first years of the twenty-first century, primarily because of the reluctance of rich countries to lower barriers to trade on agricultural goods, bowing to their farmers' insistence on having protected markets. These policies, however, ended up destroying the possibility for farmers from poor countries to increase agricultural exports and earn the income they needed to survive. Another cause for the failure of the Doha Round was the growing reluctance of developing-world countries to open their markets to manufactured goods in order to protect inefficient local industries.

In the end, most countries decided to start small, by signing bilateral free-trade agreements (FTAs), which are easier to negotiate and easier to sell to isolationist electorates because the benefits are more tangible, and domestic businesses don't necessarily have to give up their subsidies. Malaysia's first FTA, for example, was with Japan, allowing Japan to export its automobiles to the previously protected Malaysian market in exchange for reduced barriers to imports of Malaysian plywood, tropical fruit, and shrimp. Japanese rice growers, however, were allowed to keep their generous subsidies.

Once FTAs are in place, some sort of mechanism is needed to ensure that countries respect the promises they have made. In addition to commissions set up to monitor bilateral trade, the closest thing the world has to a worldwide trade watchdog is the World Trade Organization (WTO), which resolves disputes in an organized forum based in Geneva, Switzerland. Despite the fact that the WTO, much like the UN, is blamed for a wide variety of ills by populist leaders, its role is actually quite limited; the WTO was never meant to be more than a global round table where disputing parties could meet to air their grievances and try to resolve trade disputes.

Unlike the World Bank and the International Monetary Fund, which give decision-making power to a board of directors, all WTO decisions are made by consensus, with the member nations working together to decide which countries are allowed to impose sanctions. For all intents and purposes, the WTO has no power to force a country to do anything against its own national interests. Its real power lies in permitting countries that have suffered from trade barriers that exceed those authorized by existing trade agreements to erect barriers of their own, usually in the form of tariffs. For example, in 2013, the United States complained to the WTO that India was "gaming the system" by insisting that its national solar power program use only locally made solar panels, leading to a decline of 90 percent of U.S. solar panel exports to India. The WTO ruling in 2016, which allowed the United States to erect tariffs against Indian products in retaliation, led to India dismantling its illegal trade barriers and a steep increase in exports of American-made solar panels to the Indian subcontinent.

However, when the American government began unilaterally imposing tariffs on many foreign imports in 2018, the tactic was seen as a direct affront to the agreement that all trade disputes be settled around a table at the WTO. The United States claimed it was only protecting national security, a claim that was hard to take seriously since the "threat" was coming from longtime allies, such as Canada and the United Kingdom. The European Union and Canada immediately responded with calls to limit U.S. imports, targeting Kentucky bourbon, Levi's jeans, and a vast array of other American products—not necessarily tied to national security but quite strategic in the sense that many of the targeted products were from the American Midwest, an area populated by many isolationist voters.

Trade wars in the past have sometimes ended with actual military conflict, such as the Opium Wars between the Qing dynasty and the British Empire in the mid-1800s, which ended up forcing the Chinese to remove virtually all its onerous import duties as well as to give up Hong Kong to British rule; by the time Hong Kong was returned to China in 1997, it was one of the most successful trading centers in the world. Other trade wars in the recent past have included the Banana Wars between the United States and several European countries at the end of the twentieth century, centering on removing European barriers to Latin American banana producers, which were mainly owned by U.S. companies, and the Pasta Wars of the mid-1980s, when the Reagan administration tried to open up markets for American lemons and walnuts in Europe by placing punitive tariffs on imports of European-made pasta. Both disputes were resolved amicably with the warring parties gradually removing the disputed tariffs.

Despite the overwhelming benefits of trade, barriers of some sort or another have always existed and probably always will. The key is to find a way to encourage free trade with a minimum of harm to established industries and firms, while still promoting development in the world's poorer regions. Dismantling the world trading system would simply exacerbate existing problems and possibly destroy any hope for sustained global economic growth, which is essential for workers as well as captains of industry. In order for countries to increase real wages, governments need to increase productivity. And expanding access to markets abroad is one of the surest ways of forcing markets to become more efficient and more competitive, which increases the financial well-being of the country as a whole.

7

Brexit and Border Walls: Does Economic Isolation Make Economic Sense?

When the British electorate was asked to decide whether to stay in the European Union or to leave in the Brexit referendum of 2016, the people were assured by populist politicians that the billions of euros in extra funds that the United Kingdom had been paying to the EU—to support everything from agricultural subsidies to infrastructure construction in the poorer countries—would return to make Britain a better place. However, virtually every British economist, including the UK government's own Office for Budget Responsibility, pointed out that the loss of access to preferential trade with the rest of Europe would, in fact, decrease economic growth and reduce the amount of money available to pay for health care and everything else.

Around the world, electorates shaken by everything from increased immigration to interference from supranational institutions have begun taking a "Don't confuse me with facts, I know what I want!" attitude. This has led to countries from Australia to Hungary to the United States calling for limits on trade and immigration and almost everything else that seems foreign. The problem is that in the twenty-first-century economy—which is based largely on cooperation and free exchange of goods, services, and ideas—going it alone almost always has negative economic consequences.

In post-Brexit Britain, for example, one of the immediate effects of the referendum vote was a sharp decline in the value of the British pound. Investors sold the currency because of the country's diminished economic outlook. Without access to the EU market, exports were expected to decline precipitously, reducing income from foreign sales and making the country's currency less attractive. In addition, the reduced purchasing power of the local currency meant higher prices for imported goods like Middle Eastern gasoline and German automobiles. Overall inflation quickly went from 0.4 percent at the time of the referendum to more than 3 percent in less than two years.

Many pro-Brexit voters had hoped for a return to Britain's place as a kingpin in the world economy and called for a quick withdrawal from the European markets and a turn to the emerging markets of Asia and Latin America, including former colonies spread around the globe. The problem is that the European Union was Britain's major trade partner, accounting for more than 40 percent of all British exports. Countries like Singapore and Malaysia accounted for a small fraction of that. The total British trade with Malaysia at the time of the Brexit vote was approximately 10 percent of the British trade with Belgium, one of the EU's smaller economies. The entire EU trading area Britain was being asked to leave, in fact, encompassed more than thirty countries, including the non-EU members Iceland, Norway, and Switzerland.

One of the axioms of trading with other countries is that, all other things being equal, trade halves as distance doubles. Generally, trade with neighboring countries is naturally much greater than trade with countries on the other side of the world. By turning its back on its gigantic neighbor, the UK electorate was opting for an economic path with dubious potential for economic success. Even the head of the Bank of England saw the Brexit vote as an example of "deglobalization, not globalization" and predicted higher prices for consumers and the necessity of higher interest rates to keep inflation under control.

When the British government triggered the EU withdrawal process, it faced the difficult task of forging a new relationship with the EU that respected the wishes of the pro-Brexit electorate. The herculean task was made more difficult by the vague wording of the referendum. To the question "Should the United Kingdom remain a member of the European Union or leave the European Union?" voters were asked to choose "remain" or "leave." No one was asked to say how they wanted to leave, however, making the Brexit negotiations extremely difficult and leading to several years of confused, combative negotiations, provoking pressure from many voters for a new referendum.

The most extreme option considered was "no deal," which required the United Kingdom to revert to the status of a normal third-party EU trading partner, such as Bangladesh or Bolivia, where trade is organized according to a set of basic guidelines set out by the World Trade Organization. This radical option didn't include any preferential access to the European Union whatsoever—meaning that all EU borders, including the one dividing the Republic of Ireland with the United Kingdom's Northern Ireland, would have to be respected as if the United Kingdom were a foreign nation, with onerous restrictions on the movement of goods and people.

In order to have preferential access to the EU markets, three variations were considered: signing a basic free-trade agreement, continuing to be part of the customs union, or remaining in the EU single market, implying full acceptance of EU norms.

The simplest solution, being a participant in the EU free-trade

area, would involve a NAFTA-like arrangement where participant countries reduce or completely remove tariffs or quotas on
goods and/or services flowing from one country to another. Many
countries have entered into such free-trade agreements over the
years, and very few of these FTAs require participants to accept
the free movement of people from one member country to another.

The second solution was to join the EU customs union, where
members agree to have the same tariffs on imports from outside the union. The advantage of being inside a customs union
is that any imported good, once the commonly agreed tariff has
been applied, can then be sent on to any other member country.
An iPhone or a car imported into the United Kingdom from the
United States could be sent on to any other country in the customs
union without any concern for where it came from originally. But
a big factor in voting for Brexit, according to most exit polls, was to
allow Britain to set its own rules on tariffs and make its own trade
agreements. To become a full member of the EU customs union,
however, Britain would have to let the EU make these decisions.

The third and most ambitious level of participation in the EU
considered by the UK negotiating team was to become a member
of the EU single market. Under this arrangement, Britain would
not only have to accept the common external tariffs of a customs
union; it would also have to respect the principle of totally free
movement of goods, services, capital, and people. But since one
of the main reasons people said they voted for Brexit was because
they wanted to close the UK borders to unrestricted immigration,
how could the United Kingdom hope to remain a part of the EU
single market without accepting the principle of free movement
of EU citizens from one country to another? Even the fiercely independent EU holdouts, such as Switzerland, Iceland, and Norway, had agreed to allow EU passport holders to live and work in
their countries as a condition for free access to the single market.

The decision on which path to take became so intractable at one point that it was feared that the United Kingdom would exit the European Union with no deal at all, putting the United Kingdom at the same level as every other country in the world economy without any preferential trade agreement.

In other parts of the world, the movement to erect trade barriers—as well as actual border walls in Hungary and the United States—has led to many unintended economic consequences. While the reasons given by many anti-trade leaders were economic in theory, the movements to erect border walls are based on fear, including a general aversion to globalization, the fear of job losses, or blatant racism in some cases. For example, even though the U.S. economy was running at virtually maximum capacity and unemployment was at historic lows, economic woes were cited as justification for a flurry of protectionist measures, including shutting down the federal government.

Trade wars end up hurting everyone, including the countries starting them. In a 2018 letter signed by 1,140 leading economists, including 14 Nobel Prize winners, the U.S. Congress and the U.S. president were warned that protectionist measures would actually reduce jobs given that the imposition of U.S. tariffs would certainly be met by retaliatory measures from other countries. For example, putting tariffs on steel and aluminum ultimately increases their cost for end consumers and affects the production costs of a wide array of steel-based products, making them uncompetitive on the world markets—thus leading to the loss of many more jobs than those "saved."

8

———

Does Immigration Take Our Jobs Away?

Immigration has become the number one issue for many voters and governments around the world, because of the seemingly unrestricted flow of immigrants into Europe during the Syrian civil war and families crossing the Mexican-U.S. border over the past decades. The thought of millions of undocumented and illegal immigrants pouring over porous borders has been the cause of the rise of many new far-right populist parties and candidates calling for an end to immigration and a return to "order." Many observers have seen the Brexit vote and 2016 U.S. election as primarily influenced by voters' fear of immigration.

By the end of the 2010s, more than 250 million people were living in places other than their country of birth, twice as many as in 2000. Many of those immigrants, approximately 65 million by some estimates, have been forcibly displaced by war, violence, or natural disasters. Most immigrants simply move to a neighboring country, often not much better off than the one they left. Only a small fraction of the world's most vulnerable migrants succeed in moving to the rich countries in Europe, Oceania, or North America.

Table 8.1

Percentage of Foreign-Born People in Selected Countries (2018)

Rank	Country	Percentage of foreign-born residents
1.	Switzerland	28.3%
2.	Australia	27.7%
3.	Israel	22.6%
4.	New Zealand	22.4%
5.	Canada	20%
6.	Austria	16.7%
7.	Ireland	16.4%
8.	Slovenia	16.1%
9.	Sweden	16%
10.	Belgium	15.5%
11.	Norway	13.9%
12.	Spain	13.4%
13.	United States	13.1%
14.	Germany	12.8%
15.	United Kingdom	12.3%

Source: OECD

The most common complaint against immigration, especially of low-skilled workers, is that immigrants take jobs away. Secondary reasons include anything from concern for how immigrants could overwhelm schools and other public services to the nativist—if not racist—view that immigrants of a different ethnic background will threaten social cohesion and security. Many of those voting for anti-immigration parties are sometimes less worried about losing their job to foreigners than they are worried that immigrants and those of other ethnic backgrounds will surpass them on the economic ladder, leading to a decline in social status.

One of the most persistent myths about jobs is that there is a fixed number of positions available in any given economy and that that number will not change when new people are added to the labor pool. This is referred to by economists as the *lump of labor fallacy*, because in practice, more people almost always translates into an increase in jobs. It's often the case that the work immigrants perform—at least in the beginning of their careers in their new host countries—are jobs that locals simply prefer not to do. Gutting fish or working long hours picking crops under a hot sun are tasks that even those at the low end of the wage spectrum in wealthy countries tend to avoid at all costs.

Work, like most things in the twenty-first-century economy, is not a zero-sum game. When one job is taken, it doesn't mean that more jobs won't be created. The arrival of new workers tends to expand an economy by creating a need for more housing, food preparation, haircuts, and countless other goods and services.

By expanding output, immigrants tend to stimulate the economy as a whole. Most of the money that immigrants earn is recycled into the local economy, even if a portion is sent back to their families in their home country. And through the payment of payroll taxes and sales taxes, immigrants end up supporting the activities of local governments—which could, for example, use some of that money to provide skills training and other forms of additional education to enable locally born workers to move up the economic ladder. Immigrants also tend to save at a much higher rate than local workers do, and their money gets deposited in local banks, which can then use that money to extend loans to homeowners and businesses in the local economy.

Immigrants with university degrees and special skills—especially tech skills—have been shown to provide a particularly powerful stimulus to local economies. By investing in local start-ups, or even setting up start-ups of their own, highly skilled immigrants have created hundreds of thousands of jobs in North America and Europe. A Brookings Institution report has shown that while immigrants represent about 15 percent of the American workforce, they account for approximately 25 percent of the entrepreneurial investment in the U.S. economy. The same report noted that over a third of new firms—including many unicorns that end up employing tens of thousands—have at least one immigrant entrepreneur in the initial leadership team. Another study found that more than half of the U.S. tech sector's privately held companies valued at more than $1 billion had at least one immigrant founder.

Even local workers without college degrees can benefit because, like most everything in our interconnected world, what happens in one area of the economy ends up having an effect on another. A new business or factory often means an increase in a wide array of jobs at all skill levels, from flipping hamburgers to running the robots on the factory floor. In Silicon Valley and in Britain's Silicon Fen, for example, so many jobs have been created by tech firms started and staffed by foreign-born immigrants that many areas have seen consistent economic expansion, even during economic downturns in other regions.

Many economists point to Japan, which has chosen to severely restrict immigrants for social as well as economic reasons, as an example of how the fear of immigration can cause a wide array of economic problems. Japan's extremely low birthrate in recent decades has led to a shrinking population with virtually no low-skilled immigrants—only 1.5 percent of the current population was born abroad—resulting in a severe labor shortage. This, along with such other factors as deflationary monetary policy, caused the Japanese economy to seriously underperform when compared to countries with more lenient immigration policies.

A culturally diverse workforce often translates into a competitive edge for companies and businesses on an international level. A study in the *Harvard Business Review* found that businesses with a high level of diversity—including, among other things, national origin—had a higher level of innovation and consequently higher levels of profitability.

Although immigration isn't always problem-free, it's clear that, in most cases, it ends up stimulating the economy and expands a country's opportunities by providing the manpower, skills, and diversity required for companies to compete in the new global economy.

9

How Do Populist Leaders Use Our Economic Illiteracy to Gain Power?

Just as Adolf Hitler exploited the German economic crises to gain power during the Great Depression, populist leaders today have learned that exploiting economic crises and voter fears can often be the most effective way to get elected. Hitler's Munich Beer Hall Putsch in 1923 occurred at the peak of hyperinflation following World War I, and the Nazi Party's seizure of absolute power in the early 1930s occurred during a period of severe deflation. Even though solving the economic crises was presented as the reason for expanding governmental power and limiting citizens' rights, Germany's populist leader had something much more sinister in mind.

In today's complex global economy, voters are equally overwhelmed by a complex political landscape, and leaders around the world have learned that disenchanted citizens often prefer politicians who offer easy solutions, regardless of economic principles. Using economic arguments to justify "going it alone" and "putting us first" policies, autocratic rulers play on the public's general skepticism about global trade agreements and the power of the United Nations and the World Trade Organization. Even though economists can easily prove how being connected to the global economy provides major advantages, the average worker tends to blame globalization for stagnant wages and increased unemployment—at least in those industries where foreign factories or robots can do the job more cheaply. It's not by chance that four successive U.S. presidents, from Woodrow Wilson onward, used the words "America First" as their campaign slogans.

Marginalized workers usually don't want to hear arcane economic arguments when confronting low wages, unemployment, and job insecurity. For example, the average worker's wage at Walmart in the late 2010s was only 30 percent of what a worker would have earned at a Ford or General Motors plant fifty years before, so some discontent and anger is to be expected. Adding to this discontent is the propensity of populists to blame economic problems on the dysfunction of established political parties. The result has been a movement away from mainstream parties and politicians in almost every national election since the global recession, which began in 2008. From the United States to France to Italy to Mexico to Brazil and beyond, countries increasingly are being governed by radical populist politicians keen to exploit the average voter's fears and insecurities.

In some countries, economic and social turmoil have led voters to allow the democratic process to be severely eroded. By the late 2010s, many countries—including Russia, Turkey, and Hungary—held elections that were severely manipulated or, when not, functioned only to rubber-stamp current rulers. Some leaders even made attempts to remove term limits completely. In many countries, the media has become a tool of the ruling party or leader, leaving virtually no possibility of disseminating opposing viewpoints or critical arguments domestically.

The move toward populism has gone so far that countries led

by autocrats began to outnumber Western liberal democracies. One study in the late 2010s found that among the fifteen countries with the highest per capita incomes, more than 60 percent could no longer be defined as democracies. The Economist Intelligence Unit analyzed the shift away from liberal democracy since the 2007/08 financial crisis—sometimes referred to as the *democratic recession*—and found that in eighty-nine countries, democracy had deteriorated while in only twenty-seven had it improved.

Once populists have gained power, a typical tactic is to attack the press or the justice system as being part of the problem, not the solution. In extreme cases, the populists become true autocrats by stifling any form of opposition, pointing out that they—and only they—are able to solve the economic problems in a way that will benefit the average worker.

Autocratic leaders often enrich themselves and their families at the expense of the workers they are ostensibly there to pro-tect. In Hungary and Russia, for example, those with close ties to the ruling party control vast segments of the economy. "Crony capitalism" has long been an established practice in sub-Saharan Africa, but only in the twenty-first century has it found a home in some formerly liberal Western economies. In Turkey, for example, the president installed his son-in-law as the combined treasury and finance minister in 2018 at a time of considerable economic turmoil when the lira lost more than 40 percent of its value in just a few months. Since the new economic head had virtually no experience in macroeconomic policy-making, it appeared that the president was less concerned about economic progress than he was about grooming his family member to be the next ruler of the country.

In the case of the Brexit campaign, pro-leave politicians were accused of promoting Brexit—which was principally about turn-ing the United Kingdom's back on its largest market—not for economic reasons but primarily to garner long-term political advantages. When the plans for a "clean" Brexit didn't materialize, it called into question the leavers' claim that exiting the EU would allow for a new period of economic rebirth as a "global" trading nation.

As the economist Paul Krugman has pointed out, the Brexit promise was based on faulty economic reasoning, specifically the so-called *gravity equation*, which posits the idea that the size of trading partners matters a lot, but the distance between trading partners matters even more. Therefore, by turning its back on a market of 450 million people right on its doorstep, the United Kingdom had to pin its hopes on replacing that trade with markets vastly more difficult to reach.

At the same time Britain was coping with the daunting task of building an entirely new trading nexus to replace the one on its doorstep, the United States was embarking on the economically dubious effort to dismantle its trading relationships with Canada and many other major trading partners—erecting tariffs on a vast array of goods, many of which were essential to the smooth functioning of the U.S. economy. The justification for the move was the perceived reluctance of America's trading partners to open up their own economies to U.S. companies and exports.

The result was something the United States should have remembered from the effort in the 1930s to erect barriers to foreign imports: the targeted countries retaliated with trade barriers of their own. By targeting U.S. exports from states that provided the greatest support to the president's election, the retaliation hit fast and hard. The effects of the new trade war threatened to wipe out the economic gains from reduced taxes. In the end, workers were worse off, and many lost their jobs. The irony is that many workers continued to support the populist policies, saying that it was important to protect American jobs and markets at all costs.

What the supporters of the "America First" policy failed to perceive was that the U.S. trade deficit was not actually caused by other countries "cheating" with high trade barriers of their own. According to World Bank statistics, average tariffs on U.S. products before the trade war began were minuscule—1.6 percent average tariffs in Europe, 1.4 percent in Japan, and 0.9 percent in Canada. Calling for a global trade war to reduce such low tariffs seems like economic madness, especially when the economy is already running at full capacity.

Attempting to force other countries to import more when at-home factories are producing all they can and virtually everyone is already employed has the effect of increasing the prices of a country's exports, thus making them less attractive to the countries that are already buying them.

Even worse, by scorning the multilateral trade system and instigating unnecessary trade wars, populist leaders of large countries run the risk of encouraging leaders in other parts of the world to follow suit, leading eventually to global anarchy. The dirty little secret of autocratic leaders is that many are more interested in protecting their own interests, such as protecting selected political supporters or an inner circle of oligarchic businesspeople, so they play to the fears of average citizens, manipulating them into voting against the economic interests of the country as a whole.

10

Globalization—Problem or Solution?

Politicians across the political spectrum are warning of the dangers of globalization, with many calling for a return to something resembling a Depression-era isolationist system. And almost all of them are playing to our fears that the "elites" are prospering while the rest of us are suffering an inexorable decline in income and power.

The problem is that the definition of "elites" differs widely depending on which extreme the politicians are coming from. From the left, it's the economic elites, the so-called 1 percent, who, with unrestricted access to capital and markets, are profiting from globalization to amass obscene profits while the rest of us suffer. From the right, it's the left-leaning elites who, with access to education and power, push their liberal agenda of cultural pluralism and open borders, which leads to rampant immigration and soaring trade deficits.

It is easy to understand the sense of anger that pervades many middle-class workers in the developed countries of Western Europe and North America, especially when we compare our lives today to the golden era of economic growth that followed World War II. During that period, the average low-skilled worker's salary virtually doubled every generation, enabling them to buy homes in the suburbs and send their children to good colleges. But even before the Great Recession started in 2008, average workers' incomes in many countries had been essentially flat for the previous thirty years, while the top 1 percent of the population saw their incomes triple over that same period.

In most developed countries, new technology has drastically reduced the need for unskilled workers. Manufacturing now accounts for less than 10 percent of jobs in most Western economies, as robots or robot-like machines have begun to do much of the work that middle-class workers used to be paid handsomely for. While it is true that globalization has contributed to many of those high-paying manufacturing jobs moving to low-wage countries in the developing world, many of those jobs would have disappeared anyway—mainly because of new technology. And now, with the advent of an artificial-intelligence-based economy, many low-wage and low-skilled jobs are disappearing in the developing countries as well. The question facing politicians and voters of every stripe is whether closing borders is the answer. And even more importantly, who is hurt the most from a return to isolationism?

As the film star Joan Crawford once said, channeling the author Oscar Wilde, "The only thing worse than being talked about is not being talked about." In the converging global economy of the twenty-first century, it's not all that different. In many countries, the only thing worse than opening borders to trade is not opening borders. Even though there are many disadvantages to the free exchange of goods, services, and money, the advantages are almost always greater. Historically, almost all countries that chose to close their borders remained in the back of the pack during times of economic crisis as well as economic boom.

Ever since the tragedy of World War II, the world has moved to more and more cooperation and interconnectedness. This globalization effort was led by the United States—one of the few countries that wasn't completely devastated by the ravages of war. The ensuing seventy years of almost-uninterrupted economic growth provided unprecedented access to work and prosperity for rich and poor alike. One need only compare photos of war-ravaged London or Berlin to the glittering views of those cities today to appreciate the difference that access to trade and investment can provide.

For most observers, it is clear that economic isolationism was a major cause of World War II. Hitler, Mussolini, and other leaders of their ilk came to power during the Great Depression when isolationism led to the rise of authoritarian governments in previously stable democratic countries—and something eerily similar is being repeated in today's chaotic world. When the United States closed its borders to trade after the crash of 1929, it not only exported its recession to the rest of the world; it led other countries to close their borders in retaliation. Soon, an American recession became a global depression. The result? Most of the fat cats who lost money in the stock market suffered some. But most still had funds in reserve or were able to find new jobs. Ultimately, it was the farmers and the workers who faced abject poverty and starvation in those trying times.

All through history, countries that opened their doors and traded with the rest of the world prospered the most: ancient Greece, Rome, the Venetian empire, Holland in the golden age, the British Empire, Japan, and the United States over most of the twentieth century—and now many emerging-market economies are also prospering through trade. China, for example, before it opened its doors to the world economy, was a poor, struggling, backward economy. Now it's on track to become the largest economy in the world.

In the early 1990s, approximately 23 percent of the world's population was defined as being middle class—earning an income of approximately $20,000 or more. Today, more than 45 percent of the world's population fits that category, which translates into approximately 2.3 billion people who have risen out of poverty in that time. Now that hundreds of millions of the world's poor have moved into the middle class, they have become an attractive new market for goods and services ranging from automobiles to music downloads.

Globalization, by definition, opens doors. It gives us new opportunities to buy, sell, and travel abroad. Some may lose their jobs, but many will get new jobs. Statistically, trade and exchange translate into economic growth. Often, the rich tend to benefit the most when profits increase, but a growing economy also means increased demand for labor.

This doesn't mean we have to blindly accept the inequities that globalization exacerbates. But instead of blaming globalization for income inequality, why not blame the governments that allow most of the new wealth to flow into the coffers of the rich? There is a tool that governments can use, and have used for centuries, to redistribute wealth: taxes. And the way they work is excruciatingly simple: you take more money from the rich than you do from the poor. Then you provide programs that help those most in need. And with a strong and prosperous middle class, the increased consumer activity leads to an expanding economy, and almost everyone ends up being better off rather than a select few.

The functioning of free trade is relatively simple. You usually only buy from other countries if it's cheaper than it would be at home. The idea is to allow each country to sell what it produces most efficiently and then allow it to import the rest. Allowing countries to export what they have a comparative advantage in producing—French cheese, South Korean televisions, and American movies, for example—enables them to earn valuable foreign exchange, which gives them the means to import those goods and services that other countries are better at making. Think of an Ecuadorian rose producer using earnings from foreign trade to buy a new Apple computer to track all their international business.

The concept of comparative advantage is based on the idea that *every* country can compete on the world stage, even those countries that are not very efficient at producing much of anything. Simply by allowing the value of the home currency to fall, a country can make its goods and services more competitive on the world markets. Of course, this also means that imports become more expensive, which can increase inflation drastically if the currency is devalued too much.

But what about the workers who lose their jobs because of foreign competition? Obviously, it would be ideal if no jobs were ever lost, no matter what. But in a free-market capitalist system, things are in constant flux. Jobs are constantly being created and destroyed, even without globalization. Capitalism is based on change. What is important is to find a way to make sure that the new jobs being created are more valuable than those lost and that everyone has access to the improved economy. Unfortunately, many opponents of globalization see the status quo as something to be preserved at all costs.

But instead of killing the goose that laid the golden egg, why not find a way to distribute the eggs more equitably? In Sweden, for example, the government follows a policy of "protecting the worker, not the job." This *Scandinavian compromise* allows a government to tolerate shutting down certain industries—shipbuilding, for instance, which in high-wage Sweden makes little economic sense—while concentrating on helping the newly unemployed workers, providing generous social services and subsidies to help them through the difficult period after losing their jobs.

Globalization already began when the first humanoid left Africa and settled abroad. Ever since, man has been trading and exploring and fighting and preaching in other lands. Instead of using donkeys or small sailing vessels, today's global traders travel in the comfort of jumbo jets, and goods move by rail, container ships, or aircraft, but the idea is the same: opening borders opens opportunities.

Globalization, whether new or old, isn't always benevolent, however. Outsourcing jobs means jobs lost at home; immigration leads to ethnological and demographic change; transportation of goods from far lands results in pollution and increasing the product's carbon footprint. But all these problems can be addressed by using the resources of an expanding economy. In the end, we have to ask ourselves: What do we want for our future and for future generations? Basically, with a minimum of trade barriers, consumers are given the opportunity to buy the best products the world has to offer at the best prices. And by importing goods from poor countries, the rich, industrialized countries not only provide their own citizens with a wide range of products to choose from, but they also stimulate the growth of jobs in countries where people are desperate to earn enough to survive. Think of a sugar farmer in South Africa being told that a newly acquired plot of land will be foreclosed because there is no possibility to sell the produce abroad. Or a seamstress in Guatemala being told the apparel company she works for is being closed because the government of a rich country decided to force consumers to buy only locally made clothes.

Working conditions in the developing world obviously need to be carefully monitored to make sure that no worker is abused, especially children. But having access to export-oriented jobs offering salaries that usually surpass the prevailing local wage is often the best hope for families in poor countries to pay for their children's food and education and build a better future.

By giving the developing countries an economic jump start, wealthier countries are also able to expand their own economies by concentrating on information-intensive jobs with much higher salaries. In addition, as the economies in the developing world grow and their citizens have more disposable income, they can buy goods and services—such as automobiles, refrigerators, computers, and streaming media—from the more developed countries. In the end, the increased trade leads to more growth everywhere, which creates even more wealth for everyone.

The key is finding the best way to distribute this new wealth. In doing so, it's important to first distinguish between poverty and inequality. If globalization really does make virtually everyone better off, albeit in an unequal way, we should really be expending our energies on distributing the new wealth, not on destroying the machine that created it.

11

Inflation vs. Deflation

By the time the populist Venezuelan government called for new economic measures to end rampant hyperinflation at the end of 2018, the local currency had become virtually worthless. After 80,000 percent inflation over the previous year, it took more than six million bolivars to buy a loaf of bread—that is, if you could find a store that had a loaf of bread in stock. After more than a decade of economic mismanagement, the financial meltdown had become so bad that by the late 2010s, clean water distribution had slowed to a trickle, and gravely sick citizens were dying in make-shift hospitals, unable to get the treatments that were keeping people alive in almost every other country in the world.

On the other end of the spectrum, the economic crisis in Japan at the beginning of the twenty-first century was marked by se-vere deflation, where a chronic decline in prices led to decades of sluggish economic growth. When deflation was accompanied by a sharp decline in consumers—with the total population in Japan expected to decline precipitously by 2050—the crisis in Japan appeared to be just as intractable as the inflationary crises in Venezuela and other parts of the world. The problem with too much deflation, just like too much inflation, is that growth screeches to a halt because of the economic uncertainty both problems create.

In a country with persistent deflation, consumers will simply stop buying goods and services as prices decline, expecting to get a better price at some point in the near future. Likewise, companies also tend to delay investments in new plants and machinery when they think prices for their products will soon decline. In deflationary environments, companies try to find ways to reduce input costs, often leading to a reduction in salaries. The lower salaries then translate into even lower consumer spending, completing the vicious circle of deflationary economic crisis.

Like the Three Bears' porridge, an economy should be neither too hot nor too cold. And neither acute inflation nor acute deflation are positive for sustainable economic health. Despite the desire of some populist leaders to have a high inflation rate of 3 or even 4 percent, most economists recommend a "just right" inflation rate of about 2 percent per year. But how is this achieved?

First, we need to determine the level of inflation or deflation in any given economy. This is usually done by looking at the prices of items in a "basket" of goods and services that are chosen to represent the average citizen's daily needs. In some countries in the developing world, for example, more than 60 percent of the basket consists of foodstuffs. In China, it's 30 percent. And in the United States and Western Europe, only 10 percent, reflecting the fact that the average family unit spends a relatively small amount on food and the rest on other goods and services. This means that increasing food prices have a much bigger influence on inflation in the developing world.

In the United States and many other countries, the main vehicle for determining inflation is the Consumer Price Index, referred to as the Retail Price Index in Britain. This index tracks the prices of a wide range of goods and services, including milk, rent, and haircuts. This index is then used to readjust fixed incomes, such as pensions and social security payments, which are extremely important to low-income people who rely on these payments for a significant portion of their daily needs. Without being adjusted for inflation, fixed incomes can actually end up being worthless over a long period of rising prices.

According to a prominent Yale economist named James Tobin, inflation doesn't necessarily have to imply economic pain—as long as everything from salaries to social security payments is adjusted accordingly. The main cost of inflation, according to his theory, is "shoe leather," because, as long as salaries keep up with rising prices, consumers simply have to go to the ATM more often to get cash—wearing down the soles of their shoes.

But it is nearly impossible to index prices and salaries in the chaotic world of hyperinflation, and consequently, no one is left untouched by uncontrolled inflation. From the top 1 percent to the poorest of the poor, an economy in crisis eventually hurts virtually everyone. But it's the most vulnerable who suffer the most. When the cost of a loaf of bread exceeded the total monthly minimum salary in Venezuela, those at the bottom of the economic ladder had to face the worst aspect of economic hardship: starvation. Millions ended up fleeing across the border as economic refugees to Colombia and Brazil.

Hyperinflation has ravaged countries as diverse as Germany, Mexico, and Argentina—even China during the Yuan dynasty, when too much paper money in circulation led to uncontrolled inflation. In Germany's postwar Weimar Republic, in 1923, inflation became so bad that the government had to resort to issuing postage stamps worth fifty billion marks, and people had to use wheelbarrows to carry enough cash to make simple household purchases.

The main tool for fighting uncontrolled inflation is for the government and local monetary authorities to reduce the money supply. Since most easily accessed money is in the form of bank deposits, the most efficient way for a central bank to control the money supply is by regulating bank lending and reserve requirements. Essentially, when banks have more money to lend to customers, the economy grows. And when banks reduce their lending, the economy slows.

The reason central bank monetary policy works so well is because of the *multiplier effect*. Basically, money we deposit in our banks doesn't just sit there collecting dust. The bank can and does lend that money to someone else. A hundred dollars deposited in a bank in Portland, for example, may end up being loaned to an individual or a business in Key West. After setting aside a small portion of each deposit as a reserve, banks are free to lend out the remainder. The effect is to increase the money supply without any extra currency being printed. What gets loaned out ends up in another bank to be subsequently loaned again.

A bank's ability to provide loans is limited by only two things: the amount of its deposits and its reserve requirements, which are determined by the central bank or monetary authority. Most banks are required to put a minimum percentage of their funds—10 percent of deposits, for example—on reserve and are prohibited from lending these funds back to customers. If a central bank increases the reserve requirement, it effectively reduces the money supply, since banks then have less to lend to businesses and consumers. On the other hand, by reducing the reserve requirements—as several central banks around the world did during the Great Recession of 2008—they allow the country's banks to lend more, stimulating the economy and releasing even more money for lending.

Reducing interest rates has also been shown to be a valuable tool to control economic growth. When a central bank decides that an economy is growing too slowly, for example, it can simply reduce the interest rate it charges on loans of central bank funds to banks, referred to as the *discount rate* in the United States. When banks get this "cheaper" money, they are able to make cheaper loans to businesses and consumers, providing an important stimulus to economic growth. Likewise, by raising interest rates, a central bank can slow down the economy by making it more "expensive" for businesses and consumers to borrow money, consequently reducing purchases of homes, cars, vacations, and factories.

Like a locomotive pulling a long train, central-bank interest rates tend to change the interest rates throughout the economy at large. For example, the interest rate on loans made between banks—called *interbank rates* in Europe and *Fed funds rates* in the United States—will rise whenever banks have to pay more to borrow from the central bank and will fall when they have to pay less. The higher cost of money is almost always passed on to consumers and businesses in the form of higher interest rates on every other form of loan in the economy.

All interest rates are linked because money, like most commodities, is interchangeable. Banks and individuals will go wherever rates are lowest—basically, wherever money is "cheaper." A change in interest rates by the Federal Reserve in Washington, for example, will affect not only consumer and business loan rates in Miami or Minnesota but also interest rates around the world. In the global village of international money markets, interest rates have become the heartbeat of economic activity.

Just as a prudent driver keeps an eye on the road ahead, a country's central bankers try to keep an eye on leading economic indicators, which show where the economy is heading. Typical leading economic indicators are housing starts, retail sales, and spending on new plants and machinery. Lagging economic indicators, such as inflation of GDP growth, reflect only what the economy has done in the past. Both lagging and leading economic indicators, however, are useful in plotting the course of an economy—even though no one is able to predict future economic performance with certainty.

Fighting excessive deflation is in some ways more difficult than fighting hyperinflation. During inflationary times, there is basically no limit to how much central banks can raise interest rates. But in the battle against deflation, once interest rates have been reduced to zero, there is little that central banks can do to stimulate further growth. The two things that can be done once interest rates reach zero are negative interest rates or quantitative easing.

In times of negative interest rates depositors are essentially being charged to store their money in the bank; this has been the case in the past, in countries including Switzerland and Denmark. This encourages consumers and businesses to put their money in the economy at large by buying additional goods and services.

Faced with the economic meltdown following the 2008 crash, some central banks opted to stimulate their moribund economies via quantitative easing, using the unlimited purchasing power of central banks to buy large quantities of bonds in the open market to pump cash into the economy. Central banks use quantitative easing to create money where previously none existed.

How is this done? A central bank "creates" money every time it dips into its "vaults"—essentially a black hole of unlimited financial resources—to buy existing bonds from banks or other investors. These purchases, often referred to as *open market operations,* inject new money into the economy because the bank, instead of holding bonds, is now holding the "cash" it got from the central bank. This money can now be made available for loans to consumers and individuals, thereby stimulating economic growth.

In periods of crisis, however, central banks are often unable to change the perception in the minds of consumers and businesspeople that there will be no end to the vicious cycle of inexorably rising or declining prices. The solution for deflation, as for hyperinflation, essentially involves finding a way to change long-term expectations—not an easy task in an economy out of control.

12

What Is Currency Manipulation?

When the United States government initiated a trade war with China in 2018, it cited China's actions as a "currency manipulator," saying that the undervalued yuan was the major cause of the persistent trade deficits that the United States had been running with China for several decades. In fact, the United States had been running trade deficits with more than eighty nations in the world economy by that point, and the relatively low value of the Chinese yuan versus the dollar was only one piece of the puzzle. Instead of saying the yuan was too weak, the U.S. government could just as well have said that the dollar was too strong.

The value of each currency is, by definition, linked to the value of each other currency in the world economy. When the peso goes up in value against the dollar, and the dollar goes up in value against the euro, by definition, the peso has gone up in even greater value against the euro. And money doesn't just come in the form of paper currencies like dollars, pesos, and euros. From bitcoins to credit card chips to the actual cash in our pockets, anything that represents value is money. But what are all these monies worth?

Just like a street market with mountains of apples on sale one day and none the next, the value of any scarce good goes up, and a currency is a commodity like any other. The movement of goods and services from one country to another is always accompanied by a flow of money in the other direction. And since each country, or economic bloc, has its own currency, the value of goods and services sold abroad is directly influenced by the value of the home currency. And vice versa.

On the world markets, currency trading goes on twenty-four hours a day, seven days a week in computers and on trading floors scattered around the world, from Chicago to Shanghai to Paris. The price of a currency often changes several times per second. And in the twenty-first-century economy, it's the market that determines the currency's value, weighing the desires of buyers against sellers in a constantly changing environment.

There is a whole range of reasons to buy or sell a currency. One, it may be needed to pay for imports of goods or services from abroad. But speculators also may buy or sell a currency if they think the currency will change in value in the future. Who wants to buy a house in a declining market? You'd rather wait until prices start to rise and then jump in. In currency markets, it's the same story. If the view of a speculator is that the dollar will rise in value over the next few years, speculators and investors will buy, driving the price up in a sort of self-fulfilling prophecy.

Sometimes, a country can artificially reduce or raise the value of its currency on the world markets by intervening in the foreign exchange markets. By making massive purchases or sales of any given currency, governments can drastically affect its value. At the beginning of the twenty-first century, more than a hundred countries manipulated their currencies in one way or another, even though only a few admitted outright manipulation—which usually takes place by pegging, or fixing, the value of one currency to another. Examples of pegged currency systems include fourteen West and Central African countries pegging their CFA franc—referring to the Communauté Financière Africaine that they all are a part of—to the euro, and Hong Kong, the United Arab Emirates, and most Caribbean nations pegging their currencies to the U.S. dollar. Pegged currency regimes are sometimes referred to as a *dirty float* to distinguish them from the freely floating currency regimes of the advanced industrial economies such as Britain, the euro-zone countries, or the United States.

The traditional purpose of most currency manipulation is to keep the local money stable. Generally, a country with a strong currency has less inflation because of the decreased cost of imports. A strong currency also helps individuals traveling abroad and companies purchasing foreign assets. The downside of a strong currency, of course, is that jobs are lost when a country's overvalued currency puts the brakes on goods and services sold abroad, which is why many countries have kept their currency from getting too strong.

In any event, it's not always possible to keep a currency from rising or falling on world markets. Currency crashes around the world, from Britain to Argentina to Thailand, attest to the power of speculators to bring down a currency on the world's foreign exchange markets. The speculators often succeed because governments with weakening currencies are limited in what they can do to return to stability. If they raise interest rates in an effort to attract foreign investment in the country's bonds, the result can be an economic downturn, scaring away the foreign investors it was trying to attract.

Often, the efforts of central banks to control the value of a country's currency are hampered by the fact that money is being held by an increasingly large group of players in the world economy. Almost 80 percent of dollar reserves, for example, are held not by major central banks—such as those in Europe, Canada, or Japan—but by emerging-market central banks, such as those in Taiwan, China, and the oil-rich countries in the Persian Gulf region that have reinvested their massive export earnings in dollar-denominated securities such as U.S. government bonds. Emerging-market central banks were said to have more than $6 trillion of foreign-exchange reserves at the end of the 2010s, all of which could be used to manipulate and control fluctuations in their various currencies. This is accomplished by buying or selling large amounts of a country's currency in the open market, where the law of supply and demand causes the value of a scarce currency to go up and one whose supply is increasing to go down.

Being the world's most important reserve currency has had an enormous effect on the value of the U.S. dollar, and, not insignificantly, on the U.S. trade deficit. At the end of the 2010s, it was estimated that approximately 40 percent of all global trade was being denominated in U.S. dollars. When companies and countries use American currency to pay for foreign trade—even trade that doesn't begin or end in the United States—the world is inadvertently helping the U.S. economy by creating extra demand for the dollar and keeping its value up over time.

A strong currency, in addition to being useful for keeping prices lower than they normally would be, also means a lot to a country's world standing both economically and militarily. Much of the United States' military spending over past years, for example, has been financed by foreigners willing to recycle their U.S. dollar earned from trade, mainly through the purchase of U.S. Treasury securities. Having the world's reserve currency ends up giving the United States a lot of clout on the world stage as well, allowing it to impose sanctions on rogue regimes. When the United States threatened to cut off Iran—and countries trading with Iran—from

U.S. dollar transactions in 2018, for example, it ensured immediate cooperation from most countries wishing to participate in the global economy.

The dilemma of holding the world's reserve currency, sometimes referred to as the *Triffin dilemma,* posits that the extra demand causes the U.S. dollar to be stronger than it normally would be. The strong dollar then makes U.S. exports more expensive, often causing large trade deficits.

In the end, however, the biggest factors affecting a country's trade deficits are how much the country spends abroad and how much money it attracts from foreign trade partners. For example, most economists blame the United States' high trade deficits in the 2010s on the low savings rate of U.S. households and the high fiscal deficit of the U.S. government. By opting to buy that new foreign-made flat-screen TV at Target instead of saving the money in an IRA, American consumers were telling the world that we'd rather spend than save. And the American government's massive budget deficit was also sending the same message.

In essence, borrowing money to pay for excess consumption of U.S. goods and services eliminates the possibility of exporting those goods and services; basically, exports are crowded out by the behavior of the spendthrift American government and consumers. It's a bit like owning a bread shop and eating up half the loaves before they can be sold elsewhere.

When a country imports more than it exports, the current account deficit, which measures total trade in goods and services, is bound to increase. And to finance that deficit, the U.S. dollars sent abroad to pay for the extra imports have to come back into the United States somehow. This can happen in only two ways: by convincing foreigners to buy American companies and products or to buy U.S. government securities. Essentially, the trillions of dollars of government bonds issued by the U.S. Treasury have to be financed by someone, and the world's exporting nations—

flush with American dollars earned from the sales of exports to the United States—often end up being the biggest buyers of U.S. government securities. Essentially, the extra goods imported to the United States are balanced out by the purchase of U.S. Treasury bonds by foreigners.

The furor over currency manipulation in recent years has often been based more on political grandstanding than economic reality. And the practice of looking only at bilateral trade flows gives a flawed picture. Over the years, in fact, Mexico's and China's economies have been evolving from a low-wage, factory-based model to one where parts are imported and assembled and then sold abroad. By the late 2010s, for example, less than 30 percent of Chinese exports to the United States reflected Chinese content. Smartphones, among other iconic Chinese products sold to the United States, were often being assembled from parts brought in from neighboring countries where wages were even lower than in China. This led China to run persistent trade deficits with many countries, even while it was running a trade surplus with the United States.

By focusing solely on the bilateral trade deficit in goods and services, those calling for trade wars at all costs are ignoring many economic advantages inherent in a well-functioning trade system. With 1.3 billion consumers with rising incomes, for example, the Chinese market, when penetrated effectively, would be a much more lucrative market for U.S. exporters than Japan, the European Union, or other mature economies like Canada or Australia.

Also, with global markets shifting to an increased demand for more advanced products, such as self-driving cars, robotics, and other high-tech equipment—areas in which the United States excels—it becomes obvious that going to war over currency manipulation is not the most rational long-term economic choice.

13

The Fear of Investing: Is It Keeping Us Poor?

Financial ruin for many people—including those living in relatively rich countries like Spain, the United Kingdom, and the United States—is often just one paycheck away. By 2020, for example, the average American had less than $1,000 in total available savings. Around the world, most people's proverbial rainy-day funds, intended to cover unexpected costs like medical expenses or even a happy retirement, usually aren't enough to pay the next month's bills.

Despite overwhelming evidence that a diversified portfolio of stocks and bonds is one of the best ways to invest for our future, the vast majority of adults in the world economy have never owned a single share. Even young adults in the developed countries are more likely to invest in cryptocurrencies like bitcoin than in the much stabler stock markets of the world. Even today, on average, women—including those with high-paying jobs and with responsibility for overseeing their families' financial well-being—are much less prone to invest their savings in stocks and bonds than men are, which means that in virtually every developed country in the world economy, women end up with a smaller amount of invested savings. In the United Kingdom, women's nest eggs are approximately one-quarter of the amount of the average man's.

The gender pay gap can explain some of this discrepancy, but even women who earn more than men often limit their investments to cash or money-market savings accounts with low interest payments that often don't even keep up with inflation. The "real" return on these low-interest investments—when adjusted for the reduction in purchasing power caused by inflation—often ends up being negative. Stocks, however, over the last half century have provided an average return approaching 10 percent per year, well above the average inflation rate in most countries.

The reluctance of many people to invest is due to the seemingly complicated nature of building and holding a stock and bond portfolio. In reality, investing in a stock or bond is not all that different from buying a house or choosing a cell phone plan. Essentially, a share of stock is a title to partial ownership of a company. Anyone who owns a share of a company owns part of the company, referred to as *equity*. If the company makes a profit, the shareholder will benefit one way or another. Whenever a company makes a profit, for example, the managers of the company can choose to pay the profit to the shareholders in the form of a *dividend,* a cash payment that is credited to the shareholder's bank, or the money can be retained within the company, thereby increasing the total value of the company—which often leads to a rise in the company's share price.

In the twenty-first century, most stock is issued and traded electronically, but the concept is the same as it always has been: the owner of a stock owns a share of the company, and its profits, until that stock is sold to someone else. Ownership of a bond, however, is vastly different in that bond owners don't own anything except the "loan" or "IOU" that the bond represents. The issuer of a bond—a company, a government, or other organization—simply agrees to pay back the money loaned with interest at a certain point in the future.

An equity investment is generally considered to be riskier than a bond. If the company incurs a loss, or future losses loom, the company's share price can decline considerably. In contrast, a bond's return is usually known in advance; most bonds have fixed interest payments and a fixed date on which the bond's original purchase price, its nominal value, is repaid.

To reward investors for the extra risk of equity investment, stocks generally provide a higher return than bonds. Barring a major market meltdown like those that occurred in 1929 and 2008, over time, stocks provide an average return on investment that is much higher than most fixed-income securities, such as Treasury bonds or time deposits at a local bank. For example, someone investing $1,000 into the stocks that made up the Standard & Poor's Index at the end of World War II would have seen their original money rise to almost $1 million today because of the effect of exponential growth where profit is earned on earlier profits. For this reason, many financial advisers will recommend that long-term investments, such as retirement funds, be placed mainly in the stock market, where the potential for long-term yield is greater. It is generally recommended that short-term investments, such as a vacation fund, be placed in more conservative vehicles such as bonds, which tend to be less volatile.

As financial markets around the world have expanded to offer an ever-widening palette of investment options, we are increasingly required to have a high level of financial literacy. From defined contribution (DC) plans to individual retirement accounts (IRAs), from credit card borrowing to payday loans, we are being offered more and more options to save and invest. But in many parts of the world, people lack the wherewithal to make simple financial calculations.

For example, a duo of economists at the National Bureau of Economic Research in Massachusetts, Annamaria Lusardi and Olivia Mitchell, asked people from around the world three simple questions. More than half of the people in almost every advanced economy were unable to answer all three questions correctly. They were asked to perform three simple calculations related to interest rates, inflation, and diversification of investments.

The three questions were

Suppose you had $100 in a savings account and the interest rate was 2% per year. After five years, how much do you think you would have in the account if you left the money to grow: (a) more than $102, (b) exactly $102, (c) less than $102? (d) Do not know, refuse to answer.

Imagine that the interest rate on your savings account was 1% per year and inflation was 2% per year. After one year, would you be able to buy: (a) more than, (b) exactly the same as, or (c) less than today with the money in this account? (d) Do not know; refuse to answer.

Do you think that the following statement is (a) true, (b) false, or (c) do not know; refuse to answer? "Buying a single company stock usually provides a safer return than a stock mutual fund."

The correct answers were 1-**a**, 2-**c**, 3-**b**.

In the United States, only 30 percent of the respondents could answer all three questions correctly. Germany and Switzerland were the only countries where more than half of the respondents answered the questions correctly, while in Russia, only 4 percent of the people surveyed could get the right answers. Even in countries with reputations for having financially savvy citizens—such as Sweden and Japan—only approximately 25 percent of the respondents aced the quiz.

In a world where many of us are only a paycheck away from bankruptcy, every financial decision is critical. But if we aren't able to grasp that paying down our credit card debt will make a vast difference to our bottom line—with many plans charging us up to 40 percent interest annually, the amount we owe keeps compounding—we will be unable to guarantee a safe and happy future for ourselves and our families.

To make it easier to invest, stock indexes do much of the work of diversification for us, especially if we invest in exchange-traded funds (ETFs) that buy every share in an index and sell the package to us with much lower management costs than normal stock funds. A typical stock index chooses a limited number of shares, expecting that their performance will replicate the performance of all the shares in any given market. Think of a farmer who goes out to check on the progress of the crops every once in a while. Instead of checking every plant in the field, it's usually easier to take a few representative samples to get an idea of how the crop is progressing. Stock indexes use the same principle, calculating the "average" of a group of representative stocks to give investors an idea of how the market as a whole is doing.

List 13.1

List of the World's Major Stock Indexes

Australia, Sydney: All Ordinaries Index
Brazil, São Paulo: Bovespa (Bolsa de Valores de São Paulo)

Canada, Toronto: S&P/TSX (Standard & Poor's and Toronto Stock Exchange)

China: Shenzhen Composite Index

Europe: EURO STOXX 50

France, Paris: CAC-40 (Cotation Assistée en Continu—Continuous Assisted Quote)

Germany, Frankfurt: DAX (Deutscher Aktienindex)

Hong Kong: Hang Seng Index (compiled by Hang Seng Bank)

Italy, Milan: S&P / FTSE MIB Index (Standard & Poor's and Financial Times Milan Stock Exchange—Borsa di Milano Index)

Israel, Tel Aviv: TA 35 Index

Japan, Tokyo: TOPIX (Tokyo Stock Price Index)

Mexico, Mexico City: IPC Index (Indice de Precios y Cotizaciones Index)

MSCI World Index (after Morgan Stanley gave up control of the index in 2009, it is now managed independently)

Netherlands, Amsterdam: AEX Index (Amsterdam Exchange Index)

Poland, Warsaw: WIG20 (Warszawski Indeks Giełdowy—Warsaw Stock Exchange Index)

Russia, Moscow: RTS Index (Russian Trading System Index)

Singapore: Straits Times Index (index started by *Straits Times* newspaper)

South Korea, Seoul: KOSPI (Korea Composite Stock Price Index)

Spain, Madrid: IBEX 35 (Iberian Index)

Switzerland, Zurich: SMI (Swiss Market Index)

United Kingdom, London: FTSE 100 (joint venture between *Financial Times* and London Stock Exchange)

United States, New York: Dow Jones Industrial Average

United States, New York: NASDAQ (primarily technology stocks, founded by the National Association of Securities Dealers in 1971)
United States, New York: Standard & Poor's 500

The twenty-first-century economy has opened up a whole universe of possibilities for investment. And we all are investors in one way or another, even if we don't own a single stock or bond. The money that pension funds and college endowments earn from their international investments ends up financing our homes, health care, dorm rooms, or wheelchairs when we get old.

As individuals, we can also invest directly, taking advantage of a whole series of new products that make investing as easy as putting money in our bank account or using an app on our smartphone. Some apps, such as Stockpile and Bump, for example, allow us to buy fractional shares of stock, allowing us to own as little as $5 worth of stocks in companies we deal with on a daily basis, such as Starbucks and Chipotle. Some allow us to send gift cards containing partial shares of stocks. And some, such as Acorns, round up our credit card purchases to the nearest dollar and invest the change in a diversified portfolio, automatically. In a world where many shares can cost more than $1,000, the ability to break up our investments into smaller, easy-to-manage amounts allows us to invest easily and on a daily basis. And over time, these small amounts can grow enormously.

Using the "Early Money Is Like Yeast" theory, originally used in political fund-raising, money that is invested early in a person's life tends to grow exponentially. Acorns, for example, gives young investors the option of depositing an extra amount in the "piggy bank," pointing out that as little as $25 per week invested at age twenty-five would grow to approximately $300,000 by age seventy. This is made possible by *compounded returns*—where the ongoing income of a well-diversified portfolio can be reinvested and thereby generates ever-increasing returns over time. Another vastly underutilized investment option is tax-deferred retirement savings accounts, allowing the money deposited to grow tax-free. Many of these accounts, when invested in a well-diversified stock portfolio, can provide the bulk of a person's retirement funds— especially when the money deposited is matched by employer contributions.

As foreign markets have expanded their role in the world economy, smart investors have begun to expand their portfolios internationally as well. Investors can now go online and buy shares in foreign markets with little more effort than it takes to buy shares in their home country. Many web or app-based investment accounts now allow us to buy foreign shares and pay for them using our own currency. In North America, for example, you can buy American depositary receipts (ADRs), stock certificates that are created by banks that buy shares of a foreign company and place them on deposit in the United States. These ADRs give the holder the right to the underlying share just as if they owned it outright. When the foreign share changes its value, the stock certificate changes its value in tandem.

First-time investors in the global marketplace may want to choose a managed fund, benefiting from the expertise of market professionals. A mutual fund, for example, allows investors to diversify their investments across a wide range of stocks or bonds or other securities, ensuring that a sharp loss in any one investment will have little effect on the total return. Mutual funds, such as those sold by Vanguard and Fidelity, use professional managers to choose the right mix of securities for which they are paid a fee, consisting of a percentage of the amount of money under management and, in some cases, an eventual bonus if the fund does well.

There are many types of funds available for investors in the expanding world economy, each responding to a specific goal or area of interest. Some funds may concentrate investments in emerging markets, small companies, or blue chips—the top-rated companies in any given sector. Other funds may concentrate on investing in companies specializing in cryptocurrencies, or farming, real estate, or sustainability. Country funds and regional funds also provide investors with the opportunity to focus their investments in particular countries or regions of the world.

Generally, funds managed by professionals, who understand the individual markets and securities, are more successful than the average investor. The downside is that the management fees can eat into the total return, sometimes leaving only a small portion of the profit for the investor. Exchange-traded funds, therefore, have become an increasingly popular way for investors to limit volatility and reduce the fees charged by traditional mutual funds. Because most of these ETF funds are not managed per se but are based on investing in all the shares that make up a particular index such as the S&P 500, investors can avoid the loads, or traditionally high fees, that traditional fund managers charge. ETFs provide investors with a wide range of options, investing in many indexes and markets around the world. Many allow for small investors to put in as little as a hundred dollars and charge smaller fees, or in some cases no fees at all.

Politically or socially conscious investors, including many college endowment funds, prefer to invest their money in a way that corresponds to their values. A socially conscious fund manager may insist on investing only in companies that guarantee nondiscrimination for race, sex, or sexual orientation. Others may insist that the companies they invest in respect the principles of sustainability by recycling all materials or planting a tree for every one that is harvested in the production process.

Although it is difficult to find companies that are 100 percent in tune with investors' social or environmental goals, many funds choose to buy shares of companies that are the "best in their group"—doing the least amount of damage to the environment or having the highest scores for respecting workers' rights.

Just as it would be limiting to shop at only one store, it's increasingly obvious in the twenty-first century that investing solely in your local currency and local markets is financially unwise. The diversification and opportunities that investing abroad provides allow us to better ensure that we have the financial wherewithal to weather the economic turmoil of the years ahead. With the precarious financial state of some local pension plans—including national plans in countries with declining birthrates and exploding levels of retirees—it's increasingly important for us, as prudent investors, to put our assets where they can provide the best returns and ensure our financial future.

14

Comparing Investments in the New World Economy

Naked swimmers, to paraphrase the respected investor Warren Buffett, only get exposed when the tide goes out. During the disastrous crash of 2008, a lot of skinny-dippers were discovered in the world's financial marketplaces. Not least was the respected fund manager Bernie Madoff who, over decades, had been running a Ponzi scheme, using new investors' money to provide generous and stable returns to those who came before.

What made most of the investors' losses especially tragic was that they were looking for "safe" ways to invest. By providing a constant yield of several percentage points above inflation, the scam succeeded in attracting precisely those who wanted to avoid the risks of a constantly fluctuating market. Minimizing risk and still getting a high return for your investment should be the goal of any investor, whether it be a college pension fund or a single mother setting aside money for her family's future. But how do we decide what is the best investment for us?

The first question most investors should ask is this: What are the chances that I could lose some or all of my money? A bond investor, for example, needs to know not only whether the interest will be paid on time but whether the principal, or the amount of money originally invested, will be paid back as well. Leading up to the 2008 crash, those investing in mortgage-backed securities saw their investments crumble when the underlying assets became worthless and the bonds lost value; many had to be completely written off.

How can we predict what will be a good investment? Examining financial documents from diverse international companies and borrowers is a daunting task for anyone, no matter how knowledgeable. Most investors, therefore, have come to rely on ratings agencies to help them judge the risks of companies and countries around the world. The world's largest ratings agencies—Standard & Poor's, Moody's Investors Service, and Fitch Ratings—are paid by companies and borrowers to provide an easy-to-understand rating, ranging from a low grade like F or CCC for extremely risky investments to a high grade like AAA for the most reliable investments. When the United States began taking on extremely high levels of debt in the 2010s, for example, it lost its coveted triple-A rating.

After the 2008 crash, many credit ratings agencies came under heavy criticism for their failure to adequately judge the credit worthiness of the countless new and complex securities being sold, bearing such obtuse names as CDOs (collateralized debt obligations) and SIVs (structured investment vehicles). The banks that issued these securities and the credit agencies that rated them were involved in one of the biggest scams in the world of international finance. By the late 2010s, the ratings agencies agreed to pay billions of dollars in penalties for their malfeasance after having been sued by countless investors and investigated by the U.S. Department of Justice.

The credit ratings agencies originally blamed flawed computer programs that were used to analyze the new securities, saying that no one ever imagined that housing would decline in every U.S. market at the same time. As it turned out, many insiders admitted that the agencies were more interested in earning money and keeping market share than in making investors' welfare their priority. When the real estate market began to decline in the years leading up to the crash, the ratings agencies didn't change the AAA ratings of bonds containing thousands of risky subprime mortgages. Many of the securities originally rated AAA ended up being classified as *junk*, which refers to any bond rated below Baa or BBB.

Table 14.1

Rating Risk

	Moody's	S&P	Duff & Phelps
Investment grade	Aaa	AAA	AAA
	Aa	AA	AA
	A	A	A
	Baa	BBB	BBB
Speculative	Ba	BB	BB
	B	B	B
Very risky	Caa, Ca, C	CCC, CC	CCC, CC, C

When investing internationally, it's not enough to just look at the financial solvency of a company or bond issuer. We have to consider the credit risk of the country itself. Basically, a country's sovereign rating is almost always better than that of any company within the country. This is because the government, in theory, will always be the last entity to go bankrupt. If things get really bad in any given economy, a company's assets can always be seized by the government, or the company's value could be eroded by increased taxes or diminished by runaway inflation if the government prints loads of new money in a last-ditch effort to avoid bankruptcy.

A truly global company with a lot of assets abroad can often be a better credit risk than the country it is domiciled in. Nestlé, for example, has many more operations abroad than in its home country of Switzerland. Valuing and comparing companies and investments is always a difficult exercise, especially when you have to add in international variations in accounting systems, currencies, and sometimes even economic systems.

How can you compare an investment in Japanese stocks to the purchase of a vacation house in Costa Rica? How can you compare the purchase of a Brazilian corporate bond to the purchase of a U.S. Treasury security? Just as two vineyards can be compared by looking at their yield in any given year, international investments can be evaluated by looking at their total return, also referred to as *yield*. In economic terms, yield is the total increase in value of an asset over time, including payments of dividends and interest. If a bond paying a high interest rate goes up in value, it would show a higher yield than the same amount of money placed under a mattress or kept in a bank vault.

Most people prefer to compare international investments by translating all yields into a common currency. This *currency of reference* is usually the investor's home currency. For example, the Yale University endowment fund, which invests billions abroad, begins by translating all those international investments into U.S.-dollar values to see how they stack up against one another. In this way, the yield of any one investment can be easily compared to all the others.

Table 14.2

What Would $10,000 Invested in 2015 Have Yielded by 2020?

	U.S. dollar value after 5 years	Yield
Bitcoin	$336,490.11	3,264.9%
Tech stocks (NASDAQ-100)	$19,239.02	92.4%
U.S. stocks (Dow Jones Industrials)	$16,434.52	64.3%
U.S. stocks (S&P 500)	$15,622.82	56.2%
Japanese stocks (Nikkei)	$14,411.86	44.1%
Chinese stocks (Hang Seng)	$13,072.56	30.7%
Brazilian stocks (Bovespa)	$13,017.81	30.2%
U.S. single-family house	$12,662.99	26.6%
Gold	$12,630.51	26.3%
European stocks (Stoxx 600)	$11,448.34	14.5%
Emerging-market stocks (MSCI)	$11,442.27	14.4%
Oil (Brent Crude)	$10,420.37	4.2%
U.S. Treasury bonds (10Y)	$10,287.12	2.9%
Kept under a mattress	$10,000	0%
Diamonds	$9,080	-9.2%
Argentinian stocks (Merval)	$5,382.75	-46.2%

Source: Bloomberg, Diem Partner AG, UBS-AG

In a simple investment, such as gold or bitcoin, the yield is easily calculated by comparing the price at the end of a period to the price at the beginning. But what about a bond that has a fixed—or even floating—interest rate? Or a stock that provides large dividends in one year and none the next? Or a piece of property that goes down in value with a high property tax paid every year?

Most investors calculate yield by adding up all the gains and losses of a particular investment over time. Savvy investors plug all the gains and losses, or cash flows, into a spreadsheet or into a smartphone app like Personal Capital or Google Finance. The performance of any series of investments can then be compared according to yield or any other criteria. In the end, though, yields can only tell us what the past performance of any given investment has been, not what it will do in the future.

Analyzing and comparing investments also involves taking into consideration many other criteria. If the government of a country where we have invested collapses, or if new laws are passed to restrict trade or even prohibit the transfer of funds abroad—as many countries do when faced with massive outflows of money to more secure parts of the world—investments there may be seriously affected. During the financial meltdown following the recession of 2008, many international investors sold positions in well-managed emerging markets to cover losses in Europe and North America, leading to stock market crashes in parts of the world that ostensibly had nothing to do with the original crisis.

Despite the complexities of investing abroad, most investors still understand the importance of having an internationally diversified portfolio. The return from international investments can often outpace those of traditional markets like the United States, Germany, and Japan. When Latin America, India, China, and the other rapidly growing economies of Southeast Asia embarked on market-oriented reforms, for example, massive investments from abroad flowed in, buoying their already expanding stock markets and bringing the price/earnings ratios (P/E) of their companies more in line with the rest of the world.

The price/earnings ratio, which divides the price of a share by after-tax profit, has become a reliable measure that can help us determine when it's time to buy or sell a stock. Stock market bubbles can sometimes be predicted by looking at price/earnings averages in specific markets. Markets with companies with P/E levels close to historic averages—say, from 10 to 20—tend to be stable. When P/E ratios go outside normal bounds, trouble may be on the way. When the dot-com bubble burst in 2000, for example, the NASDAQ index of high-tech stocks were trading at P/E levels well above 50.

Growth stocks—shares of companies that are expected to grow significantly over the coming years—tend to have a higher P/E ratio because earnings are usually lower than for stocks of established companies. Their higher price reflects the expectation of higher earnings in the future. Health care or high-tech companies are often considered growth companies because the high-tech field is expected to grow significantly in the years to come, as opposed to "value stocks," such as those in banking or manufacturing that are based in more mature markets. The P/E ratio of some of the so-called FANG stocks, comprising four of the world's largest technology companies—Facebook, Amazon, Netflix, and Alphabet (Google's parent company)—reached astronomical levels by the end of the 2010s, exceeding P/E ratios of 300 in some cases.

In the end, investors need to pay attention to a wide array of indicators, not just ratings or yield levels, to survive and prosper in the new world economy. Balance sheets, profit and loss statements, country risk rankings, credit ratings, currency risk, and the like all play a part, and no one criterion can tell us whether an investment is wise or foolish. Even though long-term diversified investing is by far the best way to prepare for our financial futures, as the Romans said over two thousand years ago, caveat emptor: "Let the buyer beware."

15

Income Inequality: Is It Inevitable?

With the wealth of the world's twenty six richest people estimated to exceed the combined wealth of more than half of the
rest of the world's population, income inequality has become one
of the major concerns of the twenty-first-century economy. Just
within the United States, the disparity between the haves and the
have-nots reached such a level by the end of the 2010s that the average employee in many companies would have had to work more
than three centuries to earn what the average CEO earned in one
year. The political and social repercussions have only begun to be
felt. The resentment harbored by many workers and underemployed people is leading to voters taking radical stands that would
have been unheard of a few decades ago, with fringe populist parties gaining power and autocrats calling for a new world order.

Making matters worse, in many countries, the possibilities for
mobility—the ability to work your way out of poverty and move
up the social and economic ladder—are actually decreasing. It is
no wonder that *unfair* is one of the words manipulative politicians

use most when angling for the support of resentful workers. Even though many developing countries from Brazil to India to China have recently brought hundreds of millions of people out of poverty, in most developed countries, the possibility to exceed the income level of our parents' generation is disappearing.

The most common measure of mobility is called *intergenerational income elasticity*, or IGE. It indicates the probability that a child's income will be significantly different from their parents' income. An IGE of 0 implies high mobility, and an IGE of 1 indicates that the child will end up with virtually the same income level as their parent. Over the past fifty years, the IGE in the United States has gone from 0.3 to more than 0.5, indicating a severely declining level of mobility, one of the worst levels of any developed economy. The so-called Great Gatsby curve shows that income mobility tends to increase in countries with low levels of income inequality. In Denmark and Norway, for example, where there is less income disparity, it is much easier to move up the economic ladder. In countries like Brazil and the United States, with high levels of wealth inequality, being born rich means that you will probably die rich. And those born to poor families rarely are able to move up the economic ladder.

While immobility and inequality don't necessarily go hand in hand, they are often correlated. Like immobility, income inequality can also be measured, using the Gini coefficient, which assigns a score of 0 to countries with perfect equality (utopia, for most observers) and a score of 100 to a country with complete inequality—essentially one where a single household holds all the wealth. Sweden, with a relatively low level of inequality, had a Gini coefficient of approximately 24.9 at the end of the 2010s, while South Africa, with one of the highest levels of inequality (even after the end of apartheid) had a Gini coefficient of 62. The United States had one of the worst levels of income inequality seen in developed countries, with a Gini coefficient of 45.

Table 15.1

Gini Coefficient Inequality Rankings for Selected Countries
(most inequality: 100; least inequality: 0)

1	Lesotho 63.2	95	India 35.2
2	South Africa 62.5	116	United Kingdom 32.4
9	Hong Kong 53.9	117	Canada 32.1
14	Panama 50.7	121	Italy 31.9
15	Chile 50.5	134	Australia 30.3
19	Brazil 49.0	135	Switzerland 29.5
29	China 46.5	136	France 29.3
39	United States 45.0	137	Denmark 29.0
54	Argentina 41.7	141	Iceland 28.0
57	Russia 41.2	144	Germany 27.0
78	Japan 37.9	146	Norway 26.8
88	New Zealand 36.2	152	Sweden 24.9
93	South Korea 35.7		

The global income gap is much more than a Gini or IGE number, however. The disparate income levels also reflect an immense gap in quality of life. In the poorer regions of India, for example, more than a third of all women have never been taught to read. And in sub-Saharan Africa, electricity shortages affect poor areas disproportionately, causing havoc with everything from food storage to operations in local hospitals. In the United States, those living with lower income levels are three times more likely to suffer from obesity, diabetes, heart disease, and liver disease than those in the upper income levels. The so-called deaths of despair—suicides and diseases mainly caused by alcohol or drug abuse—are taking an increasing toll on those in the lower percentiles of household income.

Racial differences are also a major element of income inequality in many countries, such as Brazil, South Africa, and the United States. According to the Pew Research Center, African Americans, Hispanics, and other minorities, representing more than 35 percent of the total U.S. population, made up less than 10 percent of the top 10 percent of households ranked by wealth. To make matters worse, since minority salaries are almost always lower than white salaries in most countries—even when workers have an equivalent level of education—those at the lower income levels have to spend a much higher percentage of their money on basics such as food and transportation. In addition, many people at lower income levels are surrounded by people with constant financial needs and may feel obligated to provide short-term loans to help pay for a family member's schooling or health care, many of which are never paid back.

Most of those at the lower income levels are therefore unable to build a nest egg of their own by buying a home or investing in a portfolio of stocks or bonds. The Billie Holiday song "God Bless the Child," written at the end of the Great Depression, begins with: "Them that's got shall have / Them that's not shall lose"—words that are equally appropriate today when describing the predicament faced by many at the bottom of the economic ladder. In America, like many other parts of the world, ownership of capital—essentially owning your own home or investing in stocks and bonds—is the biggest factor in achieving lasting financial security.

Even a small nest egg, such as a gift from a person's parents at the beginning of their working career, can play a huge role in creating the wealth needed for retirement in later years. For someone today to become a millionaire in fifteen years, assuming an average return of 8 percent per year, it is estimated that they would need to save almost $3,000 per month. For someone starting with as little as $20,000 in savings, it would be necessary to save only approximately $1,300 per month, less than half of what would be required for people with no head start.

Since many low-income people don't have the extra cash to afford to purchase a home or invest in the stock market, they stay in the lower income levels indefinitely. In the United States, for example, the median net worth of white families, approximately $170,000 at the end of the 2010s, was roughly ten times the net worth of African American families. And since most extra capital is invested over the long term, it tends to grow exponentially, bringing even more wealth to those with money to invest. A typical investment in the stock market, for example, has traditionally provided an average return of almost 10 percent per year, even after factoring in the effect of inflation. Having a large capital reserve also allows families at the top of the economic spectrum to invest in other long-term ventures, such as education, insurance, and quality health care.

On a global scale, the debt trap of many low-income countries eerily resembles the problems between the haves and the have-nots within each country. The crushing burden of servicing foreign debt, representing more than the total GDP of many countries, often prevents debtor nations from investing in education and infrastructure. Funds for good teachers and schools throughout the developing world, consequently, are sorely lacking—and without a well-educated workforce, many countries are unable to compete in the new global economy.

Many countries, such as India and Brazil, have chosen to protect their economies from the uncertain forces of global trade by putting up barriers to trade. An iPhone in Brazil, for example, often ends up costing double what it would cost in New York or Miami. The result is that these countries lose out on the many advantages of free trade and consequently don't have sufficient funds to spend on education and infrastructure. Much of the money generated within the closed economy ends up in the pockets of an affluent elite controlling local banks and manufacturers, further exacerbating inequality. In contrast, China chose the path of opening its economy to the world, with a strategy based on low-skill manufacturing for export, allowing them to invest massively in infrastructure and education. By the late 2010s, China's share of the world's income had grown from 3 percent to 20 percent, bringing hundreds of millions out of poverty and reducing income inequality, at least temporarily.

For the rest of the developing world, debt reduction is often seen as the only way to allow them to grow and prosper. Making the problem much worse is the fact that much of the funds borrowed by developing countries have been squandered through mismanagement or corruption. The return to financial health is usually achieved by first reducing the interest payments on foreign debt, which often exceeds developing countries' expenditures on health and education. Canceling the debt or rescheduling it—which means delaying repayment of loans until the economy is in better health—can help governments devote precious resources to development instead of making payments to lenders. But debt reduction is only one step in the process. What happens after the debt burden has been removed? How does the country access new funds for further growth?

One of the most effective steps in encouraging economic development in the poorer countries of the world is to provide opportunities for people to sell their goods and services abroad. To reduce global inequality, it's necessary for consumers in rich countries to encourage imports from the poorer parts of the world instead of turning their backs on imports from low-wage countries. Obviously, environmental rules and respect for workers' rights need to be constantly verified. In the end, any job, even a relatively low-paying one by Western standards, is often the best hope for a worker in the developing world to start building a better life.

Proper job training is also a sine qua non for sustainable development and a reduction in income inequality. Without proper training for the children of the developing world, there can be no hope for a more equitable distribution of income. Educating girls, for example, has often been a low priority in many countries but has been shown to be one of the best development investments a country can make. In some countries, as incredible as it may seem, millions of girls are not even sent to school. Statistics show that girls who have had some schooling, even just to the primary level, are able to increase family income significantly and are also more likely to have children who survive infancy, are healthy in later years, and receive a proper education when they reach school age.

In the wealthy countries of the world, education is also one of the most promising factors in reducing inequality. In many countries, limited educational opportunity results in a poorly educated underclass sinking further and further into poverty, while those with advanced education get all the high-skilled jobs created by the new digital economy. With more than half the graduates of top universities going into extremely high-paying jobs—mainly in the areas of technology, finance, management consulting, medicine, and law—the distribution of wealth is getting worse.

In many countries, it is estimated that those at the top, especially those at the top 10–20 percent of income levels, are amassing an ever-greater share of the world's wealth. In theory, those with incomes in top income brackets should pay a higher tax rate. Those earning more than a million dollars, for example, would pay a higher marginal tax rate—say, 50 percent on the extra income instead of the lower tax rate paid on income at the lower thresholds. But in many countries, this is not the case.

Nobel Prize–winning economist Joseph Stiglitz has noted that with more than 90 percent of all income growth going to the wealthiest 1 percent of Americans, the United States at the end of the 2010s has become a country of extremes with the rich getting ever richer and the poor struggling to get by. He blames, among other factors, the demise of labor unions, the increasing role of finance and banking in the economy, and the lack of wealth-building opportunities in minority communities. With robots and artificial intelligence replacing low-skill jobs, the emphasis will have to be on educating workers to fill newly created jobs in areas such as customer service, data analysis, and so on.

Governments can help by providing tax incentives for companies to retrain those being replaced by technology. Some people—including Microsoft founder Bill Gates, among others—have proposed putting taxes on robots to provide the funds necessary to retrain those losing their jobs. In Germany, for example, the government funds extensive worker-training programs, beginning at the high school level, in an effort to prevent large-scale layoffs and, in the process, prepare the economy to be ready for everything the future has to offer.

Other possible solutions for reducing income inequality, in the United States and elsewhere, include radically altering tax policy to reduce the advantages that allow those with investments to keep getting richer while those at the bottom struggle. It is estimated that in the United States, the total federal tax expenditures on deductions for everything from mortgage interest to employer-sponsored health plans and retirement savings is more than the entire cost of Medicare or Medicaid—essential tools for providing health care to the less advantaged.

In the end, the most effective method for reducing inequality could be for governments to simply increase taxes on those at the top. This can be done mainly through the use of progressive taxation whereby some of the extra wealth of those earning more could be used to supplement the salaries of those earning less. At the extreme, a minimum income, sometimes referred to as *universal basic income* (UBI), can be used to reduce inequality even more. However, not allowing people to keep the rewards of their hard work could create a disincentive to working harder or striving to discover innovative solutions to the world's problems—important activities that may end up helping us all, rich and poor alike.

16

What Is Hot Money?

Hot money is usually defined as currency being invested abroad for short-term gains. The problem with hot money is that it can come on at a moment's notice—when interest rates in one country rise significantly higher than in the others, for example—but can leave just as quickly. Pension funds or wealthy university endowment funds—Yale and Harvard both had more than $30 billion to invest by the end of the 2010s—are constantly looking for favorable returns, moving short-term funds from Japan to India to Germany to Mexico, looking for the most lucrative investments as markets and interest rates change. It is estimated that at any given moment in the twenty-first-century economy, trillions of dollars' worth of hot money funds are being invested, easily dwarfing the total economic value of most countries in the world. For comparison's sake, the value of all the world's gold ever mined since the days of King Solomon would be only a small fraction of the value of investments in the world's short-term markets.

Like all financial players, the owners of this speculative flood of money are simply looking for a favorable return on their invest-ments. Generally, hot money investors are looking to park their funds for a short period of time in countries where the current rates or potential for currency appreciation look better than in the investors' home markets. Usually, hot money flows from rich, developed countries in times of stability—with low interest rates and slowly growing economies—to countries in the developing world with better prospects for growth. Over the past years, hot money has flowed into such diverse countries as Brazil, India, China, Turkey, and Malaysia.

Hot money inflows usually provide the liquidity for more lending in the host country, with cheaper money leading to in-creased business investment and consumer spending. With sound monetary policies and market-oriented reforms turning many developing countries into economic powerhouses, investors from around the world come running. These hot money players can include banks, hedge funds, and other high-profile investors, such as sovereign wealth funds or even college endowments. For ex-ample, the California Public Employees' Retirement System, one of the biggest single investors in the world, has billions of dollars to invest in the world's markets. Its decision to move into or out of a particular sector affects markets abroad as well as the financial well-being of retirees from Palm Springs to Sacramento.

In the short term, if all goes well, hot money investors make a tidy profit and then move on to more lucrative markets. But the macroeconomic effects in the countries receiving large amounts of hot money can be disastrous. Higher inflation and appreciat-ing currency exchange rates can lead to current account deficits, with exports falling because of the increased price of goods and services sold abroad. Like most interconnected activity in today's global economy, small investment decisions in one remote corner of the world can affect the global marketplace.

When interest rates rise in the United States—as they did in

2018, for example—a hot money investor may decide to sell shares of an emerging-market stock fund to take advantage of the changes coming out of Washington. That decision then sets into motion a chain of events that can be felt in a small village in Argentina. By giving the order to redeem $100,000 of an emerging-market stock fund, the investor—and others making the same decision—forces the fund manager to sell some of the shares in the fund to pay departing clients. This can lead to a rapid rise in interest rates in Argentina to keep the currency from depreciating further. A shop owner in the back streets of Buenos Aires, therefore, may then be forced to pay more for floating rate loans from the local bank. As more investors get on the bandwagon, the outflow of hot money can lead to a local recession or worse.

Financial panics often feed on themselves, causing foreign creditors and investors—even those without hot money interests—to pull investments out of a country in order to preserve their assets in safer areas of the world. In many cases, the only way for the host country to stop the vicious spiral is to put up barriers to the unlimited outflow of money. Capital controls, used by countries around the world from China to Venezuela, often succeed in the short term. But long-term funds may dry up when investment managers in London or New York fear that they will not be able to easily get their money back.

Some world leaders have called for the imposition of new laws to stop unlimited flows of hot money, arguing that they can cause too much political and social upheaval. Some have even called for the imposition of special taxes on hot money flows. One example is the Tobin tax, named after the Nobel Prize–winning economist James Tobin. This special tax—originally proposed only for currency transactions—could be applied to all global flows of speculative money, thereby reducing the volume of funds moving in and out of the world's markets. The money raised by this tax, theoretically, could then be used for economic assistance and social investments in the developing world.

Early proponents of a financial transaction tax (FTT), including the renowned economist John Maynard Keynes at the beginning of the twentieth century, viewed it primarily as a way to reduce volatility in the world's markets and reduce unbridled speculation. After the 2008 crash, many European Union countries called for an FTT as a way to pay back the costs of the financial bailouts of banks by EU governments. Later proponents—such as the U.S. Democratic Party candidates in 2016 and the British Labour Party in the late 2010s—called for a tax on financial transactions mainly as a way to get money from "rich" speculators, such as hedge funds and banks, to fund public services like college tuition as well as promoting growth in the developing world.

Even though approximately forty countries imposed financial transaction taxes by the mid-2010s, many were relatively innocuous "stamp duty" taxes and small fees on securities futures transactions. More extensive plans to control hot money flows, such as the proposed 1.0 percent FTT tax called for by the European Union, could have the adverse effect of reducing GDP. The amount is hard to determine, but the negative effect of a broad financial transaction tax has been estimated by some to be as much as 1–2 percent of total economic growth.

Opponents of taxes on hot money flows say that it is basically a losing battle, because the amount raised would actually be offset by reduced general taxes due to reduced economic growth, leading to a net loss for cash-strapped governments. The fear of some leaders, including the mayor of London, is that any financial center that imposes a foreign transaction tax could cause an exodus of transactions to another part of the world where there isn't one.

In any event, with economic and political turmoil occurring

around the world at a dizzying pace, the ability of any one country to control or significantly influence the maelstrom of forces buffeting the economic landscape—including the massive flows of hot money from one part of the world to another—will be increasingly limited in the years to come.

17

Barbarians at the Gate? Private
Equity Investors, Venture Capitalists,
and High-Frequency Traders

From *The Great Gatsby* to *Pretty Woman,* books, movies, and countless soap operas have portrayed financial tycoons as all-powerful
players who take advantage of capitalism to make a fortune at the
expense of others. Leonardo DiCaprio's character in *The Wolf of
Wall Street,* for example, runs a fraudulent operation to trade in
penny stocks that eventually turns him into a financial titan before
ultimately he is thrown into jail.

But who exactly are these players, and how do they succeed in
making so much money, legally or otherwise? It used to be that the
big players used "other people's money" to make tons of their own.
They did this by borrowing large sums, using leveraged buyouts to
acquire companies with only a small amount of their own money
invested. Like a playground seesaw, a leveraged buyout gets a lot
of power out of a small investment, mainly by borrowing massive
amounts to increase the original investment's purchasing power.
The idea of a leveraged buyout was usually to break up the com-

panies and sell off the parts, sometimes making a fortune in the process—and sometimes putting a lot of people out of work.

The big players of the twenty-first century still use other people's money, but it's usually in the form of long-term investments. Hedge funds, venture capital firms, and high-frequency traders all have big investors behind them—banks, pension funds, or even individuals—who put up large sums of money hoping that the experts will work their magic and make everyone a lot of money. The idea is that the experts running the funds will use their special skills to make the companies they invest in more profitable—either by increasing efficiency or by restructuring the companies' finances—making them much more valuable. Generally, hedge fund and venture capital investors are considered to be more sophisticated and market savvy than normal investors. Even banks have created hedge funds, using the enormous wealth they manage—hundreds of billions of dollars in some cases—to invest in the world economy.

What is a hedge fund? The original purpose of a normal financial hedge was to prevent losses by investing in something that would go up when other investments went down. As opposed to other investors, such as speculators or arbitrageurs who try to make a profit in the global marketplace, hedgers traditionally tried to simply keep from losing money in a rapidly fluctuating marketplace. A farmer can hedge the current year's crop of wheat, for example, by buying financial futures that lock in next year's price, allowing the farmer and the farmer's bank to sleep more soundly. The irony is that today's hedge funds are managed more aggressively than many other financial products and are primarily interested in providing investors with high returns—allowing them to benefit from, or at least weather, market fluctuations. With total funds under management worldwide of more than $3 trillion by the end of the 2010s, hedge funds have become an important subset of the investment fund universe. In recent years, however,

many top investors, such as pension funds and college endowments, have found that simpler instruments, such as exchange
traded funds—which simply invest in the stocks making up major
market indexes—can often provide better returns with significantly lower fees. Still, many believe that hedge fund managers
have a technical edge, using computers and trading algorithms to
invest in a wide array of easily bought and sold securities, consisting mainly of stocks, bonds, and derivatives. The idea is to use a
mixture of market savvy and computer power to understand markets in ways that were largely impossible before the computer age.

In some cases, hedge funds and other sophisticated traders use
high-frequency trading, making a massive number of automated
trades at extremely high speeds, spotting discrepancies and opportunities that go unseen by ordinary investors. They act on this
information by buying and/or selling securities in such volume
that they generate enormous profits—or enormous losses—for
their investors. The speed of these split-second decisions is so
crucial that many high-frequency traders put their operations in
buildings close to the major stock exchange computers, allowing
them to spot and act on shifts in the market in nanoseconds. A
high-frequency trading operation in New Jersey, for example, can
consistently beat the returns of one in the Midwest just by being
physically closer to the NASDAQ or NYSE exchanges.

Hedge funds also use such derivatives as options, futures, or
other sophisticated financial products. This allows them to make
money in both rising *and* falling markets. They find anomalies in
prices and quickly act on them, and because they buy or sell in
such large amounts, they can make big profits on small or otherwise insignificant discrepancies in the market.

Hedge funds and other high-frequency traders are often criticized for using their unique positions and computing wherewithal
to take unfair advantage of market movements. They do all of this
before the average investor can trade and benefit from new mar-

ket information, which some critics claim is tantamount to insider trading. Just as bitcoin miners with enormous computer centers have replaced small-time miners, the world's markets are becoming increasingly dominated by the big players. It has been estimated that by the late 2010s, high-frequency trading accounted for more than 40 percent of all equity trading in Europe and more than 70 percent in the United States.

Like hedge funds, private equity ventures in the twenty-first century encompass a wide range of activities, but they can generally be divided into three main areas: venture capital, growth capital, and leveraged buyouts. Basically, the words *private* and *equity* refer to the fact that almost all the ventures consist of big investors with a large amount of money to commit to purchasing privately owned companies or publicly listed companies that are being taken private. The goal of most private equity ventures is to take a large stake in companies that are perceived as good long-term investments and try to make the companies more valuable with the idea of selling the companies in the future for a hefty profit. Private equity investors usually make an up-front commitment for a certain amount of capital that can be paid out as the funds are needed.

Venture capital (or VC) investors usually take a stake in young, growing companies that are often not even on the radar of most investors in the economy as a whole. A venture capital investor that invests their own money is often referred to as an *angel*, reflecting the fact that without the investor's intervention, the fledgling company wouldn't be able to grow. Most banks and hedge funds, on the other hand, only want to finance or buy shares in companies that are publicly traded, have a track record, and, preferably, have strong earnings. Amazon, for example, took decades to show a profit and began as a small venture in Seattle funded by small contributions from friends and family of the founder, Jeff Bezos. Since many entrepreneurs don't have the money to fund their start-up's initial years of operation, they often turn to an angel investor to provide initial funding—often in the range of $50,000 to $250,000—to take the company to the next level.

The next step is often bringing in a bigger venture capital investor that can provide a much larger sum of money in exchange for a 20–30 percent share of the company. These large-scale venture capitalists traditionally use a pool of money provided by deep-pocketed individual investors or institutions such as banks or pension funds. Venture capital investors then typically provide advice and steer the company toward the holy grail of all venture capital investments: cashing out with a big profit or, even better, having the company go public with a massive increase in the value of the company's share. If everything goes as planned, the initial venture capital investors see a return of anywhere between ten and one hundred times their initial investment. Small investors don't usually have direct access to most VC opportunities, but they are increasingly being offered affordable options, such as AngelList Syndicates, which allows small investors to put as little as $1,000 into high-risk, high-return ventures that would normally be reserved for millionaires. In any event, everyone usually ends up participating in venture capital activities in one way or another since most of the world's pension funds and college endowments are turning to VC to provide the returns that pay for our retirements and our college scholarships.

Growth capital investors concentrate primarily on relatively mature companies that are looking for someone to share the risk of undertaking a major new activity, such as an acquisition, a restructuring, or a big expansion of operations. These companies may be already earning a profit, but they lack the large amounts of money required for their next step. And because banks are typically reluctant to fund risky new ventures, companies looking to grow turn to private equity funds or other growth capital investors to take them to the next level.

In many cases, private equity investors and managers ask for extensive fees for their work. These charges can sometimes reach into the billions. Like hedge funds, most private equity managers earn 1–2 percent of the money invested and a share in the profits generated, usually around 20 percent. Some countries, such as the United States, have given private equity managers an added benefit by taxing their income at the capital gains rate, which is much lower than the income tax rate. But in most cases, since the major ventures in the private equity sphere are not publicly quoted, there is no way to know how much they are really being paid.

For most private equity ventures, the investor pool is becoming increasingly public, in the sense that the major pension funds and even sovereign wealth funds investing in them are "public" entities. The Norwegian government, for example, has used its gargantuan earnings from natural-gas sales to set up a long-term sovereign wealth fund. Singapore, the United Arab Emirates, and many other cash-rich countries have done the same; even the state of Alaska has set up a fund to recycle and invest excess oil income. Many of these funds are investing large portions of their money— hundreds of billions of dollars in some cases—into the lucrative world of private equity. By the end of the 2010s, it is estimated that one in every ten U.S. workers was employed by a company in which private equity firms had major ownership, dwarfing the activities of many of the world's more traditional investors.

18

The Twenty-First-Century Company

When well-known multinationals such as the Royal Bank of Scotland and insurance giant AIG had to be bailed out by cash-strapped governments during the worldwide recession of 2008, many taxpayers complained about their governments spending hundreds of billions of dollars of their money on failing companies at a time when small companies and homeowners were allowed to go bankrupt by the hundreds of thousands. The common rationale behind "too big to fail" has been that some companies, such as General Motors, which was bailed out by the U.S. government to the tune of $10 billion in taxpayer money, are so important for the health of the economy that they can't be allowed to go out of business.

As more and more companies are surpassing in size the countries in which they do business, many are asking if companies in the twenty-first century are simply too big. A recent World Bank report listing the one hundred largest economic entities in the world has only thirty-one countries on the list; the other sixty-nine are companies. The annual revenue of Walmart, for example, is larger than the total GDP of Spain, Australia, or the Netherlands.

Table 18.1

List of World's Ten Largest Companies (Non-State Owned) by Annual Revenue (2019)

Company	Business	Headquarters	Annual revenue
Walmart	Retailer	Bentonville, Arkansas	$514 billion
Royal Dutch Shell	Oil & Gas	The Hague, Netherlands	$397 billion
British Petroleum	Oil & Gas	London, United Kingdom	$304 billion
ExxonMobil	Oil & Gas	Irving, Texas	$290 billion
Volkswagen	Automotive	Wolfsburg, Germany	$278 billion
Toyota Motor	Automotive	Toyota City, Japan	$273 billion
Apple	Technology	Cupertino, California	$266 billion
Berkshire Hathaway	Financial	Omaha, Nebraska	$248 billion
Amazon	Technology	Seattle, Washington	$233 billion

Source: *Fortune* Global 500, 2019

Most countries make a clear legal distinction between large and small companies. Generally, public companies are those that are large enough to have their shares traded on recognized stock exchanges. Smaller companies, those with their shares in the hands of a small group of investors, are usually referred to as *private* or *unlisted*. In Britain, for example, public limited companies, or PLCs, are usually quoted on major exchanges, while limited companies are not. In the United States, S corporations give businesses the advantage of limited liability without incorporation and provide investors with the advantage of being taxed only once; profits of private corporations are usually taxed only when they are paid to the company's owners.

The structure that almost every multinational uses to do business and pay taxes is based on the concept of *limited liability*, that the owners of the company are protected if the company should go bankrupt. This is reflected in the *Ltd.* that follows company names in most English-speaking countries—although in the United States, companies are commonly referred to as *LLC* and *Inc.,* or incorporated. The abbreviation *SA* in Spanish- and French-speaking countries refers to the words *Sociedad Anónima* or *Société Anonyme*, which imply the same concept as *Ltd.*—that the owners of companies are "anonymous" in that the creditors of a bankrupt company have no right to go after the shareholders' personal assets to cover the company's losses.

One of the defining characteristics of the twenty-first-century economy is how ownership of companies has shifted. It used to be that almost all investments were in the form of holding shares in publicly traded companies. Individual equity investors didn't have many other options, and the institutional investors—like pension funds and insurance companies—liked the transparency of publicly traded companies. But with the advent of private equity, more companies are moving from being quoted on publicly traded exchanges to being privately held. One of the main advantages of being privately held is that companies can avoid the problems of pesky shareholders and onerous financial reporting and run their companies in a much more private and possibly more profitable way.

Of the three entities that control a company—management, the board of directors, and the shareholders—management traditionally has been able to do things pretty much its own way, counting on tacit approval from compliant shareholders and directors. But at the beginning of the twenty-first century, things have started to change. Increasingly assertive shareholders and active board members have forced management at many companies to adapt to new ways of doing business.

After numerous scandals involving inflated CEO pay packages

and other abuses of power by corporate management, many share-holders have begun taking a more active role. For example, Volks-wagen shareholders, following the scandal of the management's directive to cheat when measuring diesel emissions in the United States and several other markets, turned on the company's direc-tors and demanded to be reimbursed for the losses incurred when the share price tumbled after the managers' malfeasance. The chief executive at the time of the scandal was even asked to return a significant portion of his salary and compensation as a penalty, in addition to facing jail time in the United States for fraud and violating the Clean Air Act.

Newly empowered shareholders are increasingly demanding a "say on pay," requiring shareholder approval of executive pay packages. Salaries and other remuneration for company manag-ers have come under increasing criticism, particularly since such company-oversight groups as the Securities and Exchange Com-mission in the United States and the European Commission now demand full disclosure of all executives' pay packages. Further-more, the European Union in the mid-2010s put a cap on the amount of bonuses that can be paid in any given year.

Stock options are another form of executive remuneration that has come under increasing scrutiny from shareholder groups. Since stock options are usually not taxed and are not accounted for on the company's books until they are exercised, the hidden value and hidden liability can be enormous. In recent years, the average total compensation of S&P 500 companies' CEOs has surpassed $10 million once stock options and other benefits were included. The average corporate executive's pay package in many companies has been estimated to be approximately four hundred times the average annual earnings of a typical production worker.

Another target of shareholder scrutiny is the issuance of "golden parachutes" to departing executives. These payments, sometimes amounting to hundreds of millions of dollars, are frequently promised to top management in the event they are removed from their jobs. The question many shareholder groups ask is why should an executive be rewarded if they are forced to leave because of poor performance?

Many shareholder groups have also insisted on having a greater say in any decision to sell the company or to take it private, and they want the option to retain shares if the company goes private. But a common criticism is that so much power being put in the hands of shareholders runs the risk of limiting the power of management to make bold decisions and increase share value over the long term. The fear of many executives is that companies in the twenty-first century will suffer from "management by referendum," where every decision is subject to the conflicting interests of the various shareholder groups. Some shareholders—political activists, for example—may force companies to make decisions that are against the interests of shareholders in general, like forcing a company not to do business in countries with human-rights violations, which may be good for the world at large but may be bad for the company's share price.

Political pressure, such as that used recently by the U.S. government to try to force companies to close far-flung manufacturing operations and "bring jobs home," may be unnecessary as companies have already reacted to recent changes in the world economic landscape. When profits began dropping in the late 2010s and the return on capital dipped to its lowest level in two decades, many U.S. multinationals began to rethink the process of doing everything abroad. Being close to your suppliers became a distinct advantage with trade and transport being disrupted by everything from rising fuel costs to such government-induced trade barriers as tariffs and quotas.

Locally based operations have also become more sophisticated, using the Internet and three-dimensional printing to replicate global firms' success in innovation and production without building costly offices and factories abroad. General Electric and Siemens, for example, have begun localizing supply chains, concentrating production and jobs into regional, or even national, entities.

In many cases, the terms *multinational* and *metanational* have to be put in the context of the evolving economic environment. Many industries no longer actually "make" anything. Uber and Airbnb are prime examples of how companies have evolved into umbrella organizations based primarily on technology rather than building something. It may be unrealistic, therefore, to ask twenty-first-century companies to create the kind of manufacturing jobs called for by many populist politicians when technology and artificial intelligence have entirely altered the economic landscape.

19

How Is the Digital Economy Transforming the World?

Since the invention of the microprocessor approximately a half century ago—which gave us the power to create everything from electronic books to streaming digital music to video chats—we have entered a truly digital age when almost everything can be made virtual.

Today, with more and more people having smartphones and access to the Internet, companies have found that they can make way more money in the digital economy than in traditional activities like making things. It is estimated that the digital economy is currently worth trillions of dollars and growing astronomically, with companies like Apple having a market cap of a trillion dollars or more. These behemoth tech firms often find themselves sitting on hundreds of billions of dollars in retained earnings, mainly because they have almost nothing else to buy—except, possibly, other tech companies.

As recently as the mid-1970s, companies had more than 70 percent of their assets in the form of real, tangible things like factories and watercoolers. Today's companies—those that make up the Standard & Poor's Index, for example—have less than 30 percent of their assets in the form of tangible goods. Other than a fancy headquarters building in California and a massive number of interconnected computers, Google is basically nothing more than a mountain of intangible assets, such as intellectual property and brand value.

Many of the things that companies used to make, like cars and jet engines, have become digitized in the sense that they churn out terabytes of data every minute and can be mined for their digital value. This often creates more bankable commodities than the product itself. The farm equipment that John Deere manufactures now provides enormous amounts of data that can be used for everything from design and manufacturing to predicting trends in food prices. Even babies' diapers, in a joint venture between Pampers and the Google sister company Verily announced in 2019, can now be equipped with sensors that allow much of a baby's activities and routines to be uploaded to an app, allowing parents—and possibly others—to have access to data from the earliest stages of a child's development. The fact that the manufacturers keep the rights to access the data their products generate—after selling the machinery to farmers or the jet engines to airlines—leads some to question whether they are not actually just renting out their equipment for a very high initial fee.

Business transacted electronically, often referred to as *e-commerce*, has grown exponentially since the beginning of the twenty-first century. And with businesses and governments accepting contracts signed digitally, taking advantage of advanced encryption technology like blockchain, any kind of transaction is now possible in cyberspace. Digital business-to-consumer (B2C) commerce began taking off when such online retailers as Schwab and Amazon created billion-dollar industries by providing consumers with products and services that were cheaper and easier to get online than by going to a neighborhood bank or shopping mall.

The low-cost structure of the Web has also allowed businesses to access many hard-to-reach segments of the public, sometimes referred to as *long-tail consumers,* who are interested in relatively rare products and services that were previously not even offered because of the high cost of traditional sales structures. Everything from indie music to kinky sex can now be accessed via the Internet in ways that were impossible just a few decades ago.

The Internet has also allowed businesses to offer tailor-made products that exactly fit the needs and specifications of their customers, providing consumers with the capability to customize anything from clothing to computers or even automobiles. Henry Ford once said that customers could buy his Model T car in any color they wanted—as long as it was black. Now, Ford can provide online customers with a complete array of options for every car it produces, including being able to choose virtually any color they like.

Business-to-business (B2B) commerce soon surpassed B2C to take the lion's share of e-commerce activity, transforming the marketplace in entirely new ways. The B2B marketplace initially was made up of companies creating online exchanges to buy materials and other goods and services from one another. These e-hubs provided a much wider range of suppliers and trading partners, leading to lower prices and increased productivity for the businesses that used them. For example, one of the companies supplying stores with the juices cherished by millennials, eJuice, has developed an online portal for its retailers with a virtual warehouse providing them with on-demand inventory. This setup allows retailers to avoid making large up-front purchases and being stuck with unsold product in the back room—one of the biggest problems for buyers.

It used to be that the vast majority of electronic and online transactions were concentrated in a few wealthy countries. But with the advent of high-speed Internet in many countries, markets from Eastern Europe to Asia to Oceania have now become e-commerce powerhouses. South Korea, for example, has universal Internet coverage at speeds that can only be dreamed of in the United States and other economically advanced countries. And after decades of being excluded from the digital economy, people in extremely poor regions of the world are now getting increased access to the Internet via smartphones. The use of mobile devices allows people in many countries, in sub-Saharan Africa especially, to leap over the fixed broadband infrastructure and use satellite technology to get Internet access in places previously untouched by the digital economy.

In countries where many people live on less than two dollars per day, tech providers realized that mobile technology had to be provided in an inexpensive manner if their markets were to continue growing. Companies like Huawei and Google in the 2010s therefore began providing Android smartphones to people in developing countries at a fraction of the price consumers would have to pay in the rest of the world. The participation of hundreds of millions of new consumers and Internet users has provided a dramatic increase in business.

New users of the Internet in the developing world have traditionally started out by using social media, sometimes at rates higher than in developed countries. The literacy rates in many countries have been shown to increase rapidly with smartphone access since most of the activity initially involves reading content on their devices. Other uses of the Internet also began to increase rapidly, with the GDP of many countries increasing as people started buying more and more goods online. Being able to buy solar panels, agricultural products, anti-malaria nets, and LED lights at greatly reduced prices has stimulated considerable new economic activity in many developing countries.

Services are also becoming a big part of e-commerce in the developing world. Farmers in many countries are using their smartphones not only to get up-to-date information on weather and commodities prices but also to access hundreds of specialized apps providing them with expert advice, sometimes using drone technology and satellites to help them plan their next crops and use their available land more wisely. In Fiji, for example, a project called *FarmEd* uses smartphones to deliver digital agricultural advice and provides access to high-tech solutions to increase productivity and help in the drive to reduce world hunger.

E-banking has also made great inroads into the brick-and-mortar worlds of finance and economics in the developing world and elsewhere. Taking advantage of the drastically reduced need for personnel and expensive real estate, online financial institutions are able to provide their services for a fraction of the cost of a traditional bank. Similar to traditional credit unions—which pool lenders and borrowers from the same company, church, neighborhood, or profession—online banks are able to bring together borrowers and lenders from far corners of the globe. After undergoing the same due diligence found in a traditional bank, customers are connected with other borrowers and lenders from distant lands. Most online banks and their affiliates are subject to the same regulation as normal financial institutions. Zopa, for example, is regulated by the British Financial Services Authority, and Prosper is regulated by the U.S. Federal Trade Commission and subject to the banking laws of the various states in which it operates—ensuring that its reliability is as high as that of traditional banks.

Social networking sites like Facebook and LinkedIn have also provided new opportunities for economic activity in cyberspace, allowing users to exchange everything from job-hunting tips to online résumés. Online advertising has become another important component of the emerging digital economy. Google has become one of the biggest companies in the world, mainly through the income from advertisers wanting access to Google's billions of users worldwide—earning the company almost $100 billion per year by the end of the 2010s. At the beginning of the twenty-first century, revenue from online advertising accounted for only about 5 percent of total advertising expenditures, but in just two decades, it has climbed to more than 30 percent. Since many consumers balk at paying fees to access websites—*The New York Times, The Wall Street Journal,* and a few other premium websites being rare exceptions—the only way for most companies on the Internet to make money is through the sale of advertising. The sale of users' data has also become an important revenue source for many sites.

Pay-per-click advertising has become one of the biggest segments of online revenue, allowing advertisers to pay a small fee to insert ads in browsers and other websites. Basing their ads on user-inputted keywords—such as *vacation* or *scuba diving,* for example—the advertiser places a carefully targeted ad in front of the person using the browser or web page. The potential for such user-specific advertising in cyberspace is almost limitless, and because information from users can be more easily refined, digital economy advertisers are getting extremely close to the holy grail of marketing: being put in direct contact with the customers—and only those customers—who are really interested in buying the product being advertised.

One of the downsides of the new digital economy is the increase in inequality, mainly caused by the job market being segregated into low-skill/low-pay and high-skill/high-pay segments. The biggest beneficiaries of the new digital economy will certainly be those who provide intellectual and physical capital rather than labor. Those innovators, shareholders, investors, and highly skilled workers who are driving the new world economy will benefit enormously, while those providing low-skilled labor, in comparison, will continue to fall behind. The pervasive feelings of dissatisfaction and unfairness among the previously blessed members of the working class have led to severe strains on the social contract that has held society together.

In some ways, the digital economy has become a victim of its own success. Since so much economic activity is now taking place online, hackers and even mischievous governments have discovered the power of manipulating the system for nefarious purposes. When Estonia began to remove a Soviet-era statue from a major square in 2007, for example, its economy was brought to a virtual standstill when attacks from Russia swamped the websites of banks, government ministries, and local companies that had become dependent on the Internet for most of their business transactions. Another form of cyberwarfare is the use of packet cyberbombs that can be sent in waves from botnets—groups of hijacked computers that are joined together in robot networks—to swamp targeted sites with unwanted activity and, in the process, bring the target's online business to a standstill.

After foreign hackers interfered in elections in the United States and many other parts of the world, authorities have attempted to find better ways to prevent cyberattacks. But when hackers and other "bot-herders" are able to commandeer computers from all corners of the globe—the attack on Estonia, for example, used hijacked computers from as far away as Malaysia and Brazil—the world's police and economic authorities are often powerless to act. Despite the trouble caused by these rogue hackers, access to the ever-expanding Internet has allowed many businesses, large and small, to thrive in the new global economy.

20

What Is the Internet of Things?

With near-universal penetration of smartphones and access to the Internet, we have entered a new age where our businesses and our lives are being altered in previously unimaginable ways. Some have started calling the transformation of the way we use interconnected technology to live and do business the "fourth industrial revolution."

It was steam in the eighteenth century, electricity in the nineteenth century, and computers in the late twentieth century that revolutionized the way we produce things and get from one place to another. In the twenty-first century, it is the interconnection via the Internet of a vast array of computing devices embedded in such everyday objects as vehicles and home appliances—called the *Internet of Things* (IoT)—that is allowing us to live and work in ways unheard of in past industrial ages. Refrigerators can now be programmed to sense when milk and egg supplies are running low and automatically order new products from an online retailer.

This revolution is possible because of cloud computing, which uses a network of remote servers hosted on the Internet to achieve the massive memory and computing power required to store, process, and analyze enormous amounts of data.

Companies have discovered that combining new technologies with access to the cloud allows them to do things in entirely new ways. In the past, production of everything from automobiles to elevators was limited to factories under centralized control using their own computers to automate single tasks, such as screwing in a door on a Nissan assembly line. Products had to be made in large numbers, called *batches,* to keep costs low and production high. Production in the new digital economy, sometimes referred to as *Industry 4.0,* uses cloud technology and the Internet of Things to automate complex tasks among a wide variety of machines, factories, and countries. With everything connected, a clothing manufacturer in northern Spain, for example, can immediately react to purchasing trends in stores in Moscow or Sydney and automatically switch production from colors and designs that are declining in sales to concentrate on those items that are becoming trendy.

Just-in-time manufacturing has now become the norm, allowing companies to avoid onerous inventory costs and get products more quickly to consumers around the world. Just as companies have learned to use data from in-store sales to adjust production, the use of high-quality sensors in machines can also help manufacturers to modify and accelerate production. The elevator manufacturer thyssenkrupp, for example, has begun installing sensors in the millions of elevators it has sold around the world, allowing the company to know which parts are getting worn out and are about to fail. By sending teams to fix a part before it breaks, manufacturers allow the end user to avoid costly downtime and disruptions.

The fourth industrial revolution was initially driven by the vast increases in computing power governed by Moore's law, which states that the number of transistors that can be squeezed onto an integrated circuit chip doubles every eighteen months. But by the late 2010s, the exponential growth of processing power in computer chips had begun to reach its limits. If Moore's law were to continue uninhibited by physics, by 2050, the components making up transistors would have to be smaller than a single atom of hydrogen.

The other key component of the fourth industrial revolution, access to the Internet of Things, means that we don't have to rely on just the computer sitting in front of us to do everything. Access to the cloud means that producers can use other people's computers to keep growth going. Better use of algorithms and software also will allow producers to keep up with the constantly increasing necessity for computing power.

The Internet of Things exhibits another law, called Metcalfe's law, which posits that the more users who are connected in a system, the better it will be. The law, formulated by Robert Metcalfe in the early 1980s, was originally applied to "compatible communicating devices," such as telephones, assuming that the more people participating in a system exponentially increases the benefits of using that system. In the digital economy, the law still applies. For instance, the more users a social media site like Facebook or LinkedIn has, the more efficiently it can function and the more valuable it becomes to its users.

In the ever-expanding Internet of Things, the number of appliances, vehicles, homes, and other devices is approaching thirty billion objects. Just as Metcalfe's law predicts, as the number of connected things has increased, entirely new cyber-physical relationships have appeared. In the health-care industry, for example, doctors are provided with our complete health records using such diverse things as heart-monitoring implants, fitness-tracking devices like Fitbit, and our smartphones, providing information on everything from our blood sugar levels to how much we've walked each day.

The advantages of connecting more and more things are numerous, ranging from increased efficiency to lower costs. But disadvantages exist as well. The security risks in having all our information accessible can be enormous, even if it is being used for benign purposes like statistical analysis. Think of the voice that informs us while waiting to be served at a call center, "This call will be monitored for quality control purposes." How will all this information be used in the future?

In the interconnected global economy, the possibilities for breaches in security are an increasing threat. And with more than 30 percent of the world using social media to share and get information, Metcalfe's law implies that the possibility for our information to be used by others—for good or for evil—is rising exponentially. We still do control—at least for the moment—the technology and processes that are creating enormous opportunities and wealth in the new digital economy. Unfortunately, many political leaders and decision-makers are trapped in old ways of seeing the world as "every man for himself" instead of finding ways to use the forces of disruption and innovation to shape a better future for us all.

21

Is Data the New Gold?

When numerous suspect political ads began appearing on Facebook at the end of the 2016 U.S. presidential campaign, no one suspected that the company paying for those ads—a relatively unknown English company called Cambridge Analytica—had secretly obtained access to the profiles of more than eighty-seven million users. The data accessed included everything from likes and clicks on interesting news stories to personal information such as users' names and addresses. A worldwide scandal erupted when the data leaks were divulged years later.

Most people were outraged that third parties had access to their personal information. Facebook and many other sites and apps have made sharing our data a requirement to being able to use their services. Basically, it isn't our names and addresses that most data analytics firms are after, and they don't really care if we like cute puppies or sunsets or articles defending the Second Amendment. What they really want is what our data can tell them about our future behavior. And once that has been analyzed and patterns and correlations have been extracted, the underlying information is no longer relevant. Which is why metadata—data that processes and describes other data—is the new gold of the twenty-first-century economy.

Data harvesters use powerful computers to go through enormous quantities of information provided by us in every possible way, from our answers to telephone opinion polls to our behavior online. Every time we search for something on Google and every time we shop online with Amazon, we are giving those companies information they can use in return. The data we provide for free is then analyzed using complex algorithms that allow the new owners of that data to understand and predict our behavior.

Through extensive questionnaires, psychologists can form a composite personality overview based on five qualities—openness, conscientiousness, extroversion, agreeableness, and neuroticism—but tech companies today make similar approximations with just a small amount of data. It is estimated that metadata analysts of people's behavior on Facebook need to see as few as seventy likes to know more about a person's personality than one's closest friends. With access to as little as three hundred likes, computers are able to tell more about our personalities than a spouse or family member can. This gives them the ability to predict how we will behave in almost any situation. This knowledge can be used for many purposes—not always benign.

In several political campaigns, from Brexit to U.S. presidential elections, supporters of both sides have used the personality profiles culled from metadata to influence and even manipulate voting behavior. By determining that a given voter has an "open" or "conscientious" personality, a targeted campaign ad may try to appeal to them—saying that the United Kingdom would save money if it left the EU, for example. But to a voter tending to have a neurotically distrustful or disagreeable personality, it would be far more effective to use scare tactics, such as saying that immigrants pose a major threat to the culture and economy.

In theory, data-driven activity can improve our lives. Products and services can be tailor-made to adapt to users' changing moods, or recruiters can match jobs to those whose personalities are most appropriate for any given job. But sometimes the use of data can feel like an invasion of privacy. Barack Obama's official 2012 campaign app, for example, allowed his metadata team to not only collect data from the person using the app but also collect data from users' friends as well. This allowed them to better allocate resources, sending campaign workers to places where voters needed more attention. But is it fair to use information from people who had never been given the option of deciding how their data is used?

Some have proposed controlling data more carefully, or even allowing users to monetize their data, letting them benefit from how their data is used. Just as a person who writes a song or publishes a book gets royalty payments every time their creation is used, a user could receive a steady stream of payments every time their data is used in the future. A grocery store / art space in Hamburg, Germany, for example, has provided a model for monetizing data by allowing people to "buy" small items of food by posting photos of the art space on Facebook. A pack of toast, for instance, costs eight likes.

Until now, most people have been willing to give their valuable data away for free or for a pathetically small reward. We have no problem using online maps or search engines to get something we need, but the information we are providing, everything from our travel plans to online purchases, is then used by companies to earn enormous amounts of money, and we see nothing in return.

In the past, it wasn't much different, however. Most people perceived network television as being free, when in fact the networks were selling our eyes that were glued to their screen. The buyers of the television service were essentially advertisers who geared their messages to the market segment of people watching—sugary cereal ads for those watching Saturday morning cartoons or Budweiser ads for those watching the Super Bowl. In the same way, we as users of free apps and free online services are being sold to advertisers. The digital economy has an entirely new currency, and it's not cash—it's data.

The idea that we have entered a new barter economy has started to attract attention from politicians and economists around the world. Just as people traded wheat for wine in preindustrial days, people today are trading data for services. And since these transactions don't have any monetary value, governments are unable to tax them, and economists are unable to evaluate the contribution of this activity to such measures as gross domestic product.

The amount being traded in the data-for-services barter economy is enormous. Five of the most highly valued companies in the world—Amazon, Microsoft, Facebook, Alphabet (Google), and Alibaba—are making trillions of dollars using and selling our data. Unlike previously successful companies like car manufacturers or oil producers, data-oriented companies get their raw materials for free. The data behemoths then charge retailers and advertisers for it. Not insignificantly, the cost of all this online advertising is then passed on to us in the form of a slightly higher price for the bottle of wine we buy at the restaurant we found on Google Maps or for that vacation we were enticed to book on Travelocity via targeted advertisements.

Some have warned that, in the future, data will be so valuable that those who control it will control us and the world in ways we can barely imagine. In ancient times, those who owned the most gold got to call the shots. The five hundred tons of gold that King Solomon mined, estimated to be the equivalent of $60 trillion today, gave him the power to rule an entire region. In medieval times, those who held the lion's share of land became rulers of entire populations. In the machine age, the owners of capital like factories, railways, and oil refineries became the modern barons. Now, with data as the world's most precious commodity, those controlling it will garner not only vast economic power but possibly even the ability to control entire segments of our daily lives.

The power of biotechnology allows for an even more intrusive form of data collection. Essentially, once enough biometric data is collected, data analysts will be able to understand human beings in ways that go far beyond using Facebook likes to determine a person's overriding personality traits. Once new technology allows computers to enter into our bodies and brains—a matter of a few decades, according to some—the companies controlling the data and the computers will be able to start altering the human mind and body in profound ways.

The power to influence thoughts and behavior already exists. Search engines today can be engineered to give predetermined answers to the autocomplete function so that the answers match the wishes of those programming the algorithms. The Google autocomplete function, for example, has been shown to give negative answers to search results about Bing and Yahoo! and, not surprisingly, positive results for searches about Google.

It is not hard to imagine a future in which data is in the hands of a monopolistic company or a dictatorial regime that could use the access to our minds and bodies to alter and control our behavior in ways infinitely more nefarious than tweaking search engine results or targeting political ads based on each user's personality profile. What will be needed is some form of control of how data is used or accessed. But who gets to decide? The people providing the data or those holding it? In the European Union, a law called General Data Protection Regulation already requires companies to get explicit consent from users for the use of their data. The penalties for companies not respecting the law range from being shut down in EU territory to a fine of up to 4 percent of global profit.

Unfortunately, companies have unlimited ways of getting us to give them our consent to use data however they please. Researchers at MIT and Stanford University once did a study where people were offered a pizza to give away their entire email contact list. Most people accepted the offer.

22

How Are Robots and Artificial Intelligence Transforming the World Economy?

Fears of robots taking over the world or of having our data and our lives controlled by nefarious dictators, governmental or otherwise, have become increasingly prevalent in the new world economy. To determine if these fears are real or imagined, we first need to understand what exactly are robots and artificial intelligence. They are, in fact, two different things that sometimes merge to become something else entirely.

Robots, in the strict sense of the term, are machines that have been programmed to do a task. The long-armed contraption that rivets car doors onto a chassis in an automobile factory is called a *robot* because it has been programmed to perform a specific function. Using sensors, it can detect the world around it and proceed to perform its preprogrammed task in an autonomous way. *Artificial intelligence*, on the other hand, is the part of computer science that attempts to replicate human intelligence. Primarily, this involves using the input of data to "learn" and develop new paths of action not planned out by the people who originally programmed the computer.

When artificial intelligence is merged with robots, it becomes something entirely new in a way resembling the mythical chimera, half-dragon and half-human. When we ask Siri or Pandora or Alexa to play us some music, it acts as a robot by simply playing a preprogrammed song list. But once the robot has had the opportunity to learn from our previous habits, it may decide to play soft jazz for us when it hears the clink of wineglasses in the background.

At the moment a robot starts to make decisions and take actions beyond performing preprogrammed tasks, it crosses the bridge separating robotics and artificial intelligence and takes us to entirely new frontiers where computers or robots use data to learn about and adapt to the world around them to make our lives safer, easier, and more productive.

The invention of the printing press in the fifteenth century granted people entry into a world of knowledge previously reserved for an elite few with access to handwritten manuscripts. We are going through a similar upheaval now that the masses have access to unlimited information through the Internet. We theoretically have the power to make another leap forward, but will it make our lives more or less meaningful?

Essentially, there are two major issues facing twenty-first-century humans as robots and artificial intelligence play an increasingly ubiquitous role in our daily lives. First, what happens when robots get so powerful and efficient that they start taking the majority of our jobs away? And second, what happens when advanced artificial intelligence becomes so powerful that it begins to approach the singularity—the moment when computer intelligence surpasses human intelligence?

The fear of robots taking our jobs away was initially scoffed at by many workers and managers. Just as the invention of the cotton gin or the steam engine led to an increase in productivity and introduced a new age of economic progress, the introduction of robots and artificial intelligence into the workplace was initially seen as leading to more efficient production methods and, consequently, a net increase in jobs. At the high-tech BMW plant in Greer, South Carolina, for example, production doubled during the decade of the 2010s, and the workforce rose from 4,200 workers to 10,000. Some jobs were replaced, of course, but they tended to be repetitive, menial tasks defined as *d* jobs: dull, dirty, dangerous, and delicate.

Initially, workers were overjoyed. Having machines take over the boring jobs often led to more interesting and less dangerous workplace experiences. Human workers left the lifting to the machines and concentrated on overseeing the production process. It was even joked that the factory of the future would consist of three things: machines, a human, and a dog. The machines to do the work. The human to feed the dog. And the dog to keep the human from touching the machines.

Currently, robots are seen as being able to replicate almost anything a human can do, such as playing chess or building a car. But getting a computer-driven robot to replicate true human intelligence, such as being able to speak naturally or sing a song, has been considered unattainable. All that has been changing, however. Combining artificial intelligence and groundbreaking advances in microtechnology, the next generation of robots will be able to do almost everything a human can, in many cases significantly more efficiently. In factories, robots can now take over almost every aspect of the production process, except, so far, those involving such higher-level skills as fine-tuning and quality control. Robots working alongside humans, sometimes called *collaborative robots*, or *cobots*, can also increase productivity and efficiency. In many cases, the machines learn new tasks from humans by imitation. Cobots are usually smaller and more agile than traditional robots. Hospitals that use cobots to assist nurses in delivering supplies and food throughout a busy hospital, for example, free up the nurses to spend more quality time with the patients. Workplace injuries like back injuries from constant lifting and repetitive use of a joint can be reduced significantly by the use of cobots. When a burger-flipping robot called Flippy was introduced in a Los Angeles burger restaurant in 2018, it not only reduced the levels of contamination by constantly cleaning its utensils, but it also dramatically reduced workplace injuries like grease burns.

Robots and AI also allow factories to tailor their production to an evolving marketplace. The BMWs produced by robots in South Carolina, for example, went from having three thousand parts to fifteen thousand after robots began taking over the assembly line. By integrating networks of robots and artificial intelligence in factories via the Internet—referred to as the *Industrial Internet of Things*—factories are able to easily shift from producing a small number of goods in large batches to a more varied mix of goods in smaller batches. Producing goods in a way that can be easily adapted to the ever-changing tastes of consumers allows for much higher production levels, higher profits, and, potentially, more jobs.

As factories become more automated, the human workers overseeing the robots are required to be increasingly well educated. The use of robots frees up human assembly line workers to spend more time on creative activities like designing the procedures and layout of their factory. At the Electrolux factory in Germany, for example, laborers who once worked with their hands building washing machines were trained to work with robots and began experimenting with the various ways robots could be used to make the assembly line even more efficient.

But what happens to those low-skilled workers replaced by robots who cannot be retrained? In the past thirty years, it is estimated that approximately 80 percent of job losses in American manufacturing were because of automation, or technological replacement. Even though the unemployment rates in most industrial countries remained low—implying rising wage prices in a normal economy—many workers with low skills saw their wages barely budge as more and more low-skill jobs were automated. Many workers were forced to take lower-paying service jobs in fast-food restaurants or convenience stores. The sea changes in employment migration seen over the previous century—workers moved from newly mechanized farms to factories, and then from newly mechanized factories to service jobs—seem to have come to a dead end. Where will the low-skilled service industry workers go when they are replaced by automated cashiers and burger flippers?

The shift from formerly prestigious blue-collar jobs with good salaries to low-paying jobs in the service industry has begun to have serious consequences in many countries. The radically altered socioeconomic environment has actually led to something unheard of in modern history: a rise in mortality rates in wealthy countries. In the United States, for example, the mortality rates of white Americans with only a high school education began increasing in the 1990s and continued well into the twentieth century, fueled in part by opioid use and suicide rates well above previous norms. These deaths of despair were principally tied to the loss of economic opportunity caused in part by technological change. Many voters in affected regions—from formerly vibrant industrial areas in northern England and France to the Rust Belt in the United States—began to vote for politicians and programs that vowed to turn back the forces of technological change.

Over the next thirty years, it is estimated that up to 50 percent of all jobs could be replaced by technology. Some business leaders predict that virtually every job will be lost if we look far enough into the future. When robots armed with artificial intelligence eventually have access to 3-D printing and unlimited computing power, it is thought that they will be able to design and build other robots—ad infinitum.

And then what? What happens when the previously "secure" white-collar professions, such as accounting, law, and medicine, are made obsolete by artificial intelligence? Eventually, the combination of machine learning and big data could end up radically altering not only our economies but our society and politics as well.

It is undeniable that the explosive growth in robots and artificial intelligence has improved the human condition. With robots doing our shopping for us, building our houses for us, and making our clothes for us, our lives have been made much better. In theory, with more and more of our jobs being done by robots, we should have more time to devote to our families and friends, take walks in the country, and compose music. But with the ubiquitousness of technology, such as work-related emails and messages appearing on our devices twenty-four hours a day, a stress-free life appears to be even less attainable in the digital age. And with the means of production increasingly concentrated in the hands of corporations or individuals with the wherewithal to glean the most profit, the rest of us may be relegated to second-class status. Technology certainly makes our lives easier, but does it make them better?

Once robots assume humanoid form and begin thinking in human ways, our role as humans becomes unclear. Driverless cars, for example, will be given the responsibility of making virtually all major driving decisions, including ones involving human life. Confronted with a choice of running over an elderly retiree or a small child, which path does the self-driving car choose?

How do we program robots to act ethically? Or can we even expect to control them once they develop genuine intelligence? As machines progress, they are beginning to manifest something roboticists call *emergent behavior,* where they begin to learn from past behavior and plot new paths that may not have been anticipated by human creators. Some high-speed trading companies, for example, use algorithms to examine patterns in the marketplace and make investment decisions that may never have been predicted by their human "masters."

Even worse, what happens when robots and artificial intelligence can be incentivized to harm us? Already, in the U.S. presidential elections of 2016, computers were unleashed on social media sites to target and influence voters in key states. Once we reach the point where we have sensors imbedded within our bodies linked to the cloud, machines will be able to intervene in almost every aspect of our lives.

The possibilities for artificial intelligence to do harm can take myriad forms but can basically be divided into three main areas: cyberattacks, drone strikes, or surveillance and propaganda. Cyberattacks are ubiquitous in today's world and typically target virtual networks, such as databases and corporate websites. Drone strikes allow humans to use advanced technology to attack physical targets and could be used to disrupt or even destroy almost any modern economy. The use of artificial intelligence to gain political advantage through surveillance or online propaganda is already being used by authoritarian leaders and honest politicians alike and will likely proliferate in the years ahead.

In the end, some sort of control will be required if we are to limit the possibilities for all this new technology to harm us. Unfortunately, many government entities are unable to keep up with the pace of technological change, making effective regulation extremely difficult to implement. The question is not only how do we control the immense power unleashed by the combination of robots and artificial intelligence but also who decides who gets to have the power to regulate the technology that is taking over virtually every facet of our daily lives.

23

What Is the Sharing Economy?

Tribal mankind traditionally shared everything from communal fires to meals to childcare. But as we got richer, we decided it was best to own our own homes, farms, and automobiles. However, in the twenty-first century, smartphones and other devices have allowed us to connect with those around us in previously unimaginable ways, creating an entirely new sharing economy.

The sharing economy gives us access to others' unused or idle assets. From sharing cars and vacation homes to sharing childcare and music, many participants in the world economy have decided that it's often better to rent than to own. The digital platforms that allow us to share have become some of the biggest players in the new world economy. Airbnb, for example, became the biggest accommodation company in the world without owning a single rental property; they simply put people in need of accommodation in touch with those who have a spare room or apartment. Uber did the same with cars, allowing those without vehicles to get rides from others, without owning a single car of its own. This "asset light" model is now being used by companies around the world, giving us access to everything from designer clothes and bicycles to airplanes and farm equipment.

Often, the sharing economy isn't really about sharing. It's about paying for access to someone else's goods and services via an online platform. When an Uber driver leases a car with the sole purpose of providing rides on demand, for example, can it really be called sharing? Whether peer-to-peer or business-to-business, most transactions in the sharing economy involve customers paying a transaction fee to a company that facilitates the exchange of anything from vehicles to workspace.

As the sharing economy evolves, the model is changing, with fewer and fewer activities involving the exchange of goods for a fee. In Barcelona, for example, the local government runs a "time bank" that allows people to provide services for free, such as taking care of a sick child or reading books to people in nursing homes. They are paid with time-bank "credits," allowing them to have someone else come by and walk their dog or water their plants when they're on vacation.

The sharing economy consists of three elements: the use of digital technology to connect "buyers" and "sellers"; access to unused or idle capacity, with such things as vehicles or homes; and trust verification, which allows us to use ratings and reviews to ensure that we're getting exactly what we want in an efficient and verifiable way. An essential element for most sharing economy transactions is to live close enough to those we are sharing with, which is why almost all the activity is based in urban areas. A notable exception is the sharing or renting of digital content, such as streaming services like Pandora and Spotify, which can be accessed from anywhere.

Another example of nonurban sharing-economy activities can be found in the countrysides of many developing countries where most farmers don't have access to mechanical equipment of any kind. In India, where fewer than 15 percent of the country's 120 million farmers have a tractor or harvesting equipment, sharing platforms—such as the Trringo service provided by the Mahindra farm equipment manufacturer—allow farmers to rent anything from a thresher to a pump. The result of this sharing economy activity has been a marked increase in productivity, leading to increased food supplies for the population at large.

Although economics is the principal driver of the sharing economy—nobody wants to rent out their apartment or spare room for free—many people simply prefer to avoid ownership altogether. And it's not just millennials who are turning away from the model of the previous generations, where it was considered essential to own your own car or home. People and businesses around the world have discovered that having access to a wide variety of homes or vehicles can actually be beneficial in its own right. Imagine trying to find one vehicle that worked equally well on a camping trip, a drive up the coast, or a fancy date night. Having access to Zipcar SUVs, roadsters, and town cars gives us something much more than economic value—it offers us a variety of experiences. In the same way, Rent the Runway's Unlimited service plan provides people with never-ending access to new fashion experiences.

The sharing economy encompasses three main types of interactions: peer-to-peer or person-to-person (P2P), such as EasyRent, which connects people looking to share apartments; business-to-business (B2B) activity, where companies share big-ticket items like cranes or even buildings; to the most emblematic activity in the sharing economy: P2B2P. In a peer-to-business-to-peer transaction, a company like Uber acts as an intermediary, bringing two peers together for a fee.

In other models, the business is not necessarily profit seeking, creating a vast collaborative economy that allows people or businesses to unlock the value of unused or underused assets in ways that bypass traditional business models. ParkFlyRent, for example, uses a community platform to connect members who park their cars at European airports with other travelers who are arriving at that airport and need short-term use of a local vehicle.

Another collaborative economy activity involves the redistribution of unused, unwanted, or unneeded goods. Instead of throwing out these items or sending them to the recycling centers, they can be given away for free using such sites as Zwaggle or Kashless. Another alternative is to swap them for something you do want, using such sites as Swap.com. There is also the possibility of getting cash for them using time-honored platforms like Craigslist or eBay, which is technically not about sharing but about buying and selling goods and services. But the ecological advantages of reusing unwanted goods instead of throwing them out can often outweigh the financial rewards.

The *gig economy* is also becoming an increasingly important part of the economy at large. Most of these gigs are part-time jobs that are constantly being changed according to the employers' needs. Platforms such as Udemy and Beastly, for example, provide a sort of peer-to-business-to-business (P2B2B) platform connecting people with businesses requiring their time and expertise for a limited period. Even though many gig workers would prefer the stability of a full-time job, some have found that they actually prefer the variety and novelty of a never-ending array of activities to the monotony of a full-time job.

The *crowd economy* is another important aspect of the sharing economy. On a crowdfunding platform like Kickstarter or GoFundMe, a simple click on the Start a Fund-Raiser button creates an online opportunity to raise a predetermined amount of money. Crowdfunded activities can range from the altruistic, such as paying for a child's heart operation, to the bizarre, such as seven thousand contributions totaling more than $55,000 to fund someone making a potato salad. By the end of the 2010s, more than $10 billion had been raised through crowdfunding worldwide.

The entrance of academic institutions and governments into the world of online collaboration has also begun to change the way we think and interact. With virtually unlimited access to knowledge, Wikipedia and some top universities are putting an increasingly diverse array of lectures and information online—not to mention the almost limitless content provided for free on YouTube, ranging from TED Talks to Khan Academy courses. The possibilities for expanding our educational opportunities through the sharing or collaborative economy are growing exponentially.

Many local and national governments have also begun sharing data online, allowing people to have access to information that was previously inaccessible. Others have begun using sharing economy platforms to distribute unused land and resources to those who may be able to make better use of them. New York City, for example, uses the 596 Acres platform to distribute vacant lots to those interested in using them for community gardens. The revolutionary changes brought by the sharing economy, in addition to disrupting entire industries, may wind up bringing a level of transparency and sense of community to our lives not seen since mankind lived in prehistoric villages.

24

BRICS and Beyond: How Emerging
Markets Are Becoming the New
Powerhouses of the World Economy

Over the last few decades, a profound transformation has occurred in the global economy, as emerging and developing countries have become the largest economic force in the world. Now that more than 60 percent of economic production is in the hands of countries that used to be derisively called the *third world,* the whole concept of an elite first world has been called into question.

From China to Brazil, from South Africa to India, the twenty or so countries that make up the list of emerging markets have become the driving force of the world economy. Over the first two decades of the twenty-first century, their economic growth has consistently surpassed the growth attained by the "advanced" industrial economies, such as those of the United States, France, and Japan.

Most economic surveys, such as those provided by the IMF and Standard & Poor's, include the following countries in their lists of emerging markets: Brazil, Chile, China, Colombia, Hungary, Indonesia, India, Malaysia, Mexico, Peru, Philippines, Poland, Russia, South Africa, Thailand, and Turkey. The four largest emerging-market economies—Brazil, Russia, India, and China—began holding their own BRIC economic summits in 2009 to plan common strategies and coordinate economic growth. When South Africa was added to the group in 2010, it changed its name to BRICS.

Some emerging-market economies, such as China and Brazil, have used their newfound wealth to undertake programs to improve growth in other parts of the developing world. Brazil, for example, in the early 2010s began investing in extensive programs to help struggling economies in Africa and South America as well as poverty-stricken Haiti. Meanwhile, China began financing more than $150 billion worth of infrastructure spending in neighboring countries. These initiatives are providing everything from high-speed train lines and modern pipelines to highways and power grids in such diverse countries as Myanmar, Pakistan, and Iran.

The eventual goal of China's Belt and Road Initiative—formally called Yidai Yilu or One Belt, One Road Initiative—is to facilitate the creation of a Eurasian trading bloc rivaling the Atlantic-oriented trading zone between Europe and North America. The *belt* in the title refers to the attempt to connect Chinese trade and production to Europe via Central Asia; the *road* refers to the expansion of maritime trade routes with modernized ports in Southeast Asia and parts of Africa. Linking Europe with Asia via modernized sea routes and efficient overland connections will depend on enormous investments from China and eventually other countries located along the new silk road. In Azerbaijan, for example, a vast infrastructure project was almost completely financed with local funds with the idea that being part of the trade route between Europe and Asia would bring enormous economic benefits in the future.

As opposed to some autocratic leaders in the West, who want to build walls and limit interaction with neighboring countries, the Chinese government has chosen to invest more than a trillion dollars to link Asia with Europe—mainly via the Asian Infrastructure Investment Bank—building countless new roads, railways, and bridges. In addition to developing new markets for Chinese exports and finding new sources for raw materials, the Chinese hope to benefit from having strategic links and friendly relations with many countries in its region and beyond.

The idea of a new international order with China as a major participant has long been a dream for many economies in the region, but a hard one to realize with the United States and Western Europe dominating the international stage. But now with some Western countries turning their backs on world trade and the continued development of emerging markets, China and the other BRICS countries have a tremendous opportunity to assert their newfound economic power. China, for example, in the late 2010s began to strongly embrace the dispute resolution system at the World Trade Organization and increased its funding—and thus its voting share—at the IMF and the World Bank. In addition, China has also begun to promote trade agreements centered on the Pacific, encompassing most major Asian economies as well as Australia and New Zealand. China also has begun to improve trade links with India and other countries located around the Indian Ocean.

Demographics often play a large part in determining a country's economic growth. In Japan and Germany, for example, growth has been hampered by a declining birthrate—and subsequently declining populations. It is expected that Japan's population will fall by a third by the mid-twenty-first century from its peak in 2010—losing more than 40 million people. In many emerging markets, however, the opposite is happening. In India, the population is expected to reach 1.6 billion people by midcentury, more than 17 percent of the world's total, and is expected to rise to 9.6 billion people by 2050. Almost all the worldwide population growth will be in the emerging and developing countries of the world.

It is estimated that with increasing GDP and increasing fertility rates, African countries such as Nigeria and Ethiopia will provide more than half of the world's population growth over the coming years, with the rest coming almost exclusively from countries in Asia and Latin America. With a GDP per head of approximately one-eighth of that in the United States, economies in countries like India will grow enormously even with marginal increases in personal income.

But sustained economic growth is dependent on a well-trained and a well-educated workforce, and in many emerging and developing economies, poor people have virtually no opportunities to obtain a good education. In Brazil, for example, only students with the money to pay for private education are able to pass the Vestibular entrance exam required to get into universities there. And in India, girls are often made to stay home to help out with chores instead of going to school. Despite the government's Beti Bachao, Beti Padhao program to save and educate young girls, more than 40 percent of adolescent girls in India at the end of the 2010s were not attending school of any kind. Worldwide, the number of school-age girls who were not taking any classes was estimated to be 150 million.

The skills gap in many emerging-market countries, where employers are unable to find qualified applicants for many twenty-first-century jobs, is severely limiting growth. In India and Brazil, more than 60 percent of new jobs in the tech industry are going unfilled, mainly due to lack of education. Some companies, such as Samsung, have even begun building a network of tech institutes to provide the training that local educational institutions are not providing. In addition, in countries like Mexico and India, the

Honeywell Initiative for Science & Engineering aims to put local students into contact with tech personnel to develop local science and engineering skills.

With more than 40 million people in the countryside earning less than a dollar a day at the end of the 2010s, China has moved to radically increase education and job opportunities in remote rural regions in an effort to include everyone in the "march toward common prosperity." Chinese efforts to improve education have shown many countries what they need to do to begin helping the rural poor in their lands—principally in Africa and Southeast Asia.

The challenge facing the BRICS and the other developing countries in the years to come will be to learn from the successes and failures of the world's developed economies. The key will be to find a way to provide economic opportunity to hundreds of millions, if not billions, of the world's underprivileged while avoiding increased environmental destruction and depletion of the world's resources. In the end, it will be important to find a way to include everyone in the rising tide of economic prosperity in the developing world, not just the rich and the relatively prosperous middle classes living in modern urban enclaves like Cape Town, Shanghai, and São Paulo.

25

What Is the Future for the European Union and the Other Free-Trade Areas?

It isn't every day that a Nobel Prize is given to a free-trade area, but in 2012, the Nobel Peace Prize committee did exactly that, citing the role the EU had played in advancing peace and reconciliation, democracy and human rights.

Most people think that free-trade agreements (FTAs) are only about removing tariffs and opening up economies to foreign trade, but, in fact, FTAs do much more than that. The 1952 decision to create the European Coal and Steel Community, the organization that later became the EU, was ostensibly about removing barriers to trade between six countries in postwar Europe: West Germany, France, Italy, Belgium, the Netherlands, and Luxembourg. By the beginning of the twenty-first century, the European Union comprised more than twenty countries joined together in a project to bring peace and prosperity to a part of the world that had seen virtually constant conflict—and catastrophic wars—for centuries.

With the signing of the Maastricht Treaty in 1992, the European Union became much more than a movement to remove barriers to trade. The treaty turned the Common Market into a sort of political and economic union that had been the dream of European leaders for centuries. By allowing the free movement of people, capital, goods, and services between the member countries, the EU was transformed into a sort of United States of Europe, where each country kept its own separate system of government and monetary and fiscal control but integrated into a much larger zone, eventually comprising four hundred million people.

After Maastricht, citizens of Portugal could live and work anywhere from London to Athens; goods could flow from Finland to Italy without any extra formalities; and money could be transferred from Madrid to Frankfurt without restrictions. The introduction of the euro in 1999 meant truly barrier-free trade among the eleven EU countries that decided to adopt the common currency. Denmark, Sweden, and the United Kingdom decided to continue to use their own currencies, as did most of the new members from the former Soviet nations to the east.

The only Western European holdouts to the EU—Switzerland, Liechtenstein, Iceland, and Norway—decided to adopt a wait-and-see policy, choosing to take advantage of access to the EU market through various bilateral and multilateral trade agreements without entering the union officially. These relatively rich nations had previously ensured barrier-free trade among themselves through membership in the European Free Trade Association (EFTA). It was thought that it was just a matter of time until all countries in Europe would become part of the expanded and ever-more-powerful EU.

The journey to a fully integrated Europe has not been without roadblocks, however. When Great Britain voted to drop out of the European Union in 2016, the plan for complete EU integration hit a major hurdle. Another challenge to EU integration was the "euro crisis" during the 2010s, when some of the member countries in the eurozone faced bankruptcy following the 2008 financial crisis.

Several of them had to be bailed out—most notably Greece, but also Ireland, Cyprus, Spain, and Portugal—when it became apparent that they didn't have the money to pay the interest and principal on their massive debts.

In the case of Greece, years of government overspending accompanied by widespread chronic tax evasion led to one of the biggest crises faced by the EU to date. The wealthier eurozone countries were asked to help in the bailouts, but many—led by Germany—insisted on balanced budgets and major austerity programs in the debtor countries before aid would be provided. The EU-mandated austerity programs led to soaring unemployment rates, as much as 27 percent in Greece and Spain, and widespread economic stagnation. With low, or even negative, economic growth, cash-strapped eurozone governments were hard-pressed to find the funds to balance their budgets and stimulate their moribund economies.

The restrictions of being in a currency union made the recovery process uniquely difficult. In other countries, economic crises are usually accompanied by a fall in the value of the local currency, leading to a surge in export income as the country's goods and services become more competitive on the world markets. But Greece and the other struggling eurozone economies had no way to devalue their currency, which limited their options enormously. The strength of the wealthier countries—especially Germany, which was running consistent trade surpluses exporting high-end goods and services like BMWs and SAP consulting—kept the euro relatively strong, while the weaker members of the eurozone faced almost unbearable economic hardship. The Greek electorate, at one point, voted to refuse to respect the austerity package imposed by Germany and other eurozone members. But the government backed down when it realized that the only alternative was the nuclear option of dropping out of the eurozone altogether, which many feared would lead to even worse economic hardships.

The political fallout from the eurozone crisis also led to power shifts in many member governments as extreme right-wing and left-wing governments came to power in more than half the countries across Europe.

The immigration crisis of the late 2010s also was a major turning point in the drive for European integration. When the German government decided to allow into the EU more than a million immigrants from Syria and other politically and economically troubled countries, it asked for each EU country to accept a share of the new "political refugees." Many EU countries, especially those in the former communist east, refused to accept their allotted share, pointing out that most were economic refugees and not in need of political asylum. The perceived chaos of the refugee crisis led to a rise in anti-immigrant parties across Europe, and in the case of the United Kingdom—according to most exit polls—the decision to drop out of the EU altogether.

Faced with electorates from Hungary to Italy to Sweden calling for more political and economic independence, the EU in the future may need to allow for more flexibility instead of less, letting EU member countries choose how far to go in integrating into the larger union. One option considered was to allow for different tiers of EU membership, ranging from an inner core that shares a single currency to those opting to become full members of the customs union to an outer circle of nonmembers like Switzerland and Norway that have close trading relations. This last group had agreed to respect EU rules even without being able to vote on EU policy. This policy of enhanced cooperation, a sort of multispeed Europe, was seen by many as the best way to ensure EU coherence.

Unlike the European Union, NAFTA (North American Free Trade Agreement)—between Canada, the United States, and Mexico—was solely based on trade and included no plan for economic, monetary, or political union. In addition, unlike the EU, no attempt was made to impose common tariffs or quotas on goods coming from outside the bloc. For the countries stretching from the cold arctic tundra to the balmy Caribbean shores, NAFTA's goal was essentially to allow each country to benefit from the others' comparative advantages. Instead of trying to grow tobacco or bananas in the Yukon, for example, Canadians figured that they would be better off if they imported these goods from their neighbors to the south, providing other goods and services in return, such as wine, timber, and banking services.

By the beginning of the twenty-first century, expanded trade in goods and services had created significantly more jobs in the NAFTA countries than those lost to increased competition. Despite the fact that some manufacturing jobs were lost in certain low-wage regions of the United States—factories in the southern and eastern parts of the country suffered disproportionately—many more were created in export-friendly sectors centered mainly in the farm belt and West Coast states. The economic gains to Mexico, with maquiladoras (foreign-owned factories) springing up across the country to assemble parts brought in tax-free, were enormous, leading to a drastic reduction in poverty and lowering the pressure for Mexican citizens to emigrate northward in search of jobs.

Despite U.S. threats to pull out of NAFTA and destroy the agreement completely, a compromise was reached in 2018 to revise certain aspects of the agreement and replace the name with *United States–Mexico–Canada Agreement,* or *USMCA.* Taking its cue from proposals in the Trans-Pacific Partnership agreement, the crafters of the new agreement included updates on protecting intellectual property rights, digital rights, environmental policies, and labor practices. The only major alteration to the original NAFTA had to do with automotive manufacturing. In order for a company to qualify for tariff-free imports, 75 percent of an automobile's parts had to be made in North America, and at least 40 percent of the automobile had to be built by workers earning at least sixteen dollars per hour. Canada and Mexico rejected U.S. attempts to alter the dispute-settlement system as well as an attempt to insert a sunset clause automatically ending the new agreement every five years in the absence of new approvals from all three governments.

Inspired by the success of the European Union and NAFTA in promoting trade, many regions of the world have moved to set up free-trade megazones of their own. In South America, for example, Mercosur (*Mercado Común del Sur* in Spanish, or *Mercado Comum do Sul* in Portuguese) brought together Argentina, Brazil, Uruguay, and Paraguay. Like the European Union, Mercosur reduced tariffs on trade between the member countries while instituting common tariffs on goods from outside the bloc. Everything from beer to fruit and banking services flowed in increasing numbers.

One of the most ambitious multilateral free-trade agreements, the Trans-Pacific Partnership (TPP), attempted to bring together twelve Pacific Rim countries accounting for 40 percent of total world trade. The TPP was intended to connect the following countries: Canada, the United States, Mexico, Peru, Chile, Australia, New Zealand, Brunei, Malaysia, Singapore, Vietnam, and Japan. Even though the agreement was constructed to ensure U.S. hegemony over trade in the Pacific zone—excluding its major rival, China—the U.S. government backed out of the agreement in 2017, highlighting the new administration's protectionist "America First" priorities. The American decision to back out of the original TPP also ended up causing the abandonment of many of the most groundbreaking aspects of the agreement, such as rules covering nontariff trade issues like establishing workers' rights, minimum wages, union rights, and prohibiting illegal logging and child labor.

In fact, many of the new free-trade agreements are focused on individual countries' domestic rules and practices, such as banning genetically modified crops or not allowing child labor to be used in local factories. And just as the trade in agricultural or manufactured goods was the primary concern of previous trade agreements, the FTAs of the future will be increasingly concerned with twenty-first-century issues like the trade of services or the role of data and artificial intelligence in the global marketplace.

26

Sharp Power: How Countries Use Economic Power to Achieve Global Clout

Military power isn't the only way countries can assert themselves in the integrated global economy. Even the ancient Romans used a combination of hard and soft power to achieve their goals, combining military strength with cultural and educational efforts ranging from the construction of amphitheaters and aqueducts to the imposition of Latin as the global language. Now, armed with multimedia prowess, cyberweapons, and hacked computer files, countries in the twenty-first century have begun to exert their power in entirely new ways.

Nonmilitary efforts to "win friends and influence enemies" abroad can be divided into two types of power: soft power and sharp power. Soft-power initiatives mainly include cultural and educational activities, such as sending ballets and orchestras on world tours or setting up libraries and cultural centers in foreign lands to showcase the country's strengths in a benign way. China has joined many Western countries in setting up cultural institutes in foreign capitals and on college campuses worldwide. In many ways, the activities of China's Confucius Institutes now scattered throughout the world undertake the same soft-power activities as France's Alliance Française or Germany's Goethe-Institut to teach languages and make each country's cultural attributes accessible and hopefully more attractive to the world at large. But when countries start to use their economic power in an aggressive, sharp-power fashion, the effect and intention is often anything but benign.

The Internet, when used to manipulate voters and skew election results in foreign lands, is probably the most commonly used medium for sharp-power activities in the new digital economy. Elections across the world—from the Brexit vote in the United Kingdom to U.S. presidential elections—have been manipulated by foreign powers in ways that would have been impossible in previous decades. Social media platforms are often paid by foreign governments to gain access to voters in targeted countries whom they can bombard with ads to shape their views and, ultimately, the way they vote.

Sharp-power access to voters in other countries is rarely achieved by a government or government agency going directly to Facebook or Twitter or LinkedIn. One of the main goals of sharp-power shenanigans is to make it appear that the information being disseminated is coming from concerned citizens and not from a foreign power. This is why sharp-power attacks use third-party intermediaries—Cambridge Analytica in the 2016 U.S. presidential election, for example—to mask the true origin of the groups attempting to alter public opinion and voter behavior. Furthermore, many governments surreptitiously fund think tanks or media outlets that are ostensibly independent, but, in reality, make carefully controlled efforts to get their desired message out to the world.

Other ways that elections can be manipulated by foreign governments include releasing compromising information, such as emails or other data stolen by hackers, at carefully selected moments in the electoral process. In some cases, foreign governments simply contribute to campaigns or referendums—or, if this is prohibited, pay a local to contribute on their behalf. In the Brexit campaign in 2016, one of the biggest contributors to the pro-Brexit side was later shown to have been involved in several lucrative business deals with the ambassador of Russia in the United Kingdom. In some countries, candidates have been investigated for receiving support from foreign governments or businesses connected to foreign governments, ranging from parliamentary politicians in New Zealand and Australia to the ultimately successful U.S. presidential candidate in 2016.

Political parties can also be subjected to various sharp-power efforts to influence their policies and platforms. France's populist Front National party, for example, openly admitted to receiving loans from Russian banks in the months leading up to the 2017 presidential elections—implying at least the possibility, if not probability, of influence by the Russian government in the party's call to exit the European Union. In many countries, governments attempt to deal with this issue by eliminating the role of special interests and foreign money in local elections by publicly funding campaigns and political parties. For example, parties in Spain and Slovakia receive 90 percent of their campaign funding from government coffers. In the United States and the United Kingdom, however, more than 90 percent of political funding comes from private, nongovernment sources, opening the door for locals as well as foreigners to further their various agendas through political contributions.

Other forms of sharp power involve direct economic aid, usually provided by a country looking to garner political or economic influence in far corners of the world. Throughout Africa and Latin America, infrastructure projects like dams, railways, or shipping terminals are paid for by countries with vast economic power

looking for political concessions. These concessions can be anything from muting criticism of the donor country's human rights
policies to influencing votes at such global forums as the United
Nations or the World Trade Organization.

In other cases, powerful nations may provide aid with economic strings attached. The United States, for example, often do-
nates money to developing countries with the mandate that the
aid money be used to purchase U.S. farm products or machinery.
The United States has also used its unique position as holder of
the world's major reserve currency to impose its wishes on everything from dismantling Swiss bank secrecy to levying economic
sanctions on Iran and Turkey.

China's Belt and Road Initiative and other aid projects are, at
least in part, intended to further economic as well as political interests in neighboring countries. After a decade of focusing on aid
and investment in Latin America, China had succeeded by the end
of the 2010s in ensuring a steadily increasing flow of raw materials, including South American oil, iron, and copper, to fuel their
industrial production at home. Faced with the success of these
and other Chinese sharp-power initiatives, in 2018, the United
States proposed spending up to $60 billion to finance new devel-
opment in Latin America, sub-Saharan Africa, and other parts of
the world, hoping to reassert economic clout in those countries.

Creating strong economic ties often goes beyond the initial
goal of gaining allies across the world. It can engender shared
political interests as well, ranging from aligning attitudes toward
abortion and climate change to converging opinions on the role
of government in the private sector. Furthermore, in the event of
military conflict, countries with strong economic ties often end up
supporting one another—for practical economic considerations as
well as political expediency.

Sharp-power initiatives have serious ramifications for global
politics. The sharp-power efforts of some countries to destroy the

cohesion of countries making up the European Union, NATO, and other alliances have been extremely successful in recent years. Brexit was just one example of how outside countries used online media and other means to destroy the cohesion of the long-standing European alliance. These initiatives and others have succeeded in undermining the prevailing assumption of Western powers that former Soviet states in Eastern Europe would become reliable and inoffensive economic partners after the fall of the Iron Curtain.

The increasing polarization of electorates around the world seems to guarantee that governments will continue to be active in shaping public opinion, at home as well as abroad. And the rise of authoritarian governments around the world—from Hungary to Myanmar, from Turkey to Venezuela—seems to guarantee that sharp-power initiatives will continue to be important tools put to use by established and emerging economic powers—no matter the cost to global cooperation and interdependence.

27

Sharing the Wealth: How Do Charities, Private Enterprise, and NGOs Promote Economic Development?

Crowdfunding, before the digital age, tended to be done the old-fashioned way—usually by asking people in a church, mosque, or synagogue for a donation. The shared interests of the congregation ensured that the money would usually be spent for the common good of the community. In today's global economy, charitable giving, like almost everything else, has been transformed by new technology. Ranging from microloans to global initiatives such as the Bill and Melinda Gates Foundation, charitable giving in the twenty-first century has become a key element in the effort to reduce inequality and improve the lives of people in the developing world.

When the United Nations was established in 1945, the founders coined the term *nongovernmental organization* (NGO) to designate the activities of nonprofit organizations working in the public sphere without direct control by national governments or intergovernmental entities. The number of NGOs in the world has been estimated to be more than ten million, and their activities range from health-care and human rights advocacy to environmental activism and education.

In many cases, large NGOs like Save the Children, Oxfam, and Doctors Without Borders play a major role in reducing poverty and increasing the quality of life for millions of people in the world's poorest countries. Many of these organizations have evolved from simply providing food or medical care to taking a more holistic approach to creating an environment where famine and epidemics can be eradicated.

The United Nations has called for charities, NGOs, and governmental organizations to work together to accomplish seventeen specific development goals by 2030. The Sustainable Development Goals project was set up in 2015 to attempt to cut in half the number of people living in extreme poverty. Other goals include ensuring access to clean water, reducing infant mortality, and guaranteeing universal primary education, gender equality, and clean energy.

The reason many developing countries fail to provide minimum services to their populations isn't due to a lack of resources. Because of the combination of weak institutions that are unable to guarantee the rule of law and a culture of corruption in many countries, the resources that could be used to alleviate hunger, disease, and illiteracy end up in the pockets of a privileged elite. Most NGOs and charitable organizations working in the developing world have discovered the usefulness of bypassing corrupt governments completely and providing tools directly to the people so they can improve their own lives in their own way. As the proverb says, "Give a man a fish and you feed him for a day. Teach a man to fish and you feed him for a lifetime."

Access to the Internet has become the single most important tool in promoting social and economic development in the twenty-first century. But even at the end of the century's second decade, more than half of the world's population lacks Internet access. In many countries, the vast majority of the population doesn't have enough money to pay for even the most rudimentary Internet service. Imagine being a bride-to-be in a remote African town needing to walk miles to get a government-issued marriage license or a rug maker in Nepal lacking access to the world's markets. Without Internet access, meaningful participation in the global economy is virtually impossible.

Given the failure of many government-run Internet services to provide access to the rural poor, several private enterprises, such as SpaceX, Facebook, and Google, have developed projects to provide free Internet to the poorest regions of the world, allowing people earning less than a dollar per day to have Internet access via smartphones and other devices that cost much less than computers. The SpaceX project is based on a new satellite network, while Facebook plans to use solar-powered planes, satellites, and lasers, and Google's parent company, Alphabet, is developing a network of high-altitude balloons.

The role of private enterprise in fostering development has become crucially important as government aid programs, charities, and NGOs find that many of the development projects are just too big for one institution or organization to handle. The United States Agency for International Development (USAID) and Britain's Department for International Development (DFID) are using their funds to hire private companies to increase the efficiency of development and aid projects in many countries around the globe. Part of the reason is that traditional aid activities like building schools or distributing food are being replaced by "technical assistance" projects to empower local entrepreneurs to manage development projects.

Projects benefiting from joint public-private-NGO partnerships often promote clean water, education, and health care. Clean water initiatives, for example, have proliferated over recent years as NGOs and charities have partnered with such celebrities as

Matt Damon and Jay-Z to find new ways to provide clean water to the world's rural poor. The scale of the problem merited the attention. More than a billion people around the world are unable to drink even a single glass of clean water on a daily basis, not to mention cooking and bathing. Infants often suffer the most from the lack of access to clean water, which leads to high rates of child mortality in many parts of the world. The World Health Organization (WHO) estimates that, even at the end of the 2010s, more than a million people die per year from drinking unsafe water.

Many investors are insisting that the money they put into the world economy support businesses that have a favorable social or environmental impact. Pension funds, college endowments, even big banks have begun including impact investments as an increasingly large part of the trillions they invest annually. Even the Catholic Church has started to consider the environmental and human impact of the money it invests. Individual investors can choose from a variety of exchange-traded funds—the MSCI World Index offers more than ten ETFs—and other investment vehicles that concentrate on companies and projects with particular emphasis on sustainability, social benefit, and governance.

An innovative twist to providing aid to the developing world is to stop relying on donations from rich countries and to move to a microcredit model, which brings together investors willing to loan small amounts of money to those who lack the collateral to get loans from traditional banks. Because they lack a verifiable credit history, many people living in poor areas cannot get a loan for a water filtration system or to dig a well. Normal bank loans in developing countries often require paying exorbitant interest rates, sometimes as much as 1 percent per week. Recognizing the problem, Nobel Prize winner Muhammad Yunus started the microcredit movement when he began providing small, collateral-free loans, sometimes amounting to less than a few dollars at a time, to those in need. The first loans were to impoverished basket weavers in India, who used the money to buy bamboo and other supplies.

When it became apparent that the repayment rate from microcredits was exceptionally high, even by commercial bank standards, many NGOs and charities began setting up microfinancing operations of their own. Grameen, Positive Planet, and Kiva are just a few of the most successful microcredit operations that provide small loans to artisans, farmers, and small-business owners in developing countries around the world.

The largest microfinance bank in Latin America, Compartamos, began with loans to high-credit-risk entrepreneurs, such as sock makers or small-shop owners. The secret to the bank's success was to create groups of like-minded entrepreneurs, including many women who were previously underrepresented in local economies. The members of these groups agreed to guarantee the debts of the other members. When big venture capital firms, such as California-based Sequoia, began investing money in microfinance operations from India to Guatemala, it was clear that microfinance had arrived on the world economic scene, providing new opportunities and promoting growth in the developing world.

Even in relatively wealthy countries, the use of crowdsourcing platforms like GoFundMe and Kickstarter have allowed individuals to help others in need. Projects have ranged from helping entire families after a catastrophic fire to covering the medical costs of individuals suffering from a life-threatening disease. The traditional charities like the Salvation Army and Goodwill have also turned to online platforms to augment funding needs, using such crowdfunding platforms as Mightycause and Crowdrise. They have succeeded in raising money for tens of thousands of charities and NGOs in the few years that they have been in operation.

Extremely wealthy individuals have also found ways to contribute to development and reduce poverty in their own way. One of the most spectacular efforts occurred in 2010 when Bill and Melinda Gates decided to donate more than half of their fortune to charitable causes. They encouraged other wealthy entrepreneurs to do the same, founding the Giving Pledge in 2010 with forty other American philanthropists. Since then, wealthy donors from more than twenty countries have signed the pledge, including investor Warren Buffett, who gave more than $32 billion, mainly to fund the activities of the Bill and Melinda Gates Foundation to fight HIV/AIDS, eradicate malaria, and promote development worldwide. The idea behind the foundation was to employ tried-and-true business techniques to tackle some of the world's most intractable development problems. Their efforts have already begun to bear fruit, as deaths from malaria worldwide have dropped from over a million at the beginning of the twenty-first century to less than half of that today.

With the wealth of the world's top billionaires exceeding the total combined wealth of virtually all the world's poor nations, their decision to give a large portion of that money to help the world's poor certainly can have enormous positive consequences—if done carefully. But as the proverb says, simply giving the money away is only a short-term solution. Charities, NGOs, intergovernmental organizations, and wealthy donors are working together with local leaders around the world to find long-term solutions to the developing world's problems, an effort that has the potential to improve the lives of the majority of people at all economic levels.

28

Corruption and Tax Evasion:
How Does Money Laundering
Work?

Corrupt politicians, even those at the very top of some of the biggest countries in the world, have discovered that the "gray" economy can be used to hide and recycle all sorts of illegally earned money. When one of the campaign managers for the winning candidate in the 2016 U.S. presidential election was indicted for money laundering in 2018, investigators cited the use of the three main money-laundering techniques—placement, layering, and integration—to make illegally earned income look legit.

Whether the money comes from illegal drug sales, gang violence, fraud, Internet scams, identity theft, or corrupt political activity, the first task is to do something with the cash. It is estimated that illegal drug sales in the United States alone generate around $60–$100 billion per year, which translates into approximately twenty million pounds (nine million kilograms) of physical cash. It would raise all sorts of red flags if drug dealers were to walk into a Ferrari dealership and pay with cash or buy a fancy Fifth Avenue apartment in New York without being able to transfer the money from a legitimate bank account. So the first step in money laundering, referred to as a *placement* process, involves finding a bank or financial institution that will believe you have earned the money legally.

A tried-and-true method to justify having so much cash is to use a cash-intensive business, such as a restaurant or a car wash. By mixing legitimate money with illegitimate money, the true origin of the funds can be disguised. By inflating the number of pizzas sold or cars washed, a legitimate business can often succeed in getting a lot of illegal money into the business's bank account without anyone noticing.

Another popular money placement scheme is to make hundreds, or thousands, of small deposits into a bank account rather than one single large deposit, which could attract the attention of law enforcement authorities. In the United States, for example, transactions over $10,000 are supposed to be reported to the government. This practice of *structuring,* or *smurfing,* multiple deposits of less than $10,000 is technically illegal, but a cooperative bank, or bank employee, can often be convinced to look the other way if the price is right.

In some countries, banks don't require any justification for large deposits. Such is the case for many offshore banking centers with lax reporting requirements, such as Grand Cayman or Vanuatu. Once an offshore bank sends money to an onshore bank in Tokyo, New York, or London, it is often too late to track the money's source.

The second step in money laundering involves using several different bank transfers to get the money into a bank account where it can actually be spent. The idea of this *layering* process is to disguise the money's illicit origin by sending it through so many banks around the world—using any number of excuses, such as trade or investment—that no one can trace it.

Some money-laundering schemes involve the use of bitcoin or

other cryptocurrencies in the placement and layering processes. Since most cryptocurrency transactions are anonymous, the origin of the money can't be traced. Defenders of cryptocurrencies point out that there are myriad legal ways to transfer money anonymously, ranging from purchasing prepaid credit cards to even Amazon or iTunes gift cards.

Launderers can also recycle illegal money through legal gambling, such as lotteries or casinos. Basically, they don't mind losing a part of the original value as long as they can get most of it back in the end. By spending a million dollars on small casino bets, for example, a money launderer can often expect to get back 80–90 percent, on average, and have the excuse of simply "being very lucky" when asked where they got the money to buy the new mansion or luxury yacht.

Offshore companies, including dummy shell companies, are often used to further disguise illegal money's origin. By sending money from a company based in Cyprus to another based on a Caribbean island with lenient tax and security systems—often under the pretext of buying or selling something at fictitiously high prices—money gradually takes on the patina of legitimacy. In the case of Brazil's *lava jato* scandal, the government-controlled oil monopoly Petrobras was found to have been inflating construction and sales contracts to the tune of hundreds of millions of dollars. The extra money ended up being sent to those running several major political parties—ostensibly used to fund political campaigns, but considerable amounts ended up in offshore bank accounts connected to corrupt politicians.

Since many offshore financial centers have no income tax or capital gains tax, companies and wealthy individuals from around the world have flocked there to avoid paying taxes. When the Paradise Papers and the Panama Papers were leaked at the end of the 2010s, it was noted that everyone from the Queen of England to Madonna and Bono had resorted to the use of offshore companies, ostensibly to minimize taxes. While the practice is not necessarily illegal, such activity raises many questions as to how much companies and individuals should be allowed to hide from tax authorities at home. Where many wealthy investors see tax optimization, others see tax evasion.

The secrecy of offshore accounts allows for many wealthy people to avoid taxes in a technically legal manner, but this offshore system of banking also facilitates illegal activity like political corruption, drug dealing, and money laundering. In recent years, countries like Switzerland and the United Kingdom have agreed to share financial information of bank clients with most major countries around the world, including the United States, to eliminate tax avoidance. The United States played an instrumental role in forcing Switzerland to give up bank secrecy and require banks to know the beneficial owner of every account—even those belonging to companies, offshore or otherwise. Ironically, in certain parts of the United States, such as Delaware and Nevada, it remains possible for anonymous companies to open accounts and transfer untold amounts of questionable money through local banks until it eventually finds its way back into the legitimate financial system.

This third step of the money-laundering process, referred to as *integration,* allows for the owners of illegal money to spend it without any questions being asked. In the case of the crystal meth–producing protagonist of *Breaking Bad,* part of the money ended up being used to pay the medical bills incurred from his chemotherapy. But in most cases, the integration stage of money laundering involves high-end purchases, such as luxury real estate, fine art, or even a yacht or two.

Real estate, in fact, has become one of the most popular places to park laundered money in the twenty-first century because of the availability of large-scale properties like golf courses, luxury apartments, or shopping centers. In addition to generating rental income and in most cases increasing in value over the years, investing in real estate allows the owners to avoid taxes on capital gains since they are only paid when the property is sold. In some countries with controls on capital being sent abroad, the purchase of real estate is still allowed. This is why many posh areas of such major cities as London, Paris, or New York—or even high-end ski resorts in Switzerland—are full of properties owned by absentee landlords. In London, for example, an estimated $6 billion worth of property is owned by politicians and businesspeople of "suspicious wealth," according to one report.

Corrupt politicians and government officials are some of the most ubiquitous money launderers in the twenty-first-century economy. In poor areas of the world, the opportunity to line your pocket with thousands or even millions is often impossible to resist, even for those who are supposed to be enforcing the law. In many countries, poorly paid policemen and government bureaucrats take bribes as a supplement to their normal income, often receiving several times their official salary from illegal transactions. In Liberia, for example, the former president was put on trial for having stashed away more than $3 billion in illegally acquired assets—a sum equivalent to the entire Liberian GDP.

Policemen and government officials who accept illegal payments often justify their actions by pointing out that their salaries are extremely low because it is assumed that their income will be supplemented by bribes, just as a waiter or a waitress in Los Angeles will accept a lower nominal salary knowing that the bulk of the day's income will be in the form of tips. *Mordida* in Mexico City, *baksheesh* in Cairo, *hongo* in Nairobi—many business deals around the world would be impossible without some sort of supplemental income.

For international businesspeople, it can seem impossible to compete abroad without getting dirty. Many countries have passed laws that make corruption illegal, even in countries where it's accepted as a standard business practice. The United States, for example, prohibits international bribery through the Foreign Corrupt Practices Act. In practice, these laws have helped reduce much illegal behavior in the international marketplace.

Watchdog groups, such as Berlin-based Transparency International, fight against corruption by providing greater visibility for international business transactions. Transparency International has teamed up with the Paris-based Organisation for Economic Co-operation and Development (OECD), which includes more than thirty of the world's wealthiest countries, to fight international corruption by agreeing to a set of rules that specifically prohibits the practice of bribing foreign public officials while conducting business abroad.

Transparency International also provides a yearly survey of 180 countries and territories around the world, ranking them from the most corrupt with a rating of 0 to the least corrupt with a rating of 100. At the top of the list of least corrupt countries in the most recent survey were the Scandinavian countries, Switzerland, and New Zealand. At the bottom were Venezuela, Somalia, and North Korea.

Table 28.1

Corruption Perceptions Index

Score 100: Least Corrupt; Score 0: Most Corrupt

1. Denmark	88	3. Switzerland (tie)	85
2. New Zealand	87	7. Norway	84
3. Finland (tie)	85	8. Netherlands	83
3. Singapore (tie)	85	9. Canada (tie)	81
3. Sweden (tie)	85	9. Luxembourg (tie)	81

11. Germany (tie)	80	45. South Korea	57
11. United Kingdom (tie)	80	87. China	39
18. Japan	73	105. Brazil	35
22. United States	71	138. Mexico	28
34. Israel	61	144. Kenya	27

Source: Transparency International, 2018

With more and more business being done over the Web and less anonymous cash changing hands, it has become much easier to trace the flow of money. Bank transfers, which are almost entirely electronic in the twenty-first century, can provide important tools for tracing the movement of illegal funds from one part of the world to another. In some countries, the salaries and income of all public officials are published online in an effort to ensure transparency and limit corruption.

Some donor countries have also begun to make international loans and aid contingent on honest banking and business practices in developing country economies. Several groups, such as the Financial Stability Forum (FSF) and the Financial Action Task Force (FATF), have made concerted efforts to investigate corruption and money laundering around the world and have even gone so far as to list the countries that are seen as being lax or uncooperative in dealing with the problem.

Unfortunately, in many countries, including the United States, the number of convictions for money laundering are minuscule in comparison to the magnitude of the problem. The United Nations Office on Drugs and Crime estimates that criminal money made up almost 4 percent of the global GDP, or approximately $2 trillion. Of that money, less than 1 percent is actually seized or forfeited. In some countries, such as the Philippines, there has never been a single conviction for money laundering.

Unfortunately, even when one country beefs up its anti-money-laundering activities, in an interconnected global economy the effect is often minimal. In many cases, the illegal money just ends up flowing to jurisdictions where the laws and practices are less stringent and where corrupt politicians are more concerned with advancing their own careers than making life hard for money launderers.

29

The Dark Web and Other Black Markets: How Big Is the Illegal Economy?

The ubiquitous role of the Internet in the twenty-first-century economy has opened a Pandora's box of illegal and semilegal activity that is difficult to control. From the hacking of politically sensitive emails to cyber-blackmail and economic espionage, the possibilities are endless. When our credit card information is stolen from Target or Blue Cross, for example, the thieves have myriad options for monetizing the valuable data, from selling the card numbers and expiry dates to using our personal information to commit fraud in a thousand different ways in a thousand different markets.

If the Internet were characterized as a gigantic iceberg, the sparkling white part we can see above the surface of the water would represent all the normal websites we visit, such as You-Tube, Google, Facebook, and other openly accessed websites and blogs. Lurking in the dark waters below the surface, however, are much bigger and much more nefarious entities referred to as the

Deep Web and the *Dark Web*—two terms that are often used interchangeably but mean two very different things.

Generally, Deep Web activities are not illegal; the people behind them just prefer being out of the public eye. Typical Deep Web functions include Internet banking, the archiving of medical records, company intranets, and other private networks where we don't necessarily want the world seeing everything we're doing.

The Dark Web—the deepest, most-hidden level of Internet activity—was given the name because activities there need to be hidden because they involve illegal or other highly secretive activity. It is also sometimes called the *Darknet*. Dark Web activity is not that different from most black-market activities, such as extortion or drug dealing, but it can also involve everything from spy communications to buying a fake ID online.

The Dark Web is accessed via a portal such as Tor or I2P, which guarantees the user absolute anonymity. By logging onto an invisible Internet browser like I2P, denizens of the Dark Web can open search engines for an almost limitless variety of illegal activity. Some of the goods for sale on the Dark Web's markets include stolen phones, stolen or hacked credit cards, counterfeit currencies, fake passports, drugs, and illegal firearms. Services can include everything from prostitution and pornography to hackers and hitmen for hire.

Payment in the Dark Web is typically made with untraceable cryptocurrencies, and delivery is often made to anonymous, number-coded boxes provided by such companies as Lelantos that don't require the user to identify themselves, similar to the delivery lockers used by Amazon and other legitimate online marketplaces. Many Dark Web sites mimic legitimate online marketplaces by providing product and trustworthiness ratings just as one would find on Amazon or Craigslist.

Before it was shut down by the FBI in 2013, the Silk Road anonymous marketplace was the world's biggest online forum for buying and selling Dark Web products—a sort of eBay for illegal, semilegal, and even legal goods and services. The individual who ran Silk Road was arrested, tried, and sentenced to life in prison without the possibility of parole. Some criticized the harshness of the sentence, pointing out that the Silk Road founder hadn't been convicted of a single violent crime. But the large number of illegal drug sales facilitated by Silk Road, estimated to be more than $10 million annually at one point, led authorities in the United States and elsewhere to ask for the harshest penalties possible.

The sale and distribution of illegal drugs is the largest black-market activity in the world, with close to half a trillion dollars traded annually. Although in some countries drug use is tolerated and even legal, in most of the world's economies, drugs like marijuana, cocaine, and heroin are strictly prohibited. The problem with most attempts to prohibit the sale of illegal drugs is that as long as a market for them exists, there will be someone willing to run the risk of selling the illicit goods to an eager client base to earn a tidy profit. When alcohol was prohibited in the United States between 1920 and 1933, for example, a vast market for illicit liquor sprang up, laying the seeds for organized crime in America and generating enormous black-market profits.

When some U.S. states moved to legalize the sale of recreational marijuana in the 2010s, vast sums of formerly illegal money began to be channeled through legitimate, government-approved businesses—generating large tax revenues for such states as Alaska, Washington, Oregon, and California. When legal marijuana sales passed the $1 billion mark in Colorado in 2017, the tax revenue generated per year was more than $200 million. This money was mainly used to fund education, public health programs, affordable housing, and, perhaps a bit counterintuitively, drug abuse prevention and treatment.

Many black-market activities are structured to take advantage of legitimate businesses and economic forums to earn illegal money. Phishing, for example, is a scam in which a party sends out emails that appear to be from legitimate business sources, such as a bank or a credit card company. They claim that they require personal information to solve a problem with a credit card account or an online purchase on a legitimate forum like eBay or PayPal. The fraudulent message sometimes can include a hyperlink, allowing the phisher to access the victim's computer from a base halfway around the world. Once the victim's information has been collected, or "harvested," it can then be used to make purchases online or can be sold to third parties over Dark Web sites guaranteeing total anonymity to the scammers.

Hackers don't trick users to get information; they steal it outright. And they have learned that a lot of money can be earned by getting access to personal data stored on business computers. This information can be used to make fraudulent purchases or sold to the highest bidder, but it is often used to blackmail the company into paying a ransom. When it was divulged in 2017 that Uber's computers had been hacked, giving Internet attackers access to the names, addresses, and phone numbers of more than fifty million Uber clients worldwide, the company divulged that it had paid $100,000 to the criminals to delete the stolen data and keep silent about the entire episode.

Other companies, including HBO and Disney, have fallen victim to similar ransomware attacks. In 2017, Netflix was told by hackers that an important upcoming episode of *Orange Is the New Black* would be released on a popular downloading site called the Pirate Bay unless a large ransom was paid. Not wanting to set a precedent, Netflix refused to pay the ransom and the episode appeared, much to the detriment of Netflix's marketing efforts. Many companies prefer to pay the money rather than suffer the embarrassment and loss of clients following the announcement that a company's sensitive data has been hacked. Some companies in the world economy have even begun keeping a bitcoin wallet stocked to be used to pay off future hackers.

More dangerous extortion attacks involve hacking into a company's or government's computer and then threatening to render the computer files unreadable—or destroy them—unless a large fee is paid. A massive attack on the computers of sixteen hospitals in the United Kingdom in 2017, for example, prevented the hospitals from accessing patients' medical records, leading many of them to cancel all nonurgent operations. Other web-based extortionists threaten to disable a business's operation or divulge client lists unless a ransom is paid. This was the case with the extramarital affairs dating site Ashley Madison where hackers threatened to divulge customers' names, addresses, and even sexual preferences until a large payment had been received by the extortionists.

As the Internet continues to evolve, new possibilities for illegal activity will emerge. It was revealed in 2018, for example, that popular digital assistants like Amazon's Alexa or Apple's Siri could be hacked by embedding inaudible commands into a music broadcast. These commands could be used to get access to users' bank accounts or make unauthorized online purchases.

And now, with much of the world's illegal online activity being undertaken on behalf of governments—or even by the government officials themselves—we are forced to confront an issue that the ancient Romans had to deal with when facing corruption and illegal activity at the highest levels. In Latin, they phrased it as: "*Quis custodiet ipsos custodes?*" In English, it's translated as: "Who will oversee the overseers?"

30

How Is Climate Change Transforming the Global Economy?

Over the last ten thousand years, the earth's average temperatures have changed very little, hovering around 59 degrees Fahrenheit (15 degrees Celsius) century after century, millennium after millennium. But the rapid global economic growth of the past decades has led to a sharp increase in the amount of carbon dioxide, methane, and nitrous oxide in the earth's atmosphere. The resulting greenhouse effect has led to a sharp increase in average temperatures, commonly referred to as global warming. Estimates vary, but generally it is expected that the earth's average temperatures—even if we pause greenhouse gas emissions—will rise to the warmest levels the earth has ever seen.

The effect of these rising temperatures will include some positive aspects, mainly in the cooler parts of the world, such as Scandinavia, where summers will be longer and warmer, leading to increased food production and a generally more agreeable lifestyle. However, in the world's warmer—and generally poorer—

regions, the effects of global warming and climate change will be nothing short of devastating. The higher temperatures will not only have a negative effect on crops and agriculture, but they will also contribute to catastrophic hurricanes, floods, and droughts. It is estimated by the International Monetary Fund that up to 20 percent of GDP per capita in the developing countries will be lost due to the effects of climate change over the next decades. In virtually every country affected, the costs of emergency relief and rebuilding after catastrophic weather events will drain government coffers.

As the world's population continues to grow and as the developing world increases consumption, greenhouse gas emissions in the future will certainly increase as well. In fact, the developing countries are already producing almost two-thirds of the world's pollution, but at an average rate per capita considerably lower than in the advanced economies. This bodes ill for the future because when countries like Mexico and China begin to approach the per capita carbon dioxide emission levels of the developed countries, global warming will get dramatically worse. Furthermore, in many developing countries with inefficient industrial production, the volume of greenhouse gases released per each $1,000 of GDP is more than three times higher than that of the more advanced industrial economies.

Table 30.1

Fossil Fuel CO_2 Emissions by Country (2017)

Country	% Fossil fuel emissions by country	Per capita fossil fuel emissions (tons/year)
World		4.9
China	29.3%	7.7
United States	13.8%	15.7
European Union	9.6%	7.0
India	6.6%	1.8
Russia	4.8%	12.3
Japan	3.6%	10.4
Germany	2.2%	9.7
South Korea	1.8%	13.2
Iran	1.8%	8.3
Saudi Arabia	1.7%	19.4
Canada	1.7%	16.9

Source: World Bank, United Nations, Wikipedia

Given that a large portion of the developing world's populations are rural and earn their living from agriculture, climate change will have a much greater effect on their daily lives than in the advanced industrial economies. It has been estimated that the rural poor in Africa, Asia, and Latin America will be the most affected by climate change over the next twenty to thirty years, with prolonged droughts in some areas and disastrous flooding in others. In Latin America, the melting glaciers in the Andes will have catastrophic effects on food production and increase the likelihood of massive flooding and other severe weather events.

Agriculture in developing countries will also be severely affected by rising temperatures. The southeastern region of the

United States bordering the Gulf of Mexico could see agricultural yields fall by more than 50 percent, according to some estimates. In many areas, energy costs will soar as people turn up the air-conditioning in their homes and offices to deal with the increased temperatures outside. With as much as 70 percent of the world's fresh water being consumed by agriculture globally, any significant change in the amount of rainfall, in rich as well as in poor countries, could have catastrophic effects on the world's food supply.

The rising temperatures will also have an enormous effect on sea levels around the world. Not only will the increased heat contribute to the melting of glaciers, polar ice caps, and the ice sheets surrounding Greenland and Antarctica, but it will also cause the ocean to expand. It is estimated that approximately half of the past century's rise in sea levels can be attributed to the increase in water temperature, because warmer water takes up more space. Not only will the rising oceans contribute to more frequent storm surges along the world's low-lying areas—similar to the flooding that crippled New Orleans in 2005 and New York City in 2012—but they will also inundate some low-lying areas permanently.

Even before the United States pulled out of the Paris Agreement in 2018, the participating countries were having trouble meeting the goal of limiting global warming to 2°C (3.6°F) over the current century. Assuming that the true level could easily be a 3°C (5.4°F) rise by 2100—not a wild assumption given current increases in economic output and greenhouse gas emissions—the rising sea levels will flood entire cities around the world, especially in Asia. More than 275 million people currently live in these areas, as estimated by the nonprofit environmental organization Climate Central. Large swaths of Osaka, Japan, would be completely flooded, with more than $1 trillion in lost value. Alexandria, Egypt, would also be almost entirely flooded, with 8 million people having to flee to higher ground. Not only would Rio de

Janeiro lose all its famous beaches, but entire areas such as Barra da Tijuca, where the Olympic Games were held, will be underwater. Miami is already experiencing periodic flooding, referred to as *king tides,* that sends knee-deep water surging through the streets of low-lying areas of the city. The city that will be the most affected will in all likelihood be Shanghai, where more than 17 million people live in areas expected to be flooded if the seas rise as much as currently expected.

Most of the affected cities in the developed world mentioned above will have the wherewithal to build seawalls and drainage systems, similar to the efforts undertaken in New Orleans after the flooding caused by Hurricane Katrina. But in many of the world's poorer regions, the effects of rising sea levels will be much more difficult to adapt to. There will be no way to protect low-lying regions of Bangladesh, which are expected to be entirely underwater if we stay on the current trajectory, displacing hundreds of millions of people. Many of these climate refugees will, in all likelihood, end up fleeing to countries in Europe and North America just like the refugees fleeing war-torn Syria and Afghanistan in the late 2010s.

The possibility of a snowball effect makes these predictions even direr. The rising temperatures are projected to cause large areas of arctic permafrost to melt at an increasingly rapid pace, releasing even more carbon dioxide into the atmosphere. Once that happens, the earth itself will begin to make a larger contribution to climate change, leading to a runaway greenhouse effect. It is estimated that the amount of carbon locked in the world's permafrost is greater than all the carbon released from the burning of fossil fuels since the Industrial Revolution began in the nineteenth century.

In 2018, the United Nations Intergovernmental Panel on Climate Change (IPCC) predicted that unless CO_2 emissions are reduced dramatically over the coming years, it will be impossible to prevent potentially catastrophic climate change. The IPCC called on nations to attempt arriving at a net-zero world where as much carbon dioxide is removed from the atmosphere as is released by the world's economic activity. But finding the land to grow enough trees to remove that amount of carbon dioxide will be virtually impossible in a world with a total population approaching ten billion people. The best solution may be to implement extensive carbon recapture processes, using anything from algae to underground vaults. At a minimum, the report urged, the amount of electricity generated by renewables such as wind and solar power would have to increase drastically over the coming years.

In the United States, some political leaders have called for a "Green New Deal" to transition the United States from an economy reliant on fossil fuels to one based on renewable energy—just as the New Deal in the 1930s attempted to deal with the Great Depression by providing massive governmental spending to jumpstart the moribund economy. In addition to moving the economy to one producing virtually no carbon emissions, the secondary goal of the Green New Deal would be to stimulate the entire economy in an effort to reduce income inequality and deal with the economic consequences of the transition to a green economy—such as major increases in unemployment in those industries producing or consuming fossil fuels. This would be accomplished through increased governmental spending to ensure that those losing their jobs are retrained and supported by government-provided health care and other services.

Essentially, the short-term effects of climate change and global warming are relatively apparent: higher temperatures and rising sea levels are already causing serious disruption to the economic activity and livelihoods of hundreds of millions of people. However, the long-term effects will alter civilization in ways that are virtually impossible to predict.

31

Economics vs. the Environment: Is It a Zero-Sum Game?

The world economy is now so big that the planet on which it is based has been permanently altered by our economic behavior. With a rapidly growing human population of almost eight billion people—increasing at a rate of approximately eighty million people each year—we need to find a way to live and work in a world of finite resources.

The traditional measure of the world economy, GDP, was devised at a time when people generally assumed the world's resources had no limit. According to the economists using GDP, you need only think about the monetary value of the goods and services produced in any given year to judge the well-being of people living in that economy. These figures ignore the cost of depleting scarce resources and creating pollution that, if continued unabated, will make vast areas of the planet uninhabitable within a century.

The "tragedy of the commons" in modern economics is that many countries, companies, and individuals don't see themselves as responsible for common areas such as the oceans and the air. Just as individuals put too many cows on the village commons and overgrazed the field in medieval times, many of today's companies and individuals don't feel responsible for the larger picture. This has led to a collective series of actions that are destroying the world's common assets.

In response, some have called for a return to a bucolic rural past with people going back to living in huts and consuming only what they can grow in their gardens. With more than half of the world's population now living in urban centers—megacities like São Paulo, Mexico City, Mumbai, and Tokyo pack in more than twenty million people apiece—a return to a rural lifestyle for most of the world's population is simply not an option. The economic and technological machine will need to continue running and growing to support these and the billions of new citizens.

In many ways, the world economy is like a bicycle: to keep from falling over, it has to keep moving ahead. And with a growing population yearning for a better standard of living, the economy will have to continue to grow—exponentially, according to some estimates—to avoid a social, economic, and political meltdown. One need only look at the example of the civil chaos that has ensued in countries like Syria or Venezuela when the social infrastructure virtually disintegrated following political and economic collapse.

Since continued economic growth comes at a greater and greater environmental cost, it has become essential for us to come up with a better measure of economic production, one that includes the costs and benefits of economic activity on the world around us. Scientists at Yale and Columbia Universities developed the Environmental Performance Index (EPI), a globally recognized index to measure a variety of environmental activities, including air and water quality, effects of fishing and agricultural activities on the environment, carbon dioxide emissions, and more. This environmental GDP is based on the idea that all factors of production—whether land, labor, or clean air and water—are scarce commodities and have an intrinsic "price" that should be factored into every business and consumer decision, allowing us to rank and evaluate virtually every country in the world economy, taking into account almost every relevant economic activity for each country.

Table 31.1

Environmental Performance Index, 2018

Score 100: Perfect Performance in Achieving Environmental Health and Ecosystem Vitality; Score 0: Worst Performance

1. Switzerland	87.42	8. Austria	78.97
2. France	83.95	9. Ireland	78.77
3. Denmark	81.60	10. Finland	78.64
4. Malta	80.90	25. Canada	72.18
5. Sweden	80.51	27. United States	71.19
6. United Kingdom	79.89	150. China	50.74
7. Luxembourg	79.12	177. India	30.57

Source: Yale University, Yale Center for Environmental Law & Policy, 2018

Basically, companies and individuals will only reduce their negative impact on the environment once they realize that it costs more to pollute than it does to clean up all the unwanted results of production and consumption. Until now, the negative externalities of pollution and other forms of environmental degradation were not priced into the cost of products. This problem, referred to as *market failure* by economists, can be remedied in several different ways. The most obvious solution would be to put a price on pollution. Unfortunately, it is extremely difficult to put a universally accepted value on clean rivers, oceans, air, or even the continued existence of polar bears.

In some countries, government authorities have been able to put a limit on carbon emissions or on the number of pollutants that can be put into the air and water. Another solution involves putting a tax on air pollutants and carbon emissions. Alternatively, a government can offer tax credits, giving companies and individuals an incentive to adopt renewable power sources. Since virtually all these solutions require political will, they are only possible in countries with an environmentally conscious electorate.

The easiest solution would be to simply put a price on pollutants that ends up making companies pay the costs of polluting directly to the government in the form of a carbon tax. An everyday equivalent is the tax that almost every country puts on sales of diesel and gasoline, even though these taxes are paid by consumers and not companies. Some countries have even called for a global price to be put on carbon emissions. The problem is how to convince all the players in the world economy to participate. We've seen how difficult this can be given that it was a struggle to get countries to simply agree to limit the growth in greenhouse gas emissions during the Paris Agreement negotiations—even with no requirements on how this was to be achieved.

A controversial but more market-oriented alternative, referred to as *cap and trade,* would require governments to cap all greenhouse gas emissions at a fixed level and then let companies and individuals buy and sell their individual "right to pollute." As strange as it may sound, the trading of pollution rights has received overwhelming support from many environmental groups because it solves two seemingly irreconcilable goals: economic growth and a clean environment. Instead of simply telling everyone in an economy that they have to pollute less, cap-and-trade schemes allow the invisible hand of the marketplace to differentiate between pollution that is economically justified and that which is not.

An efficiently run wheelchair factory, for example, generally produces much less pollution per wheelchair than an inefficient one. Under a traditional anti-pollution plan, the government would have simply called for a reduction of production at both plants. But under a pollution-rights plan, the efficient wheelchair producer could use its extra profits to buy pollution rights from the inefficient one and use those rights to produce many more wheelchairs for a given amount of pollution—making everyone in the economy better off, with no increase in total emissions.

Providing an economic incentive to reduce pollution can have far-reaching effects. Selling unused pollution rights, for example, provides the biggest incentive of all: cash in hand. Companies and individuals will naturally want to do everything they can to reduce inefficient and highly polluting activities if they can sell their unused output of greenhouse gases. And with the right economic incentive, polluters will begin to invest in new technologies to reduce pollution.

Furthermore, since many banks and investment funds are keen to invest in sustainable companies, there are considerable financial incentives for the managers and stockholders of environmentally friendly companies. Those that take extra care to reduce their carbon footprint by producing more with a decrease in pollution often see their stock prices increase faster than the market as a whole. Other companies, such as those building solar panels and wind-power generators or those developing sustainable technologies, will obviously be much more attractive to investors than those companies that are blindly destroying the environment.

Recently, many rich nations with populist leaders have chosen to turn their backs on protecting the environment and fixing climate change, with some even denying that climate change exists.

And in the developing world, environmental considerations often take a back seat to the more pressing issues of simply keeping people alive. In theory, according to the Kuznets curve, as economic activity increases, pollution increases only up to a certain point. After that, as a country has the wherewithal to pay for green technology, pollution will actually decrease with economic growth, as we've seen in countries like Sweden.

It is clear that the relationship between the economy and the environment is not a zero-sum game where one player's win is another player's loss. All the decisions we make in the twenty-first-century economy have pluses and minuses, but there is no absolute good or absolute evil. If it were simply a zero-sum game, we would all want to stop breathing in order to reduce our consumption of oxygen and the subsequent release of carbon dioxide into the atmosphere.

Essentially, we need to weigh all the costs and benefits—and our own personal preferences—carefully. If we're told that the enormous amount of methane released into the atmosphere during the production of beef is a leading cause of global warming, we might decide to become vegans. If we were then told that canceling an around-the-world trip would reduce greenhouse gas emissions by an equal amount, which one would we choose? Similarly, if we're told that taking a shower uses less water than taking a bath, it seems like an easy choice. But what about considering whether the water we're using comes from a renewable source or how much the power used to heat the water is contributing to global warming?

Basically, in addition to being economically conscientious consumers, we need to be environmentally conscious consumers as well. In the end, by looking at the environment from an economic perspective, it becomes clear that protecting the earth and its air and water is not only good for our health, but it may also allow the world economy to achieve healthy—and sustainable—growth during the decades to come.

32

What Are the Alternatives to Capitalism?

Young people from virtually every corner of the world, from Lyon to Seattle to Seoul, increasingly say they would prefer something other than capitalism to run the world economy. Confronted with a system skewed in favor of those with entrenched interests and with workers young and old suffering from declining living standards, many people in the twenty-first-century economy have begun looking at other economic systems, such as socialism or even communism, to produce and distribute wealth in a more equitable manner. The problem is that everyone has a different idea of what socialism, communism—and indeed capitalism— really are.

For the self-defined democratic socialist U.S. presidential candidate Bernie Sanders, the goal should be creating a democratic-socialist system that works for everyone, not just the lucky few holding the majority of the wealth and the means of production. As opposed to the pure capitalist model, where all production is in private hands, the socialist ideal is to have the government play a role in running the economy and deciding how the wealth that has been created is distributed. The call for free tuition and single-payer health care is just the tip of the iceberg.

Instead of giving the market free rein, under a socialist regime, the government participates in choosing an economic path that is better for the society at large. And instead of letting those at the top keep their wealth and spend it as they see fit, those at the top are taxed at a much higher rate than those at the bottom, and the money is used to help those who need it the most.

Many socialist leaders criticize the capitalist system as nothing more than "socialism for the rich, and rugged individualism for those at the bottom." They point to such discrepancies as the enormous number of government subsidies going to those at the top—tax deductions for mortgage interest and low taxes for capital gains, for example—and limited programs to help the poor buy their own homes or have access to quality education or childcare. Billionaire investor Warren Buffett has criticized the inherent contradiction of a "capitalist" system in which one of the world's richest men pays a smaller percentage of his income on taxes than his secretary does.

Many proponents of socialism are in favor of keeping the capitalist system intact but distributing the fruits of the system more equitably. This hybrid democratic-socialist model attempts to combine the benefits of capitalism with the egalitarian goals of socialism. In fact, most capitalist countries, including the United States and France, already mix the two systems and have done so for centuries. The New Deal reforms in the United States, for example, included many socialist programs, such as the minimum wage, unemployment insurance, the forty-hour workweek, and Social Security. In France, and virtually every other modern economy, a national health-care system provides the same basic care for everyone, regardless of their ability to pay.

For many proponents of democratic socialism, the holy grail is the Nordic model found in the Scandinavian nations of Denmark, Norway, Sweden, and Finland—and to a lesser extent in other such northern European countries as Germany, Austria, and the Netherlands. Leading the world rankings in almost every measure of success—from per capita income to gender equality, from anti-corruption to self-defined happiness—the Nordic model tweaks the capitalist system to provide a fully functioning market economy that is able to ensure a high level of social welfare. The Danish model of job *flexicurity*, for example, tries to find a middle ground, without going to the capitalist extreme of no job security at all and the socialist extreme of a job guaranteed for life. In many of the countries using aspects of the Nordic model, those running the companies work together with the labor force to ensure quality jobs for all and a minimum of disruption from strikes and unnecessary unemployment. In the German Mittelstand system, for instance, management and workers meet regularly to find the best way of running the business.

The blurring of the lines between capitalism and socialism and even communism allows many countries around the world to pick and choose the parts of each economic system that work best for them. When we hear the word *communism*, we think of China or Vietnam—or the Soviet Union before glasnost and perestroika. But very few countries in the world economy today completely subscribe to the communist ideal where all economic decisions are made by a central authority. The hope of creating a more egalitarian *communal* society with no class distinctions was formulated in the nineteenth century as an alternative to the abuses of the capitalist Industrial Revolution—where child labor, unsanitary work conditions, and worker abuse were rampant. Those conditions are no longer as prevalent, but the demand for a more egalitarian society is, if anything, stronger in the twenty-first century, where more and more of the world's wealth is ending up in the hands of an elite minority.

When we hear the word *capitalism,* many think only of its Western form, with its emphasis on pluralism, the rule of law, free markets, and democracy. But the success of the Chinese economy and other rising Asian stars—such as India, South Korea, and Vietnam—allows us to examine the many variations of capitalism more closely. Economists have noted that countries often tend to blend at least two different varieties of capitalism. The United States' economy, for example, is a mixture of big-firm capitalism and entrepreneurial capitalism. The combination of these two types of capitalism—with Apple and Google existing alongside thousands of dot-com start-ups—has allowed the United States and other similar economies to create unprecedented prosperity by generating significant increases in productivity, on which most economic well-being is based.

In contrast, China—although nominally communist—has succeeded in blending entrepreneurial capitalism with state-guided capitalism, where major economic decisions are made by the central government. This hybrid system has been so successful that, in addition to bringing hundreds of millions of previously impoverished people into the burgeoning middle class, China is on track to soon become the largest economy in the world. Meanwhile, Russia has based its economic growth on a mixture of oligarchic capitalism, where the bulk of power is held by a small group of entrepreneurs with a state-guided economic system not all that different from that which existed under the czar at the beginning of the twentieth century. Some other countries in Eastern Europe, such as Hungary and Poland, have slipped into an economic system that some have dubbed *crony capitalism,* where business elites benefit from their close connection to the political elite, often to the detriment of the rest of the population as a whole.

Every system has its advantages and disadvantages. The oligarchic capitalism of Russia succeeded in bringing order to a chaotic post-Soviet economy, but growth has been slower than in the other BRICS countries. In Japan, where the government and big companies form complex networks of interlocking relationships, economic growth slowed markedly in the beginning of the twenty-first century despite the efforts of Abenomics, named after the innovative prime minister Shinzo Abe, to jump-start the economy with fiscal and monetary stimulus packages. In the case of China, the "social harmony" that allowed it to become an economic superpower has depended largely on an authoritarian regime that would be completely unacceptable in most democratic societies. But China's openness to the world, at least in the areas of trade and development, may be the main reason for its economic success.

Alternative or fringe economic systems can take many forms and, in some cases, provide viable alternatives to the pure capitalist model. In Israel, for example, some have opted to participate in an alternative communal economic system that has been built around the kibbutz—an economic community based on a mixture of collective labor, love of the land, and no-frills egalitarianism. When members of some of these communities began leaving to earn higher salaries and own their own homes outside the kibbutz, many kibbutzim began to lure younger residents back with the promise of being able to purchase homes and keep a greater share of the income they generated. Some of the kibbutzim even began selling off plots of land to nonmembers, who were allowed to take advantage of some of the communal services, such as childcare, schools, and access to the organic food produced on the farms.

On the other side of the Atlantic, countries like Venezuela and Bolivia have attempted to create a socialist utopian system modeled on Cuba's Marxist-Leninist regime, where the central government controls all major means of production. Under this system, in theory, the pain and inequities of capitalism would be replaced by an economy organized on the principle "from each according to their abilities, to each according to their needs." The collapse of the Venezuelan economy in the late 2010s, however, led the authoritarian government to blame not the model but foreign meddling and a collapse in oil prices, its major source of income. But in the end, with people lacking any incentive to work and with companies lacking access to markets, Venezuela had become an economic disaster case, with millions going hungry and thousands dying in hospitals bereft of twenty-first-century medications.

Almost all successful economies end up using a mixture of various models. What needs to be decided is: What is the right mix? The "creative destruction" of the pure capitalist system has certainly succeeded in bringing unprecedented prosperity to billions around the world, but it has also caused a lot of collateral damage along the way. The key is finding the system that works best for the people who live within each country. Vast cultural and economic differences ensure that not all countries will thrive under any one particular system. In the end, it's up to the people to decide on the right mix.

33

Are Trade Unions Becoming Obsolete in the Twenty-First Century?

When the Deliveroo bike and moped delivery workers went on strike in London in 2016, their main demand was to be assured of a minimum living wage. When the service's customers—mainly the owners of Pizza Express and Wagamama—refused to meet their demands, the UK Labour Party condemned the move as a return to "Victorian Britain," infamous for the blatant exploitation of workers and abhorrent workplace conditions that were prevalent in the nineteenth century.

In the twenty-first-century economy, with its emphasis on flexible working conditions and new technology, trade unions have been forced to reconsider their role. In the past, unions have focused mainly on safety, working conditions, fewer hours per week, and compensation. But over past decades, laws in many countries were passed to ensure safer working conditions, leaving unions to focus on workers' benefits and compensation. But now in the new sharing economy, businesses like Deliveroo, Uber, and many others refer to their workers as *entrepreneurs* and say they shouldn't receive the same benefits that full-time employees do, such as pension plans and health care. Many twenty-first-century workers prefer the flexibility that their jobs provide, allowing them to decide when and how much to work in a given week, even though that means forgoing the traditional guarantees that union membership promotes.

The decline in union membership in the twenty-first century can be attributed to a variety of reasons, not just the propensity of many younger workers to work in short-term or gig economy jobs. Technological change has also played a major part. A visit to almost any modern factory today presents a stark contrast to factories of the past—think of a Ford Model T assembly line at the beginning of the twentieth century, with thousands of semiskilled workers on assembly lines stretching as far as the eye can see. In today's modern factories, the use of robots and other forms of mechanization has made semiskilled industrial workers, and their unions, an increasingly rare factor in the manufacturing process. Few of the newer automobile factories in the southern U.S. states, for example, have unionized employees.

Service industries, the fastest-growing segment of the twenty-first-century economy, also present unions with a challenging environment because the jobs can usually be filled by tapping the workforce at large, most of whom are not unionized. Generally, any employer of low-skilled workers, such as a hotel or a corporate cleaning service, can simply outsource or replace employees.

The influence of unions to be able to lobby on behalf of laborers is increasingly jeopardized in a world where skilled and semiskilled workers can be replaced by robots and increased mechanization, and unskilled workers can be replaced by a virtually unlimited supply of nonunion employees.

Over the last half century, the percentage of employees belonging to unions has declined drastically in most industrial economies. In some Scandinavian countries, the number still remains high partly because unions there provide unemployment insurance whereas in many other Western countries, governments provide the safety net through taxes. In the United States, union membership is approximately half of what it was fifty years ago, one of the lowest levels among OECD member countries.

Table 33.1

Union Membership as a Percentage of Total Employees, Percentages by Country

Iceland	90.4%	Germany	16.7%
Sweden	66.1%	Australia	13.7%
Belgium	54.2%	Mexico	12.0%
Italy	34.3%	South Korea	10.5%
Canada	25.9%	United States	10.1%
Ireland	24.2%	Turkey	8.6%
United Kingdom	23.2%	France	7.9%
Japan	17.1%		

Source: OECD/Statista 2019

Many labor leaders blame the fall in union membership on globalization, citing the move of many manufacturing jobs to overseas markets with lower labor costs. Others point out that the advances in technology would have destroyed many manufacturing jobs regardless of globalization. Outsourcing, the practice of paying outside firms to do part of a company's business, has resulted in many jobs being moved to low-wage countries. This has led to the loss of many jobs—and union members—in high-wage countries over the past decades.

Unions have consequently become increasingly reliant on service-industry workers and government employees. In some countries, all employees of government entities, such as municipal employees, are forced to join the relevant union—or, at least, pay union dues, regardless of membership. It was argued that the work of the unions made all employees better off, so all employees should pay a part of the union's costs. In the United States, this was the case until 2018 when the Supreme Court ruled that forcing people to join unions or pay union dues violated their First Amendment right to free speech since one activity of the unions was to lobby for worker-friendly laws and support specific candidates who were in favor of higher salaries and benefits for government employees.

In addition to judicial and political headwinds, unions in many countries are suffering from demographic change. As older workers who were generally more amenable to unions and union membership retire, they are being replaced by younger workers who tend to be less willing to let unions get involved in their employment choices and job conditions. Instead of going on strike, disgruntled young gig economy workers can turn to social media to shame abusive employers and highlight unacceptable business practices.

Only in those countries where unions have reinvented themselves, adapting to the twenty-first-century marketplace, is union membership strong—and in some places actually increasing. In Germany, for example, unions and work councils take an active role in determining the direction of the companies their members work for. This codetermination model makes unions active partners in running companies, helping promote high-performance work systems that increase productivity and profits. In many cases, these extra profits find their way into the workers' pockets—a huge incentive for unions to be a force for innovation and change.

Forward-thinking unions also have become more involved

in promoting workers' competitiveness, insisting on professional training as an individual right for all workers, allowing them to benefit from increased automation and digitization. The emphasis will have to be on ensuring the viability of future workers, instead of insisting on preserving the status quo. By concentrating on being as low-cost and digitally savvy as the companies they are involved with, the unions of the future may still have a role to play in the twenty-first-century economy.

34

Health Care: Ways That Work

Unlike almost everything else in the world economy, you really can't put a price on health. The traditional measures of GDP, therefore, don't include health or happiness in their measures of a country's economic well-being. We can put a price on health care, however.

Compared to almost every advanced country, the cost of health care in the United States is more than double the average cost elsewhere. Many reasons are given for the high price of health care in the United States: the high rate of obesity, the high rate of diabetes, the tendency of Americans to go to the doctor more often, and so on. But a close look at the statistics shows that Americans, on average, go to the doctor considerably less often than people do in most other wealthy countries. And the high obesity and diabetes rates in the United States—in 2017, 38.2 percent of all Americans over the age of fifteen were obese and 10.8 percent had diabetes—are not much higher than the rates in Canada, Mexico, Hungary, and the United Kingdom, all of which have much lower levels of health-care spending.

How do other countries keep health-care costs low? Most of the world's wealthy countries have a single-payer system that can negotiate with the hospitals, drug companies, and other health-care providers to keep prices low. In Canada, for example, with the government paying for the majority of health-care expenses nationwide, the pressure is on health-care providers to agree to a low-cost deal rather than lose out on the business.

In the United States, the part of the health-care system that is paid for by government programs—such as Medicaid, Medicare, and the Department of Veterans Affairs—has much lower average costs than does the rest of the market. The approximately one-fifth of U.S. health-care expenses negotiated by the U.S. government entities cost on average less than half of those charged to patients with private or employer-provided health care.

To make matters worse, by the end of the 2010s, more than 10 percent of Americans, approximately thirty million people, did not have any form of insurance to cover health-care costs. An emergency visit to a hospital, therefore, could end up bankrupting the patient. By charging uninsured patients much higher fees than those charged to Medicare patients, hospitals are able to recoup the money they lose elsewhere. According to a Harvard study, more than 60 percent of personal bankruptcies in the United States have been caused by medical expenses. And in the vast majority of those bankruptcy cases, the person filing had some form of health insurance; it just wasn't enough to cover all the costs. The sky-high prices of most health-care services in the United States are the result of relatively inefficient markets and the lack of a strong price-setter, such as a government-run health-care system like Medicaid or the British National Health Service.

Transparency of prices, an essential factor in choosing how to spend our money in almost every other sector of the economy, is severely lacking in the health-care industries in many countries, not just in the United States. When you're being wheeled into the emergency room with a heart attack, the costs of the hospital's services are not a high priority. This phenomenon of inelastic demand means that most patients are simply willing to spend whatever it takes to get the medication and care to return to good health. For example, some drugs that sell for a few dollars in countries around the world end up costing hundreds, if not thousands, in the United States. Because the plethora of insurance companies and health-care plans in the United States are unable to work as a unified block, they have no leverage to force a health-care provider to lower their prices—allowing health-care providers to charge as much as they want.

Despite being at the top of the list in terms of per capita health-care costs, the United States is often at the bottom of the life expectancy lists among advanced industrialized countries.

Table 34.1

Health-care Costs for Selected OECD Countries

Rank	Country	Health-care spending (per capita spending US$)	Health-care spending (as % of GDP)	Life expectancy
1.	United States	9,892	17.2%	79.3 years
2.	Switzerland	7,919	12.4%	83.4 years
3.	Luxembourg	7,463	6.3%	82.0 years
4.	Norway	6,647	10.5%	81.8 years
5.	Germany	5,551	11.3%	81.0 years
6.	Ireland	5,528	7.8%	81.4 years

Rank	Country	Health-care spending (per capita spending US$)	Health-care spending (as % of GDP)	Life expectancy
7.	Sweden	5,488	11.0%	82.4 years
8.	The Netherlands	5,385	10.5%	81.9 years
9.	Austria	5,227	10.4%	81.5 years
10.	Denmark	5,199	10.4%	80.6 years
13.	Canada	4,644	10.3%	82.2 years
17.	United Kingdom	4,192	9.7%	81.2 years
23.	Israel	2,776	7.3%	82.5 years
25.	South Korea	2,729	7.7%	82.3 years
29.	Hungary	2,101	7.6%	75.9 years
31.	Chile	1,977	8.5%	80.5 years
35.	Mexico	1,080	5.8%	76.7 years

Source: Bloomberg, 2017

While life expectancy is subject to many factors, such as diet, climate, or even the national murder rate, the role of health care in longevity is by far the most important factor. In some countries in the developing world, where basic health care is virtually nonexistent—and where billions of people don't have regular access to effective treatment for malaria, HIV, and tuberculosis—the life expectancy of local populations is very low.

The countries that provide the best health-care results, as judged by high life expectancy and efficiently provided health care, usually combine a government-provided single-payer system with ample private insurance options to provide complete coverage. Almost all the countries with the best health-care systems require that virtually every citizen be covered in one way or another. The London-based Legatum Institute, in its 2017 Global Prosperity Index, cites the following ten countries where health care is the most successful.

List 34.1

Best Health-care Systems in the World,
Legatum Institute Ranking

Ranking Country

1.   **Luxembourg**   **Average life expectancy: 82.2 years**

Universal health care. Even though virtually everyone in this small country is covered by the compulsory tax-funded health-care plan, approximately 75 percent pay for supplemental insurance policies to cover extras. Free choice of health-care providers. Costs are fixed for almost all health-care services.

2.   **Singapore**   **Average life expectancy: 84.7 years**

Universal health care. Mixture of state-run and private hospitals. All Singaporean workers are required to put approximately 37 percent of their salaries into a mandated savings account that can be used on health care, among other things. The government uses its authority to keep drug and other medical costs down.

3.   **Switzerland**   **Average life expectancy: 82.5 years**

Universal health care. Every citizen is required to have private health insurance, and approximately 30 percent receive government help to pay for it. Health care is provided by a combination of private and government-run hospitals. Insurance companies provide basic services on a nonprofit basis, but make money on extras such as single-room coverage.

4.   Japan   **Average life expectancy: 84.7 years**

Universal health care. Compulsory purchase of public health insurance, usually paid for by the employers. Patients pay 20 percent of their medical costs up front.

5.   Netherlands   **Average life expectancy: 81.2 years**

Universal health care. Mandatory insurance is required for all, mainly for primary care. Long-term care and care for the elderly is covered by a tax-supported government insurance system. Private insurers are required to charge the same price for all patients, young and old, sick or healthy.

6.   Sweden   **Average life expectancy: 82 years**

Universal health care. Tax-supported health care system puts caps on the amounts each citizen pays in any twelve-month period. Prescriptions are subsidized, and prices are controlled by the government. Fewer than a million Swedes pay separately for private health insurance giving them priority for certain procedures and operations.

7.   Hong Kong   **Average life expectancy: 82.8**

Universal health care. A mixture of public and private health-care providers. Those with private health insurance use the private hospitals. Most use the state-supported public hospital and health-care system, however. The Chinese territory's women have the longest life expectancy of any demographic group in the world.

8.   Australia   **Average life expectancy: 82.2 years**

Universal health care. Approximately 50 percent of Australians have private health insurance while the rest are covered by a national Medicaid system. Prescriptions are subsidized by the government via a Pharmaceutical Benefits Scheme. Health care is provided by a combination of private and government-run hospitals. Treatment in public hospitals is free while people with private insurance policies usually choose to pay for private upgrades.

9.   Israel   Average life expectancy: 82.3

Universal health care. All Israeli residents are required to join one of four national health insurance organizations, known as Kupat Holim. They are run as nonprofit organizations and are required to provide health-care services to all residents, regardless of their income or medical history.

10.   Germany   Average life expectancy: 80.7 years

Universal health care. Every citizen required to have a semiprivate health insurance called Krankenkasse. Those with higher incomes can purchase more extensive private health insurance. Those unable to pay have their insurance plans paid for by the government. Health care is provided by a combination of private and government-run hospitals.

Source: Legatum Institute, 2017; CIA World Factbook, 2019

Despite many negative aspects—such as lack of choice of hospitals and doctors, longer wait times for treatment, and the high cost to the government of providing some or part of the services— the advantages provided by universal health care could help solve many problems in the poor countries of the world where doctors and basic health-care services are sorely lacking. It has been shown that even rudimentary health-care systems in developing countries can reduce many diseases and complications that keep citizens and workers from realizing their full potential. And by combining the advantages of public and private components, many systems don't have to rely only on extensive government funding and overly onerous taxation.

Realizing that affordable health care is actually pro-growth, countries like Costa Rica and Chile have developed universal health-care systems that provide services for approximately one-eighth of what it costs in the United States and end up with populations that have almost equal, if not better, life expectancy rates. With healthy workforces providing necessary labor and managerial skills, countries with well-functioning health-care systems are able to produce more goods and services for the country, providing the economic wherewithal for even broader health-care coverage in the future.

35

How Is the Behavior of Millennials and Other Generations Changing the World's Economic Landscape?

At one point during the late 2010s, millennials became the world's largest generation—the exact year depends on the country you're looking at. For decades, the baby boomers, those born during the demographic surge in the two decades after the end of World War II, had been the dominant cohort and pretty much got to call the shots, making economic choices that neither their parents—and certainly not their children—could match.

The almost unlimited zeal in the postwar years to buy new homes and cars stimulated economies around the world. This led to levels of economic growth unheard of before or after. During the boom years of the 1950s and 1960s, for example, economic growth in the United States and many other countries was almost double the growth in real GDP figures of later generations. Much of this economic activity was influenced by the unique behavior of the dominant demographic group.

Basically, the various demographic groups can be broken down as follows:

- 1945 to mid-1960s: baby boomers (boomers)

- Mid-1960s to mid-1980s: generation X
  (gen X, MTV generation)

- Mid-1980s to 2000: millennials
  (generation Y, the me generation)

- 2000 to 2020: generation Z
  (iGen, the smartphone generation)

It's always difficult to generalize, but once you remove the many exceptions in any given population, there is almost always a set of basic core beliefs and behaviors that can be used to define a given group—and economic groups are no less definable than any other. Baby boomers, for example, were seen as being particularly optimistic, buying new cars and homes with glee, reassured by the strong economic growth and prosperity following the end of World War II.

The following generation, gen X, was seen as being much more skeptical about the power of the markets. The gen Xers' insistence on finding a life-work balance reflected the economic skepticism they acquired during the economic turmoil of the 1970s and the subsequent 1980s economic boom that accompanied the Reagan-Thatcher push for freer markets.

Millennials, the generation born in the years leading up to 2000—greatly influenced by the terrorist attacks on September 11, 2001, and the Great Recession of 2008—are seen as taking an even more skeptical view of the value of unlimited economic growth, calling for a greater emphasis on social equality, a sustainable environment, and quality of life.

Digital technology—basically the use of computers, tablets, and smartphones—has had a pervasive influence on the economic behavior of millennials—and even more so on the following generation, tentatively called *generation Z*. The new generation's constant use of smartphones—and the many forms of social media accessible via smartphones—has led to a tectonic change in behavior that is only beginning to be understood.

Not only are young people around the world forgoing real-world social interaction for countless hours nurturing online virtual friendships, their economic and social behavior is being altered in countless other ways as well. Since the 1990s, for example, alcohol and drug use has dropped significantly. Cigarette use has fallen by more than half in many countries, while the percentage of high schoolers having sex has fallen by more than 25 percent. The switch from TV watching to time spent in front of smaller screens has changed the behavior of advertisers and media companies as well. The move to media streaming, such as that offered by Netflix, Amazon, and Apple, has led to a complete change in the way media is produced and distributed in the twenty-first century.

The technological savvy of the new generations has destroyed many of the old paradigms for producing and marketing goods and services. Where boomers once were keen to have the latest cars or television sets to keep up with the Joneses, and where gen Xers and even millennials were keen to have the latest item of clothing or CD, the trend among young consumers is to "have it their own way," insisting on brands and products that reflect a turn away from mass market economic behavior and toward more individual style and content.

The move away from economic behavior geared to a standardized American dream has led to the decline of companies that relied on selling a "ticket to acceptance" with their products based on a perceived "elite" status. Not only has this affected traditional companies like Sears and Kmart—in 2017, Sears closed three hundred stores in the United States—but it also affects newer companies like Abercrombie & Fitch, which have relied on a classic model of branding, stressing conformity to a fashion ideal rather than a more individualistic outlook. The new generation's emphasis on individualism and independence has led to the development of entirely new ways to produce and sell products and services in the twenty-first century.

Social media has played a big part in the move toward products and services tailored to the individual consumer and niche audiences. Where boomers and gen Xers grew up getting their news from standardized network TV programs and newspapers meant for a broad audience, the new way to stay informed is to use online filtering tools, such as Reddit, Facebook, podcasts, and even comedy news programs to get an individualized information stream—a model that has also been embraced by older generations.

The fear of many political and economic analysts is that the new focus on the individual is leading us to a world where people are treating opposing viewpoints or behavior as invalid or "wrong." The pluralism of previous generations, such as the commingling of hippies and entrepreneurs in the 1960s, is being replaced by a focused, distilled world where no one wants to hear opposing views and alternative behavior. Exacerbating this phenomenon is the tendency of many young people to forgo traditional news sources, such as network television, newspapers, and magazines, and rely on social media for learning about and understanding the world at large. The result is a world of increasingly one-sided viewpoints. The political correctness of twenty-first-century economic behavior—such as refusing to buy products from countries with extremely low minimum wages, for example—is leading many people to refuse to look at the benefits provided by increased economic cooperation. Another example is the idea among many that buying locally is always the best way. If not undertaken in an appropriate way, however, buying and growing locally can have unwanted environmental consequences. Using greenhouses to grow tomatoes in the Netherlands or Canada instead of importing them from sunny Spain or Mexico can lead to a much higher carbon footprint for each tomato produced, even when you factor in the cost of transporting the tomatoes by ship or cargo plane.

Clearly, the economic behavior of earlier generations—such as the baby boomers' rampant destruction of forests and farmland to build all those new houses—has provided a cautionary tale to the generations that followed. The result has led to the tendency of millennials to live in smaller homes and apartments closer to town centers, meaning that they have to spend less time in traffic and emit less pollution to have access to the workplaces and other amenities that cities offer.

Even baby boomers, as they get older and reach retirement age, are forsaking the large homes with expansive yards to move into smaller homes and apartments as well, increasing their living standards and lowering the carbon footprint of their economic activity. Retiring baby boomers are bringing their concern for a high quality of life to the final stage of their lives—opting for luxury and respect for alternative lifestyles—ranging from golfing or cricket-themed retirement homes to those exclusively catering to the LGBTQ community.

The population shift away from traditional suburbs to dense urban areas has both positive and negative repercussions. The move away from building oversized McMansions in the suburbs not only means less expenditure on furniture and fixtures and lawn care, but it also means less need for those who earn their living by building the homes and cars needed to get suburbanites to work. The loss of many of these blue-collar jobs may tend to make the divide between rich and poor even larger. On the positive side, in addition to considerable environmental advantages like the reduction in air pollution from automobile exhausts, the move to a more urban lifestyle can lead to considerable increases in economic productivity. For example, the propensity of millen-

nials to move closer to their workplaces, as well as to their favorite bar or coffeehouse, has led to an interesting phenomenon
referred to as *synergy*. Many studies have shown that productivity
can be significantly increased when density leads employees to
be in closer contact with one another, leading to a more efficient
exchange of new ideas and more possibilities to work together.
With an increasing number of millennials choosing to move into
smaller apartments—many of which have small living spaces but
share ample common spaces, allowing them to interact with other
residents—the opportunities for positive collaboration increase
exponentially.

The main plight of millennials—earning less than their parents did at their age and being saddled with large amounts of
student debt—has forced them to turn to technology and tech-
nologically enabled activities, such as car sharing and online
platforms to exchange everything from clothes to housing. In the
United Kingdom, for example, home ownership for young millennials is approximately half the level it was for baby boomers at the
same age. Car ownership is also plummeting for young workers in
many countries as well.

The increased emphasis on access over ownership has led such
companies as automobile makers to radically rethink their business plans. Ford Motor Company, for example, decided to supply Zipcar's fleets on 250 college campuses across North America
with the ulterior motive of introducing millennials to their products in the hopes that, once familiar with a particular model, the
user would opt to purchase it in later years. But many millennials,
and an increasing number of people in the previous generations,
have decided that it's simply easier and more economical to share
rather than own.

Macroeconomic policies, such as stimulating the economy by
lowering interest rates, are also being transformed by the altered
economic behavior of new generations. The "Reagan Recovery"

after the recession of the early 1980s, for example, was fueled by baby boomers rushing to buy new homes and cars when the Fed lowered interest rates and the anti-tax government drastically increased spending, leading to large budget deficits. In today's world, however, it's not obvious that deficit spending and lower interest rates will have the same effect on millennials' spending patterns. Many say they simply prefer the convenience of ride sharing and even public transportation and have no interest in saddling themselves with even more debt. By the end of 2010s, the estimated combined student debt in the United States had exceeded $1 trillion, with the average loan balance owed exceeding $37,000 per student.

In many European countries, home ownership is also seen as an option, not a necessity. In Germany and Switzerland, for example, home ownership rates are considerably lower than in the United States and Canada, and the economy doesn't seem to be any worse off because of it. The extra level of disposable wealth resulting from low home ownership rates is, in many cases, used to invest in things that are more important for the millennials and others, such as additional education. In an ideas-based economy, the value of technological and other relevant skills can be of immense value to the individual as well as to the economy at large.

Instead of buying a home or car, many millennials and even members of the younger generation Z are opting to use their money to make the world a better place—choosing, for example, to contribute to a food bank or even fund charitable causes on a crowdsourcing website. Given that the major purchase of many millennials is a smartphone—relatively expensive in many cases—they have the option of reducing work hours and spending the time working for a nonprofit or a political campaign or even a start-up that doesn't have the wherewithal to pay a high salary or any salary at all.

Some have chosen to travel abroad or donate their time and

energy to charitable activities in developing countries, such as building new schools or digging wells in parts of the world suffering from drought caused by climate change. In most cases, this economic activity doesn't fit the traditional measures of economic growth, such as GDP or even Environmental GDP, sometimes referred to as Green Gross Domestic Product (GGDP), but that doesn't mean that the activities of millennials or even retirees of previous generations don't have an enormous effect on the world economy.

The most obvious option for the new generations to use their disposable income—since they're not buying cars or homes—is to invest it. But the vast majority of millennials around the world don't have any investments at all, in part because of their lower relative salaries and higher levels of student debt. And those who do choose to invest sometimes opt to invest in such nontraditional investments as bitcoins, which may or may not go up in value in the tumultuous years ahead. Long-term financial security, however, requires careful financial planning and a steady flow of savings into investment accounts.

The view of many millennials is that investing is only for the wealthy or that it can wait until they are closer to retirement age. Instead of hoping for short-term gains from cryptocurrency price fluctuations, millennials and all those coming of age in the subsequent generations could use their extensive tech savvy to start investing small amounts via smartphones or use online platforms like Nutmeg, Moneyfarm, and Wealthify—many of which allow small amounts to be invested, easily and securely, without having to go to a bank or investment house to set up the accounts. Given the enormous resources offered by an evolving digital economy, millennial investors have the power to make exciting and economically viable lifestyle choices and investment decisions in ways that previous generations could only have dreamed of.

36

New Ways of Working and Living in the Twenty-First Century

With data, robots, and other forms of artificial intelligence revolutionizing the twenty-first-century economy, countries and individuals are being forced to rethink previous economic models. In past decades—indeed, centuries—work has been considered one of our most important activities, even man's "highest calling" in some economies. But with much of mankind's work now being done by machines, we are being required to rethink what it means to be human. We are finally able to ask the question: Which economic model will bring us the most happiness?

The new generation of workers entering the world economy is coming in with entirely new expectations and priorities, and almost all are related to the desire to find the right work-life balance. As opposed to earlier generations who had the sole aim of earning as much money as possible, many of those entering the workforce today are choosing to work less, even if that means earning less. The previous model, sometimes called *turbo-capitalism*, where people were expected to work ever-longer hours to serve the economy—and where increasing economic output and increasing wealth were the main goals—is becoming increasingly obsolete in today's world.

In Denmark, for example, people have begun trying to balance their professional lives with other pursuits, giving them more happiness even if it means less wealth. This Danish *hygge* philosophy is based on the notion that once all our basic needs are met, more money doesn't necessarily lead to more happiness. Essentially, when all our necessities have been taken care of—such as all those basic needs provided via free health care, free university education, efficient public transportation, and so on—earning more money may not be seen as the most important thing in life.

Other countries have developed similar systems to integrate the various aspects of our lives in ways that don't necessarily revolve around money. In Japan, for example, *ikigai* is a concept roughly translated as "a reason for being" that attempts to pinpoint the place where the four major parts of our lives converge—bringing together "what you're good at," "what you can be paid for," "what the world needs," and "what you love." The point of convergence of the first two, for example, is *profession*. The first and last converge at a point called *passion*. When all four coincide—when what you're good at is what you love and also happens to be something that the world needs and is willing to pay for—you have found true happiness, or *ikigai*. Everyday examples could include anything from a successful food critic who is paid to visit and write about top restaurants to a talented musician who has been able to make a career of giving sold-out concerts around the world.

Other countries have developed similar holistic views of the combination of life and work in the twenty-first-century economy. In Sweden, for example, *lagom* is all about living simply and in harmony with the environment. The Swedish furniture maker IKEA has introduced this idea quite successfully into many of its products sold worldwide. In the Netherlands, *gezellig* is a philosophy extolling the value of surrounding yourself with comfortable people, places, and things. *Gezellig* literally means "companion" or "friend." In Finland, *päntsdrunk*, or *kalsarikännit*, praises the value of solitary relaxation. The humorous translation of *kalsarikännit* in the popular Homer Simpson meme is: "Drinking alone in your house, in your underwear, with no intention of going out."

Finding the right work-life balance has become, according to many observers, the most important concern of workers in the twenty-first-century economy. And with some futurists predicting that robots will end up making us all redundant, the major question may be whether there will even be a role for human work in the new machine-driven age. Already today, intelligent machines are performing an increasingly wide variety of human-based tasks, from driving cars to reading chest X-rays to ordering our favorite food to restocking our Wi-Fi-linked refrigerators. What will we do when machines and artificial intelligence combine to such a degree that almost everything will be done by them?

One possible scenario is that although machines will most probably replace most of the tasks performed by low-skilled workers, they will also create many new, more complex tasks for humans to perform—designing the robots, for example. Under this scenario, virtually all the jobs performed today by relatively low-skilled workers—such as assembling refrigerators on the factory floor or chopping up food in restaurant kitchens—will fall by the wayside in the years to come. For example, some analysts have predicted that over the next two to three decades, more than 60 percent of jobs in the accommodation and food services industries will disappear, along with the probable loss of 50 percent of jobs in manufacturing, transportation, warehousing, and retail.

In the short term, many low-skilled workers will be able to find work in the areas where employment is expected to grow, such as home health, personal care, and customer service. But the high-salary jobs, which usually require extensive technical and digital expertise, will probably not be an option for most of those who will lose their jobs to automation. Instead of reducing income inequality, the technological age may, in fact, end up increasing it.

What can be done? For many, getting the right education is becoming an increasingly critical decision. A traditional college or university education has long been seen as a sure path to getting a good job and succeeding in the marketplace. This is still the case in many fields, but with colleges and universities churning out more and more graduates with "practical" skills, such as those with traditional business degrees, employers are finding it harder and harder to find employees with all the diverse skills they require to succeed in the rapidly evolving twenty-first-century economy. The employees most sought after in the future will, in all probability, be those with a combination of technical skills supplemented by skills that require more creative nontraditional ways of thinking. An essential requirement in the future will be an ability to embrace change—including the ability of workers to reinvent and reeducate themselves many times throughout their careers.

In addition, those most likely to succeed will without doubt be those who not only have the ability to interact with technology but also have the skills that machines can't easily accomplish, such as creativity, critical thinking, emotional intelligence, adaptability, and the ability to cooperate in teams. Paradoxically, one of the most effective ways of gaining these skills is by turning our backs on machines and spending time getting a broad cultural education.

In some countries, such as Germany, Austria, and Switzerland, young people are encouraged to forgo traditional colleges and universities altogether and enroll in apprenticeship programs that are often a mixture of classroom learning and on-the-job training. The idea is to bring private enterprise and public support together to provide the workforce with exactly the kind of workers

it needs—a mixture of technical skills and a traditional education. The programs have resulted in all three countries achieving some of the lowest rates of youth unemployment in the world
and have provided the opportunity for many to work their way up
the corporate ladder through constant retraining. In Switzerland,
more than two-thirds of students leaving secondary school opt for
this hybrid form of vocational and traditional classroom learning.
Even the head of the Swiss bank UBS, Sergio Ermotti, began his
career as an apprentice at a small bank in Lugano and in the early
2010s became the CEO of one of the largest banks in the world.
Unfortunately, in many countries, a vocational education suffers
from the stigma of being only for those who are unable to get into
a traditional four-year college or university.

In some cases, automation ends up increasing the demand for a
company's products and creating a need for more employees, not
fewer. These new jobs are often in the areas of administration and
tech support. Those workers who are able to add new skills, such
as human resources or organizational behavior, have been able to
take advantage of the many new jobs created when machines make
production more efficient and companies grow. The more workers
can reinvent themselves—becoming hybrid workers with several
different skills—the more they will be able to find gainful employment in the years to come.

The ability to program, design, and work with the machines
that are taking over the twenty-first-century workplace will also
be increasingly sought-after skills in the years ahead. Unfortunately, many of those who are already in the workplace or those
who have lost their jobs—older workers, usually—are not being
given the training to keep up with the changing demands of the
fusion economy. Most employers are reluctant to provide extra
training for employees because they fear that competitors will hire
them away, and they will have lost their educational investment.

Paradoxically, with more machines doing more of our work,

many humans are confronted with the need to actually work more instead of less. Those who are losing their jobs in their early fifties, for example, are finding it necessary to begin a second career to supplement insufficient retirement savings or the inability of public pension schemes to provide a livable income. In the United States, for example, more than half of families have virtually nothing set aside for retirement—for a wide variety of reasons ranging from low income to unexpected health-care costs to a fear of investing. The necessity for so many to continue working well past the traditional retirement age has created a whole new phenomenon in some modern economies: the end of the concept of retirement as we know it—with some people forced to keep working until they become incapacitated or die. And with advances in biotechnology, life expectancy is expected to increase dramatically in the decades to come. Saving enough over the forty-five-year span of a traditional career will therefore be increasingly difficult, if not impossible, as we begin living past one hundred.

The gig economy has also become a viable work alternative for many people in the twenty-first-century economy, ranging from those looking to supplement retirement income to young people turning their backs on the traditional idea of work. Apps and online platforms like Snag Work and Wonolo provide a steady stream of part-time employees to help companies—ranging from retailers to restaurants—with temporary gaps in their schedules. One gig economy platform, Directly, even provides companies with temporary customer service personnel. Expert users become at-home call centers and are paid a small fee to answer questions coming in from fellow customers. Even the car-sharing companies like Lyft and Uber have a large share of employees who work part-time, choosing to work only on the weekends, for example. Some cite the possibility of using a temporary job as a gateway, an on-ramp of sorts, to more permanent employment.

The downside of the gig economy is that temporary workers

often tend to have fewer rights and protections, such as job security or health-care benefits. But many gig employees—young workers, especially—say they are not looking for job security per se. Some point out that working a constant stream of gig jobs can actually provide more security than working for a single employer who can fire you on a moment's notice. By the end of the 2010s, nearly one in four Americans earned money from the gig economy, according to the Pew Research Center.

One thing is certain: in a world dominated by technological breakthroughs, we will have opportunities to work and live in ways never before possible. With driverless cars becoming viable transportation alternatives, for example, we will be able to rethink the entire process of transportation and car ownership. While cars previously sat idle in our garages for an average of twenty-two hours a day, they can now be sent out into the sharing economy to provide transportation to many others and provide a nice source of extra income for ourselves. And the entire concept of work—once defined as going to a factory or office and working an eight-hour shift day after day—has been transformed by the ability of workers to take advantage of entirely new technologies, such as videoconferencing and cloud computing. Today's workers can now work almost anytime and anywhere, even on a Caribbean beach or in a Swiss ski chalet.

The recognition that time is as valuable an asset as money, leading to the increasing decoupling of wealth and well-being in the twenty-first century, is manifesting itself in many other ways as well. *Smart working,* for example, responds to the wish of many employees to have complete control of their time, choosing when to work and when not to and destroying the prevailing notion that work can only be done during the usual business hours and in the company's offices.

Basically, the top-down business model, with managers telling a docile workforce what to do and how to do it, is increasingly becoming a thing of the past. Productivity is becoming less a question of efficiency and more a question of outcomes, however they are achieved. For many millennials and other tech-savvy workers, it makes no sense to spend countless hours in office-based meetings when they have learned how to use social media to interact with people in an almost unlimited variety of formats.

Work environments are also being upgraded across the world to make the work experience a more enjoyable and fulfilling experience. With everything from the biodome botanical garden at Amazon's Seattle headquarters to sleep pods and childcare facilities in workplaces from Denmark to Singapore, innovative new workplaces have been created to respond to employees' desire for a higher quality of workplace life.

In the end, future models of work will have to adapt to entirely new social, technological, and economic influences. *Work* will cease to be a place to go or a thing to do; it will increasingly be seen as an activity with a purpose—hopefully one that ends up making the world a better place.

Glossary

In today's world, we are being bombarded with a plethora of economic terms: *bitcoin, escalating tariffs, data mining costs, gig economy, Dark Web,* and more. This glossary provides a list of the most commonly used terms that can be referred to periodically to refresh your memory and improve your economic literacy.

401(k). Many governments allow individuals to set aside some income for retirement—tax-free. In the United States, this deferred income is put in special accounts called 401(k)s. In the United Kingdom, it's referred to as a *self-invested personal pension* (SIPP), and in Switzerland, it's referred to as the *dritte säule,* or "third pillar." All these plans are meant to supplement retirement funds coming from the government or from company-financed pension plans.

Abenomics. In Japan, where the government and big companies form complex networks of interlocking relationships, economic growth slowed markedly in the beginning of the twenty-first century. Abenomics, the economic plan named after the innovative prime minister Shinzo Abe, attempted to jump-start the moribund economy with fiscal and monetary stimulus packages.

Acquisition. In the mergers-and-acquisition game, a company can acquire another in two ways: by using its own stock and merging the two companies' assets, or by using cash or borrowed money to acquire the company by buying enough stock to give the investor control. An acquisition is often referred to as a *takeover* and can occur in two ways: as a friendly takeover, one that takes place with the acquired company's approval, or as a hostile takeover, where the acquired company is taken over by the investor buying enough of the company's shares to gain control—usually against the wishes of the acquired company's board of directors.

Affiliate. A company that is related to but not specifically owned by another is referred to as an *affiliate*. In the virtual economy, affiliates are entities that group together for mutual gain. Many retailers on the Amazon website, for example, are affiliate companies, not owned by Amazon but benefiting from access to the Amazon platform.

AI. See Artificial Intelligence.

Algorithmic Trading. In a few milliseconds, large preprogrammed computers buy or sell stocks before the market has had a chance to react to new events. This allows them to take advantage of discrepancies in the market and to react to new events quickly. By the beginning of the twenty-first century, algorithmic trading was already responsible for 30–50 percent of all trades on America's stock exchanges.

Alpha. *Alpha* is the term used to describe the extra return that fund managers say they provide to investors. Compared to standard market indices like the Dow Jones Industrial Average and the S&P 500, many fund managers provide higher returns, for which they feel they are justified in asking for several percentage points in fees for providing the extra alpha they provide to investors.

American Depositary Receipt (ADR). ADRs are repackaged shares from foreign stock markets, sold in the United States as dollar-denominated securities. The idea is that investors in North America can invest in foreign stocks in the same way they buy domestic ones. Even the dividends are paid in U.S. dollars.

Amortization. See Depreciation.

Angel. See Venture Capital.

Appreciation. A rise in an asset's value. Appreciation is the opposite of *depreciation,* which describes the decline in an asset's value over time and is accounted for as a loss in the company's books. Appreciation is accounted for as income or capital gain (see Capital Gain).

Arbitrage, Arbitrageur. An arbitrageur attempts to spot discrepancies in world markets and then acts quickly to buy where a product is sold cheaply, selling it in another market where prices are higher. Many arbitrageurs use high-frequency trading, making a massive number of automated trades at extremely high speeds, spotting discrepancies and opportunities that go unseen by ordinary investors.

Artificial Intelligence / Robot. *Artificial intelligence* and *robots* are often used to describe the same thing, but they are, in fact, two different things that sometimes merge to become something else entirely. Robots, in the strict sense of the term, are machines that have been programmed to do a task. The long-armed contraption that rivets car doors onto a chassis in an automobile factory is called a *robot* because it has been programmed to perform a specific function. Artificial intelligence, on the other hand, is the part of computer science that replicates human intelligence. Primarily, this involves using the input of data to "learn" and develop new paths of action not planned out by the people who originally programmed the computer. The combination of robots and artificial intelligence creates machines that can actually "think." Already today, intelligent machines are performing an increasingly wide variety of human-based tasks, from driving cars to reading chest X-rays to ordering our favorite food to restocking our Wi-Fi-linked refrigerators.

Asset. Like gold, cash, or a valuable building on a company's balance sheet, assets are seen as positive—as opposed to *liabilities,* such as debt, which are seen as negative. The assets of most companies are divided into financial assets, such as cash and securities; fixed assets, such as buildings and computers; and intangible assets, such as goodwill and patents.

Asset Stripping. Sometimes, two plus two is more than four. Asset strippers acquire an undervalued company and sell off its assets, such as real estate or undervalued subsidiaries, often making more money than was needed to acquire the company to start with. Asset stripping usually allows takeover artists to generate the cash that is needed to pay off the debt incurred to acquire the company.

B2B/B2C. Transactions on the Web limited to businesses (a car supplier selling mufflers to a Detroit automaker, for example) are referred to as B2B—business-to-business transactions. A transaction involving a consumer buying over the Web (an individual buying a book at Amazon.com, for example) is referred to as B2C—business-to-consumer transactions.

Balance of Payments. The sum of a country's international trade and investment is called its *balance of payments.* This measure includes all the country's transfers of goods, services, and money. It is called a *balance* because purchases and sales of goods and services to and from other countries are always compensated by transfers of money flowing in the opposite direction. This measure is often confused with *balance of trade,* which is not the same—the trade balance only measures the trade in goods, excluding services and investments (see Merchandise Trade Balance).

Balance Sheet. The snapshot of a company's assets and liabilities. A balance sheet looks at a company's financial well-being at a given point in time. The balance sheet has two sides: assets—what the company owns—on the left, and liabilities— what the company owes—on the right. Whatever's left after subtracting liabilities from assets is called *shareholder's equity,* the extra value of a company that belongs to the company's owners.

Bank for International Settlements (BIS). Based in Basel, Switzerland, the Bank for International Settlements is often referred to as the central banks' central bank. It serves as a clearinghouse for transactions between the world's central banks in addition to regulating the international banking system.

Bankruptcy. A company that can't pay its debts on time is said to be bankrupt. In many countries, bankrupt companies are given an opportunity to try to pay off their creditors. This is called Chapter 11 in the United States. If the company can find no other solution to its problems, it goes into liquidation (chapter 7 in the United States), and its assets are sold to pay off the debts.

Barter. Exchanging one good for another—like trading vodka for Pepsi in the former Soviet Union—barter allows businesses or consumers to avoid problems posed by unconvertible or hard-to-exchange currencies. In most developed countries, barter is unnecessary because it's much easier to use money as a go-between.

Basis Point. A hundred of these make up a percentage point. Financial markets have become so finely tuned that it is no longer enough to talk about interest rates changing one-quarter or one-sixteenth of a percent. They now move by as little as one-hundredth of a percent, or one basis point. Using this system, a half of a percent rise in a bond's yield, or 0.5 percent, would be fifty basis points.

Bear Market / Bull Market. A bear market, like the proverbial grouchy ursine, is said to be one headed down. A bull market, roaring ahead, is used to describe markets headed up.

Bearer Bond. Like a cashier's check, a bearer bond is the payment of choice for villains in James Bond movies because it, in theory, will be cashed with no questions asked—there is no owner's name or registration required for a bearer bond. The holder of the bond owns the right to receive the full value of the bond, plus interest payments. This issuance of bearer bonds was banned in the United States in 1984, mainly to combat their use in money-laundering schemes.

Big Bang. In Japan, the term *big bang* was used to refer to a package of financial reforms undertaken in the late 1990s. The earlier deregulation of London's securities markets was referred to as the *big bang* as well. This led to an explosion in banking and financial services that caused many international banks and trading houses to move to London to take advantage of the opportunity to trade large blocks of international securities with no restrictions or taxes imposed by local authorities.

Bilateral Trade Agreements. Two countries agreeing to liberate the trade in goods and/or services (see Multilateral Trade Agreements).

Bitcoin. See Cryptocurrency.

Black Market. Whenever a desired good or service is prohibited by law, black markets tend to spring up to satisfy frustrated consumer demand. In some countries, currency exchange is prohibited, so black markets—sometimes called *parallel markets*—are set up to take over the normal role of banks or currency traders. The black economy consists of all those underground transactions, such as prostitution, illegal drugs, pornography, and gambling, that, because of their illegality, are out of the control of local officials.

Black Swan Theory. A completely unexpected event that has a major impact on the world economy is sometimes referred to as a *black swan*. Most black swan events, such as severe market drops, are usually seen in hindsight as having been predictable, but in most cases they take everyone by surprise. The black swan theory was formulated by the Lebanese American author Nassim Nicholas Taleb in an attempt to help people and businesses plan for the unexpected while still concentrating on events that can be predicted and, eventually, beneficial.

Blockchain. Blockchain is a type of encryption technology that ensures that the information we are receiving is exact and hasn't been tampered with. It can be used for everything from keeping track of cryptocurrencies like bitcoin to tracking commodities like chickens from infancy in the coop to the frying pan in our kitchens. The advantage of blockchain is that the information that is encrypted is virtually impossible to alter once it has been put into a string of code.

Blue Chip. AAA, top of the line. A blue chip stock is one that is considered the best in its field. The term originated in the game of poker, where the most expensive chips are usually the blue ones.

Blue Collar / White Collar. Workers who perform manual labor and earn an hourly wage are generally referred to as *blue collar* in reference to the color of shirt many manual laborers used to wear. White-collar workers, professionals earning a salary, usually have higher levels of education and usually earn more money than blue-collar workers.

Bond. The ultimate IOU. A bond is a piece of paper that says, "I, the borrower, promise to pay you, the bond owner, a certain amount of money in the future." Originally, bonds had little slips of paper attached to them, called *coupons,* that gave the owners the right to periodic interest payments. Bonds around the world are now traded on electronic exchanges, but the payment of interest is still often referred to as *coupon payments.*

Botnet. Shortening the words *robot network,* the term *botnet* is used to describe a network of hijacked "zombie" computers that can be joined together to send waves of unwanted traffic, swamping the target's site and bringing online business to a standstill.

Brady Bond. Named after the former U.S. Treasury secretary, Brady bonds were repackaged debt from developing countries, mainly in Latin America, that had fallen on hard times. The advantage of Brady bonds was that they had the backing of U.S. Treasury securities, which made them more attractive to international investors.

BRICS. The term *BRIC,* first used by the investment bank Goldman Sachs, is an acronym for the four largest developing countries of the twenty-first-century economy: Brazil, Russia, India, and China. South Africa was added to the group in 2010, necessitating a change in the name from *BRIC* to *BRICS.* The five member countries, representing more than 40 percent of the world's population, hold periodic summits to coordinate economic policy.

Bridge Loan. Like a bridge over troubled waters, bridge loans are meant to cover short-term borrowing needs. The idea is to help bridge the gap for the borrower while they arrange more long-term financing. The International Monetary Fund and the Bank for International Settlements in Basel often provide bridge loans to poorer countries trying to arrange bailouts with the World Bank or other long-term lenders.

Broker/Dealer. Just as a real estate broker brings together buyers and sellers for a nice commission, a securities broker acts as a go-between in financial transactions. Most brokers—stock brokers, for example—receive a fee that is based on the volume of securities traded. A securities dealer, like a car dealer, has an inventory of securities that can be sold to investors for a fixed price. Some investment bankers fill both roles and are called, not surprisingly, *broker/dealers.*

Brownfield. See Greenfield/Brownfield.

Bubble. Economic bubbles, also referred to as *market bubbles,* are defined by hugely overpriced stocks or other items of value. Bubble economies have existed since the beginning of markets. In Holland, during the Dutch Golden Age, there was the tulip bubble, and in America in the late 1990s, there was the dot-com bubble. Even the Great Depression of the 1930s was partly the result of the crash of greatly overpriced shares in 1929. The housing bubble in the United States and other countries at the beginning of the twenty-first century led to sharp losses, especially in subprime mortgages when the housing bubble burst (see Irrational Exuberance).

Budget Deficit. A country runs a budget deficit when revenues, usually in the form of taxes, are exceeded by spending. Just like anyone spending more than they earn, a country running a budget deficit has to make up the difference by borrowing money. In the case of the United States and other creditworthy countries, deficit spending is allowed to go on virtually unchecked—as long as there are enough domestic and foreign investors willing to subsidize the nation's spendthrift ways by buying government debt.

Butterfly Effect. See Chaos Theory.

C2C. Transactions on the Web between consumers. Consumer-to-consumer transactions (like buying and selling DVDs or football tickets) are essentially limited to transactions between individuals, not businesses (see B2B/B2C).

Call Option. A call option gives the holder the right to buy something at a certain price. Like other options, a call option can usually only be exercised for a certain length of time. An investor who thinks the price of an asset will go up will want to buy call options because when the underlying asset goes up in value, the price of the call option increases vastly more. Investors can buy put and call options (see Put Option) on such diverse instruments as stocks, commodities, and foreign currencies.

Cap and Trade. See Emissions Trading.

Capital. Capital and labor are the two main inputs into economic production. In accounting, capital consists not only of the cash a company owns but also physical assets such as property, buildings, and machines—including robots. Capital can also include such intangibles as managerial expertise and the firm's brand names.

Capital Account. All international flows of money-related investment are grouped together in a country's capital account. Capital accounts typically include foreign direct investment (see Foreign Direct Investment) and such portfolio investments as purchases and sales of stocks and bonds. The capital account and the current account (see Current Account), when added together, determine the country's total international economic activity, referred to as *balance of payments* (see Balance of Payments).

Capital Gain. When securities or real estate are sold at a profit, the difference between the sale price and the original purchase price is called a *capital gain*. Capital gains are usually taxed at different rates from other income, such as interest and dividend payments. In some countries like Switzerland, capital gains are not taxed at all.

Capital Market. Where investors go to buy or sell securities. A capital market is an exchange or a group of exchanges where bonds and other debt instruments are traded. Most capital market trading is done on trading floors in banks scattered around the world and connected electronically to form one big international market.

Capitalism. The economic system that lets people and the markets make the decisions on how much to produce and at what price. Capitalism is based on the idea of private ownership, as opposed to command or communist economies where the assets are in the hands of the state (see Communism).

Carbon Footprint. The amount of greenhouse gases released by a specific action or series of actions is referred to as a *carbon footprint*. Even though they may include emissions of other greenhouse gases, such as methane or sulfur dioxide, most carbon footprint calculations translate emissions to their carbon dioxide equivalent to make it easier for us to understand and compare. Concerned citizens of the world economy can calculate their carbon footprint by going to web-based carbon footprint calculators, such as the one provided by the Conservation Fund, an environmental organization based in Arlington, Virginia.

Carbon Tax. A tax on fossil fuels that generate carbon dioxide emissions, like almost any other tax, tends to reduce the item's use. Typical carbon taxes are gasoline taxes, which are meant to discourage consumers' use of the polluting fuel. Some countries have called for a global tax to be put on all carbon emissions. The problem is how to locate all the polluting activity and to convince all the players in the world economy to participate in the scheme.

Carry Trade. The practice of borrowing money in one currency, where interest rates are low, and investing it in another currency, where interest rates are high. The idea is to earn money on the *spread*, the differential between the two interest rates.

Cartel. A group of companies or countries that bank together to control production and prices. The most famous example of a cartel in the global economy is the Organization of the Petroleum Exporting Countries (see OPEC), which was set up in the 1960s to coordinate the production of oil, thus allowing them to better control the market.

Cash Cow. A company or a stock that generates a continuous flow of cash is often called a *cash cow*. Cash cow industries or products usually don't need any marketing or special attention; they just keep churning out the profits.

Cash Crops / Food Crops. In many developing countries, a food crop is often used just for feeding the farmer's family. If there is a surplus, it can be sold for cash—hence, the name *cash crop*. This surplus can provide income that allows the family to buy clothing, shelter, and other items necessary for survival.

Cash Flow. A quick measure of the money coming into and going out of a company. Cash flow tells investors what the company has done over a specific period of time without accounting tricks like depreciation and other write-offs.

Centrally Planned Economy. Where the bureaucrats get to make the decisions. In a centrally planned economy, the state has the authority to decide who produces what and at what price it will be sold. Resource allocation is also decided by the central decision-making bodies. Centrally planned economies are also called *command economies* or *planned economies*.

CEO. The big cheese. The chief executive officer is the person who runs the company—as opposed to the *chairperson*, who oversees what management does.

CFO. The chief financial officer is in charge of the money coming into and going out of a company. The CFO usually reports directly to the CEO. A CFO is typically in charge of overseeing financial accounting, financial planning, and managing financial risk.

Chaebol. In South Korea, many companies are grouped together in conglomerates, or *chaebols*, that sometimes become quasi-monopolies. After the economic crisis of the late 1990s, the Korean government moved to dismantle them.

Chairperson. The person in charge of overseeing what a company's management does. The chairperson and the board of directors are supposed to look after the best interests of the company's shareholders, who appoint them for fixed terms—and pay them a yearly fee.

Chaos Theory. The classic view of chaos theory is that many events in the world are simply impossible to predict or control. Nonlinear events like the weather, stock market fluctuations, or how our brains work depend on such a wide array of factors that no one—not even someone armed with the most powerful computer—is able to say what will be the future effect of current actions. The butterfly effect, as explained by Edward Lorenz, the MIT meteorology professor who first studied chaos theory, is the idea that something as insignificant as a butterfly flapping its wings over the Amazon or elsewhere could eventually cause a severe thunderstorm in a far corner of the world.

Chapter 7 / Chapter 11. The two most important concepts in the book of bankruptcy (see Bankruptcy). In the United States, Chapter 11 (called *administration* in Britain) allows a bankrupt company to try to work out its troubles. Chapter 7 (called *receivership* in Britain) is when the struggling company is liquidated—the assets are sold off to pay as many of the company's debts as possible.

Climate Change. The effect of a drastic increase in greenhouse gases in the atmosphere has led to an increase in the percentage of the sun's rays being trapped in the earth's atmosphere, leading to increasing temperatures in many parts of the world—in addition to severe storms and changing weather patterns. Transportation, industrial production, and agricultural activities have all contributed to the increase in particles in the earth's atmosphere and subsequent global warming. The economic effect of global warming, when such catastrophes as hurricanes and floods are included, is expected to reach into the trillions of dollars.

Collateralized Debt Obligation (CDO). Collateralized debt obligations are loans with an asset or a bundle of assets attached to them. The assets can be anything from a flow of money— from mortgage payments, for example—to a flow of goods, such as a farmer's future crops or an orange juice factory's future production. The loan and the assets are usually grouped together and sold as a single instrument. Investors in CDOs are provided with guaranteed access to revenue generated by the underlying assets. If the underlying assets stop generating revenue, as the defaulted mortgages did in 2007, the CDO can become worthless.

Commercial Bank. A bank that takes deposits and loans is commonly referred to as a *commercial* bank. Although commercial banks—at least in Japan and the United States—have traditionally been prohibited from getting involved in such investment banking activities as selling stocks or underwriting new issues of securities (see Initial Public Offering), by the beginning of the twenty-first century, they were allowed to do almost everything their investment banking brethren do (see Investment Bank / Investment Banking).

Commercial Paper. Short-term securities, or loans, issued by banks, corporations, and other commercial entities. Commercial paper is a relatively safe investment because of the short-term nature of the risk. Commercial paper is normally not used to finance long-term investments but for short-term uses, such as financing the purchase of inventory or to increase working capital. Commercial paper can consist of promissory notes, drafts, checks, or certificates of deposit.

Commodity. Raw materials, such as oil, gas, or soy beans, are referred to as *commodities*. Most commodities are easily traded on the world markets because they are relatively homogenous: gold from Siberia is basically the same as gold from Nevada. Commodities can be traded in many ways: in spot transactions, for immediate delivery, or in the futures market, where they are traded at a fixed price that will be effective at some later date. Other commodities include corn, silver, tin, beef, wheat—and the proverbial pork bellies.

Commodity Money. See Fiat Currency.

Common Market. The former name of the European Union (see European Union). The idea, at the time of the EU's founding, was to allow goods and money to flow, unrestricted, across member countries' borders. When the European Economic Community became a political as well as an economic entity, it was decided to change its name to the more generic *European Union*.

Communism. Communism's goal is to create a society with total equality. This utopian idea, developed during the nineteenth century by such economic philosophers as Friedrich Engels and Karl Marx, was based on the desire to remedy the abuses of the capitalist system, especially egregious during the early years of the Industrial Revolution, when child labor, unsanitary work conditions, and abuse of workers were rampant.

Comparative Advantage. The law of comparative advantage is based on the synergies produced when each country in the world is allowed to produce and export the goods and services it produces most efficiently. In the end, the theory goes, everyone will be better off.

Consumer Price Index (CPI). The index of prices in the U.S. economy. Referred to as the *Retail Price Index* (*RPI*) in Britain, the CPI summarizes the prices of a basket of goods and services that a typical citizen would buy over the course of a given year.

Convention on International Trade in Endangered Species (CITES). Along with the United Nations Environment Programme (UNEP), the CITES organization regulates the trade in endangered species of fauna and flora. By controlling the sale of ivory, for example, CITES is able to reduce poaching to a minimum. CITES makes a distinction between animals that need to be protected by a total ban on trade and hunting, called *Appendix I,* and those species that can be "harvested" in sustainable numbers, called *Appendix II.*

Convergence. Individual countries often have divergent economic needs in different areas, so governments try to homogenize the economy as a whole by converging economic policy. Just as it's hard for the Fed to balance the needs of each region of the United States—California could be booming, for example, while the Midwest stagnates—it is extremely difficult for the European Central Bank to accommodate the needs of the various countries of the European Union. Central banks try, therefore, to make the different economies converge as much as possible, especially in the areas of inflation, growth, and unemployment.

Convertible Bond. To make bonds or other securities more attractive to investors, companies sometimes make them convertible, allowing investors to exchange them for something else of value, usually the issuing company's shares. A convertible bond is often comparable to a stock option: the owner has the right, but not the obligation, to trade the bond for a company's shares at any time.

Corporate Finance. When companies or governments need large amounts of money, they usually turn to investment banks to help them find financing at an attractive price. The goal of a corporate finance adviser is to find the right mix of bonds, equity, swaps, or other forms of financing that allow the corporation to secure funding at the lowest possible cost.

Corporate Governance. The rules that govern the way corporations are managed and controlled are referred to as *corporate governance*. It basically refers to the relationship among the company's stakeholders—shareholders, management, and the board of directors—but may include the company's relationship with customers, employees, suppliers, banks, regulators, and the community at large.

Corporate Social Responsibility. See Socially Conscious Investing.

Correction. A temporary market drop. As opposed to a crash, which is expected to last over a longer period of time, a market correction is the way economists describe a short-term decline in the value of stocks or bonds.

Creative Destruction. New technologies tend to push out old ones. Joseph Schumpeter's theories, developed back in the 1930s, were based on an idea that economies grow by leaps, and if businesses don't adapt to new technologies, new products, and new ways of producing and distributing goods, they will be destroyed. Or, more mildly put, go out of business—allowing new companies to take their place.

Crony Capitalism. See Oligarchy.

Crowdsourcing. Using the Internet to outsource specific goods and services is referred to as *crowdsourcing*. Using the Internet's access to large networks of possible providers of goods and services, individuals and companies are able to accomplish a wide variety of tasks. The possible uses of crowdsourcing are almost limitless, ranging from astronomy (where online users helped NASA organize space photographs) to genealogy (where individuals collaborate to create a database of family members, worldwide). The term was coined in 2006 by Jeff Howe in the magazine *Wired*.

Cryptocurrency. Cryptocurrencies are digital assets, such as bitcoin or Ethereum, that serve the same purpose as other forms of currencies. They can be used as a medium of exchange or used to store value. Almost all cryptocurrencies use a form of encryption technology, usually blockchain, to ensure authenticity and other forms of technology to control the creation of additional units. When the owner of a cryptocurrency decides to purchase something—a good or service, for example—the

entire system is updated to reflect the transfer of the cryptocurrency from buyer to seller. Usually, once a cryptocurrency
is transferred to its new owner and verified, the transaction
cannot be retracted (see Blockchain).

Cum. In Latin, *cum* means *with*. A bond with a warrant still attached to it is referred to in the markets as *cum*. A stock sold
with the dividend still to be paid is traded as *cum dividend*.

Currency. A euro, a yen, a buck, or a pound—printed money is the
currency of all advanced economies. Currencies are printed by
central banks and monetary authorities and are usually backed
by nothing more than the good faith of the issuing authority.
In the United States, the Treasury used to provide the option
of exchanging dollar bills for gold. Since 1973, this is no longer the case. Nowadays, most major currencies are only worth
what other people or businesses are willing to pay or trade for
them.

Currency Peg. Sometimes, a country can artificially reduce or
raise the value of its currency on the world markets by intervening in the foreign exchange markets. By making massive
purchases or sales of any given currency, governments can
drastically affect its value. At the beginning of the twenty-first
century, more than a hundred countries manipulated their
currencies in one way or another—even though only a few
admitted outright manipulation—which usually takes place
by pegging, or fixing, the value of one currency to another.
Examples of pegged currency systems include fourteen Central African countries pegging their CFA franc to the euro, and
Hong Kong, the United Arab Emirates, and most Caribbean
nations pegging their currencies to the U.S. dollar.

Current Account. The measure of a country's international trade in goods and services over a given period of time. Current accounts measure "visible" trade, such as rice and television sets, as well as "invisible" trade, such as banking services and movies. The current account also includes financial transfers, such as money sent home by citizens working abroad and interest paid on foreign debt. The current account is balanced by the country's capital account, which adds up all the financial transfers, including international purchases and sales of financial assets like stocks or bonds.

Customs Union. A trade union where members agree to have the same tariffs on imports from outside the union is called a *customs union*. The advantage of being inside a customs union is that any imported good, once the commonly agreed tariff has been applied, can then be sent on to any other member country. An iPhone or a car imported into Italy from the United States, for example, can be sent on to any other country in the European customs union without any concern for where it came from originally.

Dark Web / Dark Net / Darknet. Lurking in the dark waters below the surface of the world economy are nefarious entities referred to as the *Deep Web* and the *Dark Web*. The two terms are often used interchangeably but mean two very different things. Generally, Deep Web activities are not illegal; they just prefer being out of the public eye. Typical Deep Web functions include Internet banking, the archiving of medical records, company intranets, and other private networks where we don't necessarily want the world seeing everything we're doing. The Dark Web—the deepest, most-hidden level of Internet activity—was given the name because interactions there need to be masked, most often because they involve illegal or other highly secretive purchases or exchanges. It is also sometimes referred to as the *Darknet* or the *Dark Net*.

Data. Data is information that is used by organizations and institutions to analyze everything from people's spending habits to their political preferences. Once data is coded in a format that can be used easily by the analyzing entity, it can provide a vast amount of information useful for everything from economic forecasts to consumer marketing. Raw data is data that has been cleansed of ancillary or unneeded information, such as the user's name, address, and telephone number. Data that provides information about other data, allowing users to find relevant information in the amassed data at users' disposal—similar to a card catalogue in a library allowing users to find relevant books—is referred to as metadata.

Datsu-sara. The Japanese had to invent a new word to describe the once rare event of a manager who left a company to go work somewhere else. With today's global economy, however, employees are not expected to be a *sarariman,* working for the same company, forever. *Datsu-sara* literally means *corporate dropout.*

Davos. See World Economic Forum.

Dealer. See Broker/Dealer.

Debenture. A debenture is a bond backed only by the good credit of the company issuing it. The purchaser relies on the full faith of the issuer to be paid back, which means that they are only paid off after other, more senior debt has been paid off. Subordinated debentures naturally provide a higher rate of interest to reward investors for the higher risk.

Debt-to-Equity Ratio / Debt Ratio. A good way to judge a company's health is to look at how much it owes and how much it owns. The basic idea of a debt ratio is that if a company owes too much money to creditors, it will have a hard time staying afloat in troubled times. In many new economy companies, debt ratios are extremely high, often because assets and income (in the beginning, at least) are relatively low. A start-up company often needs many years to begin showing a profit.

Debt Glut. During the meltdown of the credit markets following the subprime mortgage defaults of 2007 and 2008, many banks were faced with a glut of commercial paper that investors refused to buy (see Commercial Paper). Some banks took this debt onto their own balance sheets, in effect buying the short-term bonds and other instruments that they had issued on behalf of corporations and other entities.

Default. When a company—or a country—is unable to pay its creditors on time, it is said to be in default. Interest payments on notes and bonds are usually the first to be stopped by a cash-strapped borrower. If no solution is found, the borrower is forced to declare bankruptcy. A country in default sees its credit rating plummet and often finds it difficult to get more money from international investors.

Deficit, Deficit Spending. Almost too good to be true, deficit spending allows you to pay out more than you earn. In the world economy, there are two kinds of deficits: budget deficits and trade deficits. A government is said to run a budget deficit when tax revenues are not enough to cover spending. To overcome this, governments issue debt—such as Treasury bonds—to provide the funds they need to continue their profligate ways. In a worst-case scenario, a government can simply print up more money. A trade deficit occurs when a country spends more on imports than it earns from exports.

Deflation. The opposite of inflation. Deflation occurs when an economy slows down to the point that prices—usually measured by a basket of goods and services—decline. It is an extremely rare event because most producers are reluctant to lower prices. Japan is one of the few countries during recent years to suffer from deflation.

Demand. Demand is an important aspect of economics, relating primarily to consumption. Essentially, demand tells us what consumers or businesses will buy at a given price. Economists use supply-and-demand curves to explain that when producers raise prices, consumers lower their purchases and demand falls. Conversely, when prices are reduced, demand increases. Similar to depreciation, amortization is the way companies account for the reduction in value of intangible assets over time.

Depreciation. Accountants refer to the reduction of a tangible asset's value over time as *depreciation*. For example, as a car or computer loses its value over time, its value is depreciated in the company's books. Tax authorities often allow companies to treat depreciation as a cost of doing business, thus reducing taxable income. Therefore, companies prefer to depreciate as much as they can, as early as they can, to take advantage of the opportunity to reduce their tax bill.

Depression. A prolonged economic slowdown is defined as a depression if it lasts for more than two or three quarters. A depression is usually marked by a steep decline in production and demand. As a result, stock markets drop, companies go bankrupt, and unemployment usually rises. Governments try to avoid depressions by providing economic stimuli, such as increasing government spending or allowing the money supply to rise.

Deregulation. *Que sera, sera*—"Whatever will be will be." When governments want to encourage competition and make economies more productive, they often deregulate, removing restrictions on companies' behavior. After deregulation, previously cosseted companies like airlines or cable service providers are allowed to make their own decisions on prices and markets, regardless of the effect on consumers.

Derivative. A financial instrument that gets its value from other financial instruments. A derivative, such as an option or an index-tracking future, will increase in value whenever the value of the underlying security or securities on which it is based goes up. It may sound like a house of cards, but derivatives allow people to invest in profitable ways. Derivatives tend to be risky investments, however. Investors get more bang for the buck when the underlying instrument goes up, but they can lose big in a declining market.

Devaluation/Revaluation. The decision to raise or lower a currency's value is not taken lightly. Governments use open-market purchases and sales of a currency or altering interest rates to regulate their currency's value on the international markets. However, when speculators and other international investors begin dumping a currency they perceive to be weak, a government is sometimes forced to devalue, letting the currency fall to a new, more-sustainable level. Devaluations have occurred everywhere over the past years, from Argentina to China and from Turkey to Thailand.

Developing Economies. From China to Brazil, from South Africa to India, the twenty or so countries that make up the list of emerging economies have become the driving force of the world economy. Over the first two decades of the twenty-first century, their economic growth has consistently surpassed the growth attained by the "advanced" industrial economies, such as those of the United States, France, and Japan. Most economic surveys, such as those provided by the IMF and Standard & Poor's, include the following countries in their lists of emerging economies: Brazil, Chile, China, Colombia, Hungary, Indonesia, India, Malaysia, Mexico, Peru, the Philippines, Poland, Russia, South Africa, Thailand, and Turkey.

Diminishing Returns. Consumers and producers tend to pay a lot for their first purchase—the first bottle of Coca-Cola, for example, or a new tool for the factory. But the law of diminishing returns shows how subsequent purchases need to be encouraged by ever-declining prices to keep sales from declining. Offices and factories are also subject to the law of diminishing returns. When the first new machine is installed, productivity increases rapidly—just imagine the result of installing the first computer in an office that previously used hand calculators—but when additional machines are installed, productivity still increases, though not as quickly.

Dirty Float. See Managed Float.

Discount Rate. The interest rate that the U.S. Federal Reserve, America's central bank, charges on loans to member banks. This rate is set periodically by the Fed in an attempt to influence interest rates throughout the economy, thus allowing the Fed to control economic growth. The discount rate is often confused with the federal funds rate, although only the first is directly determined by the Fed.

Disinflation. A bit of an oxymoron, disinflation refers to a slowdown in the rate of inflation, which is a rise in the prices of a basket of goods and services. Basically, under disinflation, prices still rise, but not as quickly. Not to be confused with *deflation*, which is a decline in prices (see Deflation).

Dividend. A payment to the company's shareholders. A dividend occurs when a company has made a profit and instead of investing the money back into the company, it decides to pay it out to the company's shareholders.

Division of Labor. A butcher, a baker, a candlestick maker—when an economy divides up work, letting each worker do what they do best, things usually get done more efficiently. The same concept can be applied to the world economy, letting some countries excel at making one thing and others something else (see Comparative Advantage).

Doha Round. The World Trade Organization's attempt to organize a global trade agreement was initiated in Doha, Qatar, in 2001. The primary purpose was to get the rich, industrialized countries in Europe and North America and Japan to remove barriers to trade in agriculture and the developing countries to remove barriers to trade in manufactured goods.

Dollarization. See Currency Peg.

Dormant Account. An inactive bank account. In most countries, after a few years, dormant accounts are closed, and the money is handed over to a government agency. In Switzerland, however, many accounts left dormant after World War II were left inactive, earning little or no interest until the 1990s, when international pressure forced the Swiss banks to reveal that thousands of these accounts were still around. The Swiss banks made a billion-dollar settlement with international authorities to get part of the money to Holocaust survivors and their heirs.

Double Deficit. When a government overspends, it is said to run a budget deficit. A trade deficit occurs when a country imports more than it exports. When both occur simultaneously, it is referred to as a *double deficit*. A double deficit is also referred to as a *twin deficit*.

Dow Jones Industrial Average (DJIA). The "Dow" is one of the most watched market indexes in the world. Even though it tracks the prices of only thirty or so stocks, it is seen as one of the best indicators of how the market as a whole is doing. It used to include only "old economy" stocks from the New York Stock Exchange. Then it began to add NASDAQ "new economy" shares, such as Intel and Microsoft. The Dow Jones group also produces indexes for many other types of stocks, including transportation and utilities.

Downsizing. The term *downsizing* was first used in the 1970s to describe the practice of companies laying off large numbers of employees, usually in an effort to reduce costs and, consequently, increase profits. Unfortunately, it doesn't always work. Losing experienced employees often leads to decreased productivity, and lower morale often leads to losses instead of profits.

Dumping. The sale of goods or services at a price below cost. Dumping doesn't really hurt anyone since the consumers buying the product are certainly happy to pay less than they normally would. But when a foreign producer is found to be engaged in dumping, local producers cry foul and usually get the government to provide sanctions (see Tariff) to get the offending country's producers to stop selling products abroad too cheaply. The American government has often used dumping as an excuse for high tariffs on everything from steel to ethanol.

E-Commerce. Business transacted electronically, referred to as *e-commerce,* includes the purchase and sale of products or online services over the Internet. E-commerce transactions can range from the purchase of online books from Amazon to the use of gig economy platforms providing such services as childcare or online tutoring. Philanthropic activities, such as crowdfunding or crowdsourcing platforms, are also defined as e-commerce activities. With businesses and governments accepting contracts signed digitally, taking advantage of advanced encryption technology like blockchain, almost any kind of transaction is now possible in cyberspace.

Earnings / EBIT / EBITDA. Earnings are a company's proverbial bottom line. Earnings are what is left after subtracting all expenses from revenue. Earnings are sometimes also referred to as *net income* or, more simply, *profit. EBIT* refers to earnings before interest and taxes. *EBITDA* refers to earnings before interest, taxes, depreciation, and amortization (see Depreciation).

Econometrics. The scientific use of statistics and mathematical formulas to develop and test economic theories. Econometricians use complex models to simulate real-life situations and test the effects on economic behavior of a wide range of variables, such as interest rates, taxes, and investment incentives.

Economy of Scale. "Many hands make light work." *Economy of scale* describes the benefit of making a lot of something at one time. The Industrial Revolution was based on the idea of producing in large numbers, which meant that the costs of producing something were spread out over a large number of products or services (see Division of Labor and Comparative Advantage).

Elasticity, Elasticity of Demand, Elasticity of Supply. The economic term that refers to the propensity of a behavior to change, or "stretch," over a given period of time. Elasticity of demand, for example, describes how much the demand for a given product will change if there is a change in the product's price. A shopper with a high elasticity of demand would tend to rush out and buy a product as soon as it goes on sale. A shopper with low elasticity of demand tends to keep buying the same products at the same store—even when they could be had at a lower price in another store down the street.

Emerging Economies / Emerging Markets. See Developing Economies.

Emissions Trading. The basic idea of emissions trading is to provide economic incentives to reduce carbon dioxide and other greenhouse gas emissions—the major cause of global warming. The idea behind emissions trading is to cap and trade, which means setting limits on the volume of greenhouse gases that can be emitted by a sector or the total economy, and then allowing individual players to trade their pollution rights, achieving a rational and economically viable approach to reducing pollution.

Equilibrium. Economics is based on the theory that all forces in an economy move toward equilibrium. When the price of a product is too high, for example, people tend to reduce their purchases. To sell more inventory, therefore, producers have to lower the price until demand and supply match each other. Equilibrium exists for most economic concepts, such as savings, investment, and employment.

Equity. Equity means ownership. On a company's balance sheet, *equity* refers to the part of a company that belongs to the shareholders—after all the liabilities have been subtracted, of course. A company's net worth (see Net Worth) is also referred to as *stockholders' equity.*

ETF. See Exchange-Traded Fund.

Euro. The euro was created by the European Union on January 1, 1999, when eleven countries fixed their currencies to a totally new unit of exchange. From that point on, the national currencies of Germany, France, Italy, Spain, Portugal, Ireland, Austria, Finland, Belgium, Luxembourg, and the Netherlands existed no more. Euro notes and coins were put into circulation. Britain, Denmark, and Sweden opted to retain their own currencies. By the end of the 2010s, Cyprus, Estonia, Greece, Latvia, Lithuania, Malta, Slovakia, and Slovenia had given up their national currencies to join the eurozone. Several countries, such as Kosovo and Montenegro, have decided to use the euro as their national currency even without becoming full members of the European Union.

Eurodollar. A currency abroad. Eurodollars are U.S. dollars that are held in bank accounts outside the United States. The prefix *euro* is used to describe any currency held outside its country of origin, even if the country isn't in Europe. Japanese yen held in Singapore, for example, are referred to as *euroyen,* just as British pounds held in Canada are called *europounds*. And what do you call a euro that is held outside Europe? A *euro-euro*, of course.

European Central Bank (ECB). Based in Frankfurt, the European Central Bank was set up when the euro was created in the late 1990s. Its mission is to oversee economic and monetary policy in the countries that have adopted the euro. The ECB has supplanted most of the activities of the various countries' central banks (such as the Bundesbank and the Banque de France). It was clear that without a common interest rate and monetary policy, the individual member states would all tend to go their own way in charting economic policy, and the new common currency would have little chance of success. The head of the ECB is appointed to an eight-year term by the countries that make up the eurozone (see Eurozone).

European Free Trade Association (EFTA). The four Western European holdouts to the European Union—Switzerland, Liechtenstein, Iceland, and Norway—decided to form their own free-trade union and adopt a wait-and-see policy to joining the EU, choosing to take advantage of access to the EU market through separate trade agreements.

European Union (EU). The European Union—previously called the *European Economic Community, European Community,* or *Common Market*—began as a simple customs union in the 1950s. The original idea was to do away with barriers to trade between the member countries. Eventually, this "community" evolved into a broader "union" with common political, social, and economic policies.

Eurozone. The eurozone is made up of the nineteen countries that use the euro: Austria, Belgium, Cyprus, Estonia, Finland,

France, Germany, Greece, Ireland, Italy, Latvia, Lithuania, Luxembourg, Malta, the Netherlands, Portugal, Slovakia, Slovenia, and Spain.

Ex. The Latin word meaning *from* is used to describe bonds or other securities that have had their warrants removed. A stock that is sold *ex* is one that has already had its dividend distributed to a previous owner (see Cum).

Exchange Rates. The value of currencies worldwide is determined by their exchange rates. Since currencies have no value other than what they're worth in terms of other currencies, the exchange rate tells you what each currency is worth at a given point in time. A Norwegian krone, for example, is worth a fixed amount of euros—or dollars or yen. Exchange rates are constantly readjusted to keep them in line with the other currencies' values.

Exchange-Traded Fund (ETF). Investment funds that are not managed per se but are based on investing in all the shares that make up a particular index like the S&P 500 are referred to as *exchange-traded funds,* or ETFs. They allow investors to avoid the loads, or traditionally high fees, that traditional fund managers charge. ETFs provide investors with a wide range of options, allowing them to invest in many indexes and markets around the world. Many allow for small investors to put in as little as a hundred dollars and charge smaller fees, or in some cases no fees at all.

External Debt. See Foreign Debt.

Fair Labor Association (FLA). One of the many human rights organizations that are active on college campuses, the FLA attempts to build coalitions of companies, consumers, and social activists to find solutions to the sweatshop conditions in factories in many developing countries. The idea is to get consumers to support the group's efforts to establish rules governing such areas as freedom of association, minimum wages, maximum working hours, sanitation, and worker safety.

Fairtrade / Fairtrade Labelling Organizations International (FLO). "Fairtrade" certification, provided by the nongovernmental organization FLOCERT, identifies products that meet previously agreed upon environmental and labor standards. FLOCERT uses independent auditors to ensure that everything from bananas to sugar and tea is produced according to standards set by a sister organization, Fairtrade International.

FANG, FANG+. The FANG index is the stock index that tracks the prices for four of the world's largest technology companies: Facebook, Amazon, Netflix, and Alphabet (Google's parent company), all of which are traded on the NASDAQ stock exchange. The FANG+ index includes many other high-tech companies, such as Alibaba, Tesla, and Twitter. These indexes are particularly useful for valuing twenty-first-century companies, as virtually none of the original FANG companies have a significant number of traditional assets, such as assembly lines or factories.

Fed Funds Rate. The interest that banks in the United States charge on overnight loans to other banks. It's called the *Fed funds rate* because the money being loaned between banks is usually kept at the Federal Reserve. When a bank has excess reserves at the Fed, it can loan this money to other banks that may need it to meet the Federal Reserve's strict reserve requirement. The Fed funds rate is often confused with the discount rate, which is, in fact, set by the Fed (see Discount Rate). Although heavily influenced by the Fed's policies, the Fed funds rate is actually set by the banks themselves.

Federal Open Market Committee (FOMC). U.S. economic and monetary policy is controlled, in large part, by a small group of Federal Reserve Board members who meet on a regular basis to chart the course of the nation's—and often, the world's—economic growth. The FMOC sets certain growth targets, including money supply, inflation, unemployment, and so on. The minutes of FOMC meetings are released to the public on a regular basis.

Federal Reserve Bank / Fed. The United States' central bank, the Federal Reserve, manages the money supply, regulates the banking system, and acts as a lender of last resort to banks in trouble. The Fed is independent: it answers to no one, except in periodic reports to Congress. The seven members of the Federal Reserve Board are appointed by the president.

Fiat Currency. A currency that relies on people having faith in the government that issued it is called a *fiat currency*. Most major currencies in the world economy are fiat currencies: the U.S. dollar, Japanese yen, and euro are solely backed by the government banks issuing them. Other currencies are sometimes underpinned by reserves of physical goods backing them, such as gold or silver. These currencies are referred to as *commodity money*.

Financial Action Task Force (FATF). Based in Paris, the Financial Action Task Force is an independent organization that examines tax havens around the world and issues regular reports on which countries are cooperating in the fight against money laundering. It is an arm of the Organisation for Economic Co-operation and Development (see Organisation for Economic Co-operation and Development).

Financial Stability Forum. Based in Basel, Switzerland, the Financial Stability Forum was set up by the world's biggest free-market economies (see G7) to promote financial stability and address other matters of concern to the international markets. One of their tasks is to keep an eye on money laundering worldwide.

Fiscal Policy. In contrast to monetary policy, which is mainly in the hands of central bankers around the world, fiscal policy is in the hands of each country's government, which gets to decide how much to tax, how much to spend, and how much to borrow (see Monetary Policy).

Flash Crash. With computer algorithms guiding them, powerful investment firms buy and sell billions and sometimes trillions of dollars' worth of securities around the world on any given day. Sometimes, a sell order provokes a flood of sell orders from computer-guided traders around the world in a matter of minutes, if not seconds. These flash crashes—rapid, deep falls in the price of a traded security, such as a stock or cryptocurrency—sometimes occur in the blink of an eye, moving whole markets without any rational explanation.

Flextime / Flexitime. Instead of requiring their employees to work fixed eight-hour days—from 9:00 to 5:00, for example—some companies allow them to choose their hours. Often, they are required to be at work during a core period to facilitate interaction with other employees but are otherwise free to come and go as they please.

Flight Capital. Fearing impending economic turmoil or government policies that may threaten savings, citizens and companies often send money to financial havens outside a country in times of crisis. This flight capital sometimes amounts to a large percentage of a country's total wealth. Latin American citizens, for example, during times of high inflation, have bought U.S. dollars and euros and sent them to bank accounts abroad—sometimes in defiance of currency exchange laws. Attempts by governments to limit the transfer of money abroad often end up encouraging capital flight—exactly what they are trying to avoid.

Floating Rate Note (FRN). Just like a home loan with an adjustable interest rate, a floating rate note is a security that has its interest rate adjusted periodically, usually reflecting changes in interest rates in the economy at large. Most floating rate notes use LIBOR, the London Interbank Offered Rate, as a reference for determining the interest rate to be paid to the holder. Adjustable-rate home loans usually are tied to the prevailing corporate loan rate (called the *prime rate* in the United States). Banks and investors prefer the price stability of floating rate notes because, during periods of widely fluctuating interest rates, the prices of FRNs remain relatively stable.

FOMC. See Federal Open Market Committee.

Foreign Debt. Sometimes called *external debt,* a country's foreign debt consists of all money that is owed to creditors abroad. This debt can be owed by individuals, companies, or even the government.

Foreign Direct Investment (FDI). When a foreign firm buys a domestic one, or even a controlling share of a domestic company's stocks, it is accounted for as foreign direct investment. FDI often provides needed capital to companies and countries that is more long-lasting than hot money investments (see Hot Money), which come in and go out at a moment's notice. FDI can often provide needed foreign expertise and new business practices. In some countries, FDI accounts for up to half of all company ownership.

Foreign Exchange / F/X. Currencies are traded on a twenty four-hour-a-day basis on "forex" marketplaces, usually located on bank floors in major financial capitals around the world. Foreign exchange trading is unique in that there is no intrinsic value for the items being bought and sold. Each currency is quoted in terms of other currencies. A dollar, for example, is quoted in terms of how many euros or yen or pounds or yuan it is worth (see Currency).

Foreign Reserves. Foreign exchange reserves, or forex reserves, are the foreign currency and other reserves like gold and special drawing rights (see Special Drawing Right) held by a country's central bank. Traditionally, most countries have held the bulk of their foreign reserves in U.S. dollars that were used to back such liabilities as local currency that has been issued or reserves put on deposit by financial institutions or the country's government. Since the beginning of the twenty-first century, however, many central banks have diversified their foreign reserves positions to include large portions of euros, yen, and other international currencies.

Forest Stewardship Council (FSC). The watchdog of the world's forests. The Forest Stewardship Council was set up by the

WWF (see World Wide Fund for Nature) to provide consumers and businesses with an official seal of approval for purchasing tropical woods. The FSC seal certifies that wood or wood products have been harvested in ways that ensure sustainability. Instead of clear-cutting, for example, the FSC encourages selected harvesting, cutting only selected trees in a forest to keep the forest and the surrounding biosphere intact.

Forward Markets / Forward Trading. A forward contract fixes the price of a transaction to be executed at a specific date in the future. A wheat farmer, for example, can sell next year's harvest by going to the forward markets to find someone who will agree to set a price today. Unlike futures contracts (see Future Contract), which are traded on exchanges with fixed prices and dates, forward contracts are tailor-made to accommodate the needs of both the buyer and the seller.

Free-Market Economy. Where the decisions are made by the market, not the government. The idea of a free-market economy is to provide consumers and businesses with the best products at the best prices. In contrast to centrally planned economies, where decisions on how much to produce and how to distribute that production are made by the government (see Centrally Planned Economy), a free-market economy lets the markets decide everything, from prices to production.

Free Trade Area of the Americas (FTAA). In 1994, Western Hemisphere leaders decided to join together all the disparate economies and trading groups, from the Yukon to Tierra del Fuego, and create a Free Trade Area of the Americas, which would eventually encompass all the free-market economies of North, Central, and South America. Unfortunately, political infighting and entrenched special interests have kept the venture from becoming much more than a well-intentioned idea.

Friction. *Friction* refers to impediments that may interfere with consumers or businesses buying a particular good or service. In economic theory, less friction leads to higher demand. Online music sales, for example, languished for many years because the songs purchased were subject to restrictions like DRM (digital rights management), which limited the number of times consumers could recopy them or share with their friends. When these restrictions were done away with, sales soared.

Friedman, Milton. The most well-known free-market economist. Milton Friedman, Nobel Prize winner and University of Chicago economist, did more than almost anyone to promote the idea that free markets are the best way to make difficult economic decisions. "Free to choose" is the goal of Friedmanian economics. Theoretically, if consumers are allowed to buy what they want and producers are free to sell what they want, the world will be made a better place for (almost) all.

Future Contract / Future Trading. A future is a security that can be bought or sold, just like a stock or bond. It is, essentially, a contract to buy or sell a commodity or a financial instrument at a fixed price and at a fixed time in the future. Futures are unlike forward contracts (see Forward Markets) in that their terms are standardized. Because the time and date on future contracts correspond to other contracts, they can be traded on exchanges around the world.

G7/G8/G20. The first group of nations set up to coordinate economic strategy was the Group of Seven, or G7, which included

Canada, the United States, Japan, France, Germany, Italy, and the United Kingdom. The leaders of the seven countries meet regularly to discuss a wide range of political and economic issues. When Russia was included in the group, from 1997 until 2014, it was referred to as the G8. A larger group, encompassing the G7 nations and the other major world economies, including several developing countries (see BRICS), was formed in 2008 following the world financial crisis (see Great Depression / Great Recession). The twenty members of this group are Argentina, Australia, Brazil, Canada, China, the European Union, France, Germany, India, Indonesia, Italy, Japan, Mexico, Russia, Saudi Arabia, South Africa, South Korea, Turkey, the United Kingdom, and the United States. Spain is a permanent guest invitee.

GDP/GNP. See Gross Domestic Product.

Gearing. Gearing gets you more bang for your buck—allowing companies to borrow money to supplement the funds provided in the form of share capital. Gearing is also referred to as the *debt ratio.*

Generations X, Y, and Z. The generations following the baby boomers ("boomers")—who were born between 1945 and the mid-1960s—were given letters, awaiting evocative names. Members of generation X (also referred to as *gen X* or the *MTV generation*) were born between the mid-1960s and the mid-1980s. Members of generation Y (widely referred to as *millennials* or the *me generation*) were born between the mid-1980s and 2000. Members of generation Z (alternatively referred to as the *iGen* or the *smartphone generation,* or even *lingling hou* in China—meaning "after two zeros") were born during the two decades following 2000.

Gig Economy. The gig economy encompasses those jobs that are basically temporary and consist of flexible working hours. Gig employers usually hire independent, freelance workers who are unable or unwilling to be employed on a full-time basis. While some gig economy workers are forced to take temporary jobs by a dearth of full-time jobs in their respective markets, others have found that they actually prefer the variety and novelty of a never-ending array of activities to the monotony of a full-time job.

Gini Coefficient / Gini Ratio. Income and wealth inequality can be measured in many ways, but the most commonly used measure is the Gini coefficient, which assigns a score of 0 to countries with perfect equality (utopia, for most observers) and a score of 100 to a country with complete inequality—essentially one where a single household holds all the wealth. It was developed in the early years of the twentieth century by the Italian statistician and sociologist Corrado Gini.

Going Public. See Initial Public Offering.

Gold Standard. It used to be that a currency's value was either fixed by the government or linked to some other item of value, such as gold. In the United States, for example, before 1973, you could convert U.S. dollars into gold at a fixed exchange rate. The gold standard was meant to ensure that the currency would always have a minimum value. Most currencies now use a system of floating exchange rates (see Currency) that lets the market decide what each currency is worth.

Golden Parachute. Fearing a hostile takeover, many top managers incorporate huge guaranteed bonuses into their severance packages to ensure that they'll land on their feet—with their pockets full of money—should they ever be forced out of their job by new owners.

Goodwill. The part of the company that can't be attributed to tangible assets and liabilities is referred to as *goodwill,* even though it may have nothing to do with the company's benevolent intentions. A typical example of goodwill is a brand name. Since many twenty-first-century companies, such as dot-com startups or websites, have no tangible value, their goodwill is said to be worth millions, if not billions.

Great Depression / Great Recession. The economic downturn following the Wall Street stock market crash in 1929, referred to as the Great Depression, lasted through most of the 1930s. It was the deepest and severest depression the world experienced in the twentieth century. Worldwide gross domestic product (see Gross Domestic Product) fell by approximately 15 percent. The Great Recession, in contrast, saw a decline of worldwide GDP of less than 1 percent between 2008 and 2009. It began after the collapse of the housing market in the United States in 2007 and lasted for several years, affecting virtually every country in the world economy.

Greenfield/Brownfield. Similar to building something new in an open field of grass, a greenfield project is one unconstrained by prior work. Rolling out a new cell network, for example, uses entirely new technology, and no adaptation to preexisting networks is required. A brownfield project is one where the work has to be adapted to previously constructed systems, such as altering computer code in an existing database. Many previously constructed brownfield construction sites bring additional problems to the builder, such as polluted land or decaying infrastructure.

Greenhouse Gases. Without some particles in the atmosphere, the earth's temperature would sink below freezing. The presence of certain particles in the atmosphere—mainly water vapor, carbon dioxide, methane, nitrous oxide, and ozone—cause a "greenhouse" effect, trapping some of the sun's rays and warming the earth just as a greenhouse creates a healthy environment for plants to grow (see Climate Change).

Green New Deal. Just as the New Deal attempted to end the 1930s depression in the United States with massive governmental spending to jump-start the moribund economy, many political leaders have called for a Green New Deal to transition the United States from an economy reliant on fossil fuels to one based on renewable energy. The resulting economic consequences, including enormous unemployment in those industries producing or consuming fossil fuels—the automobile industry, for example would be mitigated by massive governmental spending to ensure that those losing their jobs would be retrained and supported by government-provided health care and other services to reduce income inequality in the post–fossil fuel economy.

Gross Domestic Product (GDP) / Gross National Product (GNP). Gross domestic product and gross national product both measure economic activity. While GDP adds up all the goods and services produced within an economy over the course of the year, GNP adds some international components, such as income from foreign operations. Neither GDP nor GNP tells the whole story, however. Many economies have considerable unreported activities, including unpaid housework, volunteer work, and such illegal activities as drug sales and prostitution. Another word for GDP/GNP is *output*.

Growth Capital. As opposed to most other venture capital investors who concentrate on young, start-up companies, growth
capital investors concentrate primarily on relatively mature
companies. Growth capital investors generally help companies
looking for someone to share the risk of undertaking a major
new activity, such as an acquisition, a restructuring, or a big
expansion of operations. The companies may be already earning a profit, but they lack the large amounts of money required
for their next steps. And because banks are typically reluctant
to fund risky new ventures, companies looking to grow turn to
private equity funds or other growth capital investors to take
them to the next level.

Hedge. A hedge provides a protection from an uncertain event in
the future. Homeowners, for example, feel safer during inflationary times, knowing that their house's value will probably
also increase in value, hedging other eventual losses. An owner
of a stock portfolio can hedge by buying put options, which
give them the right to sell the shares at a relatively high price
should the market drop precipitously.

Hedge Fund. Only remotely related to the original practice of
hedging, hedge funds are large investment funds run by savvy
managers for a highly sophisticated clientele. They are often
associated with risky bets, investing clients' money in speculative instruments, such as derivatives and securitized loans
(see Algorithmic Trading). Some hedge funds, however, have
been quite successful in providing a consistently high return
for their clients, which include many college endowments and
pension funds.

High-Net-Worth Individual. The kind of client whom most banks
dream about. A high-net-worth individual is one who has a

lot of disposable assets and few liabilities. Banks around the world have discovered that serving this type of client can be a lucrative business. Operations catering to the needs of high-net-worth individuals can be found all around the world—in New York, London, Paris, Geneva, Luxembourg, Tokyo, São Paulo, Singapore, and Zurich.

Hot Money. Money invested internationally for short periods of time is often referred to as *hot money.* In developing countries, billions of dollars can come flooding in, in search of high returns. But when economic fundamentals change, or a world financial crisis occurs, the money can flow out again at a moment's notice.

Human Development Index (HDI). Economic statistics only tell part of the story. The United Nations Development Program (UNDP), therefore, has set up a Human Development Index to track member countries' progress in improving the standard of living of their citizens. They examine such factors as infant mortality, average age, literacy, and death rates.

Hyperinflation. Prices rising out of control. Hyperinflation usually occurs in countries with severe economic and political problems, such as Germany in the 1920s and Argentina in the 1990s. In some hyperinflationary countries, prices can rise by more than 1,000 percent per year.

iGen. See Generations X, Y, and Z.

IMF. See International Monetary Fund.

Impact Investing. See Socially Conscious Investing.

Import Substitution. Governments sometimes use protective tariffs or quotas to force businesses and consumers to substitute imports with locally produced goods and services. This policy of import substitution is often used in developing countries in an effort to avoid spending precious foreign currency reserves as well as to stimulate local economic development. The problem is that many countries can't produce all goods at the same level of quality as imported goods. When a government forces farmers to buy poorly made domestic tractors, for example, it reduces crop yields, and everyone suffers.

Incomes Policy. Incomes policy is an inflation-control plan that countries use to reduce consumers' real disposable income. Freezing wages is one way of accomplishing this; by reducing spending, it is hoped that the economy will slow down and inflation will be brought under control.

Industrial Revolution. The rapid industrialization in Britain during the late eighteenth and early nineteenth centuries, when steam power allowed the economy to expand and grow enormously, is referred to as the *Industrial Revolution*. The transformation from an economy based on agriculture to one based on the mass production of goods led to a rapid increase in wealth, albeit unequally distributed. This "industrial" revolution soon spread throughout the rest of the developed world.

Inflation. Inflation is, simply put, a measure of the percentage increase in prices. It is usually given as an annual figure, although sometimes it is difficult to tell if the figures announced refer to the annual rise in prices or the rise over a quarter or an even shorter period of time. Since the 1970s, inflation has become the biggest concern of central banks; stimulating growth without unduly increasing prices is the goal but is not always realized. In most economies, inflation is measured by an index of consumer prices, which measures a basket of goods and services (see Consumer Price Index).

Initial Public Offering (IPO). When a company goes *public,* its shares are allowed to be sold and traded on a recognized exchange. This allows the company to have access to a large investor pool and provides the original owners with a lot of money when they sell their shares to the new investors. An IPO has become a rite of passage for many start-up companies.

Insider Trading. A company's insiders are those who have access to the company's financial statements or other company secrets. Normally, insiders are the company's top managers. The activities of insiders are carefully watched by the markets and by financial oversight authorities. Insider trading is illegal in most countries.

Institutional Investor. Unlike small retail investors, institutional investors invest large amounts of money—billions of dollars or yen, pounds, or pesos—in the world markets every day. Typical institutional investors include insurance companies, banks, pension funds, hedge funds, and sovereign funds (see Sovereign Fund).

Interbank Rate. The interbank rate that banks charge for loans to other banks is usually the lowest interest rate in the market. These interbank rates are then used as a benchmark, or standard, for other lending.

International Development Association (IDA). The arm of the World Bank that lends to the world's developing countries.

The IDA provides loans at generous interest rates and under generous conditions using money provided by wealthy World Bank member nations.

International Labour Organization (ILO). Based in Geneva, the ILO is responsible for overseeing all aspects of the world economy that relate to labor. One of the major goals of the ILO is to make sure that workers in developing countries are provided minimum workplace standards.

International Monetary Fund (IMF). The International Monetary Fund was established in 1945, at the same time as the World Bank (see World Bank). Its first job was to regulate the world's exchange rates. It has now assumed a leading role in restructuring debtor countries' economies and providing short-term loans to economies in need.

International Standards for Organization (ISO). Although it defines itself as a nongovernmental organization, the Geneva-based International Standards for Organization sets industrial and commercial standards that often become law in most countries in the world economy. The ISO 9000 family of standards, for example, defines how companies produce and deliver goods and services; it covers everything from quality control to recordkeeping.

Internet Corporation for Assigned Names and Numbers (ICANN). ICANN oversees the system of domain names on the Web, including those ending in .com, .org, .gov, and so on. Some of the ICANN directors are chosen by Internet service providers, and some are elected by *netizens,* ordinary Web users from around the world.

Internet of Things (IoT). With tens of billions of devices connected to the Internet via voice-controlled Alexas and Siris and other controls strategically placed in hundreds of millions of homes and businesses across the world, the Internet of Things has become a major force in the new world economy. Devices ranging from refrigerators and front door locks to cars and tractors around the world now are connected to one another and to data processing facilities allowing the devices to interact and exchange data twenty-four hours a day.

Inverted Yield Curve. Traditionally, investors insist on higher interest rates for longer-term loans—essentially to cover the increased risk of loaning money over a longer period of time. The thinking is that a solvent borrower may go bankrupt in the future, and the more time that goes by implies higher risks. Most yield curves, therefore, slope up: with short-term bonds providing lower interest rates than those further along the timeline. But when investors fear that their other long term investments— such as those in the world's stock markets—look like they will decline in the future, the tendency is to put their money in more stable investments, such as government bond markets. Just as in a street market, where prices go up when everyone wants to buy the same item, the prices of long-term bonds will therefore go up when the world's money comes flooding in. And since bonds' yields decline when their price increases, yields on long-term bonds can decline rapidly in a market where investors feel that the stock market is headed for a precipitous fall. An inverted yield curve, where long-term bonds provide a lower yield than short-term deposits, is therefore seen as a warning sign that the stock market is headed for a crash.

Investment. Economists use the word *investment* to refer to the part of economic production that is not saved or consumed.

Accountants, on the other hand, use the word to refer to a company's purchase of productive assets such as factory buildings, equipment, vehicles, and computers.

Investment Bank / Investment Banking. As opposed to commercial banks, which take deposits and loan out money to earn income, investment banks are primarily occupied with issuing and trading securities and providing financial advice to companies. In some countries, investment banks are referred to as *merchant banks.* In the converging twenty-first-century fusion economy, many banks have put investment banking and commercial banking activities under one roof—commonly referred to as *universal banks.*

Investor Relations. The area of corporate communications related to a company's relationship with its investors is referred to as "investor relations." The idea is to communicate effectively with the investment community at large, presenting a positive image for the company and, hopefully, encouraging new investment.

Invisible Hand. The idea of an invisible hand of the marketplace, guiding consumers and businesses to make the right economic decisions, was developed by the economic philosopher Adam Smith in the eighteenth century. His theory was that markets, if left to themselves, would find the most efficient way of doing things.

Invisible Trade. Exports and imports of services—such as banking, insurance, and media—are referred to as *invisible* by economists because they aren't actually shipped abroad. Invisible trade can be anything from the sales of movies to consulting services to online music downloads. In many economies, invisible trade has become more profitable than the trade of visible goods like commodities and automobiles.

Irrational Exuberance. Originally used by the U.S. Federal Reserve chairman Alan Greenspan, the expression *irrational exuberance* is used to describe any market that is overvalued—in comparison to traditional prices, at least. The first bubble to burst after Greenspan's words was the dot-com bubble, during which companies with no profit and no assets—only promise for future earnings—were rated at values that ranked them alongside some of the biggest and most important companies in the world. Paper millionaires can become paupers overnight when their shares or holdings of companies are reduced to more realistic levels (see Bubble).

Joint Venture. Two or more businesses joining forces to get a competitive advantage in a particular market. Joint ventures are particularly useful in foreign countries where partnering with a local company allows a foreigner to take advantage of the partner's local knowledge and skills.

Junk Bonds. Companies with low credit ratings—usually below BBB (see Rating)—often have to issue bonds with high interest rates to get needed capital for expansion or takeovers. These lower-than-investment-grade bonds are usually referred to as *junk bonds,* but the companies that issue them—along with their investment advisers—prefer to call them *high-yield securities.*

Keiretsu. Another way of saying *Japan Inc. Keiretsu* describes the tightly organized system of interlocking companies in the Japanese economy. It involves multiple layers of businesses, banks, wholesalers, distributors, and brand-loyal retailers that group together, often limiting the penetration of foreign companies and brands in local markets.

Keynesian Economics. British economist John Maynard Keynes was one of the most influential economic thinkers of the twentieth century. Keynes's ideas on using government spending (see Fiscal Policy) to combat economic recession revolutionized modern economic science. Basically, Keynesian economics calls for overspending, or deficit spending, during an economic slowdown, and underspending, or running budget surpluses, during times of too-rapid economic expansion. Most politicians are easily convinced to use deficit spending to stimulate the economy but are decidedly un-Keynesian when it comes to spending less during periods of rapid economic growth.

Kleptocracy. A government or a state with corrupt leaders who use their power and influence to exploit the economic system—taking control of companies or accepting bribes, for example—for illicit gain. Kleptocrats are most often found in countries where the rule of law is limited and oversight is kept to a minimum—usually in countries ruled by dictatorships, oligarchies, or military juntas. But even in some modern democracies, kleptocratic leaders take advantage of their office to further their business interests in many different ways, especially when institutions that are charged with overseeing their activities, such as courts or the legislative branch of government, are unable or unwilling to take action.

Kuznets Curve. Pollution and wealth inequality, according to the curve devised by the economist Simon Kuznets in the 1950s and '60s, initially increase as an economy grows and then decrease as per capita income rises. The Kuznets curve has been criticized by some for not predicting the effect of the technological revolution, which increased world per capita income to record levels but also increased the disparity in wealth and income. By the end of the 2010s, the thirty richest people on the planet had an amassed wealth equal to the entire lower 50 percent of the world's population.

Laffer Curve. Rumor has it that an American economist, Arthur Laffer, drew a curve on a restaurant napkin to show that a reduction in taxes would lead to more taxes coming in, not fewer. His idea was that if a government reduced taxes, it would free up money that people would use more efficiently than the government, thereby stimulating the economy. This new economic activity would then bring in even more taxes than before. The curve headed down at the beginning, showing lower taxes in the short term, but rose toward the end, showing the expected positive effects of reduced taxes.

Lagging Economic Indicators. Unemployment and GDP growth are called *lagging economic indicators* because they tend to tell you where the economy has been, as opposed to information like new home starts (see Leading Economic Indicators) that tend to tell you where the economy is going.

Laissez-Faire. The French term *laissez-faire* means, literally, *let them do it.* It is used to describe a government policy that lets the markets decide what is best. Consumers and producers, in theory, will usually come to the right decisions if they are left to decide on their own.

Leading Economic Indicators. Statistics that help economic and political leaders plot the future course of the economy. Leading economic indicators include such things as retail sales, spending on new plants and machinery, and housing starts.

These indicators tell us where the economy is headed, not where it's been (see Lagging Economic Indicators).

Letter of Credit. In international trade, importers often are required to prove that funds are available to pay for an incoming shipment of goods. This letter of credit is usually provided by a bank that guarantees to the seller that the import will be paid for once it arrives.

Leveraged Buyout (LBO). A leveraged buyout uses borrowed money to take over a company. The buyer puts up a certain amount of capital and borrows the rest, either in the form of bank loans or high-yield securities (see Junk Bonds) that give the investor the leverage to acquire the desired company.

Liability. On a balance sheet, liabilities are listed to the right of the assets. Liabilities typically include debt or other anticipated obligations—money that the company has to pay back sometime in the future. Current liabilities are those that have to be paid off in twelve months or less. Longer-term liabilities are referred to as *long-term debt.*

Limited Liability. Almost every company in the world uses a structure based on limited liability, meaning that owners of the company are protected if the company should go bankrupt. This is reflected in the *Ltd.* that follows company names in most English-speaking countries—although in the United States, companies are commonly referred to as *LLC* and *Inc.,* or incorporated. The abbreviation *SA* in Spanish- and French-speaking countries refers to the words *Sociedad Anónima* or *Société Anonyme,* which imply the same concept as *Ltd.,* that the owners of companies are "anonymous" in that the creditors of a bankrupt company have no right to go after the shareholders' personal assets to cover the company's losses. In some parts of the United States, companies are allowed to pass the profits directly to the shareholders without paying taxes at the corporate level. The shareholders of these S corporations are taxed every year on their share of the company's profits regardless of whether dividends are actually distributed.

Liquidity. In the trading world, *liquidity* means being able to execute trades with ease. Essentially, it means that there are enough buyers and sellers to guarantee a steady market. In the corporate world, liquidity describes a company having enough cash on hand to meet debt payments.

Listing. See Initial Public Offering.

Living Wage. See Universal Basic Income.

Lombard Rate. The interest that central banks in many European countries charge on collateralized loans is called the *Lombard rate*. The banks borrowing the money usually have to put up top-rated government bonds as collateral to receive the preferential Lombard rates. The name is based on Europe's early bankers, who often came from Lombardia, the northern Italian region where Milan is located.

Long Tail. Instead of concentrating on selling large volumes to the masses, long-tail business models are based on the idea of selling small volumes of hard-to-find items to customers who may have been excluded before the advent of e-commerce. With Internet-based businesses using data and targeted marketing, customers who were previously ignored—such as those looking to buy rare vinyl LPs or unique clothing items—have now become major sources of income. The concept of the long tail refers to the small part of a graph that plots sales per custom-ers, extending well beyond the sweet spot targeted by main-stream retailers.

M&A. See Mergers/Mergers and Acquisitions.

Macroeconomics. The big picture. Macroeconomics is the study of an economy's aggregate factors, such as unemployment, growth, inflation, and government spending. The other side of the economy, called *microeconomics,* looks at the more detailed aspects of an economy, primarily related to the behavior of businesses and consumers.

Managed Float / Dirty Float. As opposed to a free-float currency regime, many developing countries use a managed float, or dirty float, to peg their currencies—keeping their value stable, relative to a chosen reference currency or basket of currencies. For example, Hong Kong, China, and Saudi Arabia have tra-ditionally kept their currency pegged to the dollar. And many Eastern European countries, including Hungary, Lithuania, Estonia, and Bulgaria, have kept their currencies pegged to the euro. At the beginning of the twenty-first century, more than one hundred countries in the world economy used a managed float to keep their currency exchange rates stable.

Margin. Margin trading is a way of getting more bang for your buck. In a margin account, banks or brokers loan money to in-vestors so they can buy more stocks and bonds. The client puts up some of the money; the bank puts up the rest. Essentially, the client uses what's already in the account as collateral to borrow money to buy more securities. The reward to the cli-ent is huge if the market goes up. But when markets go down, the client can lose a lot as well. If the market drops too much, the bank gives the client a margin call, asking for extra money or more collateral. If none is available, the securities the client has are sold immediately, before the market has a chance of going down any further.

Marginal Analysis. The study of economic behavior at the edge. Marginal analysis examines how people or firms behave when given the option of having or producing "one more" of something. The additional "one thin wafer" is not so appetizing if it follows a big meal. Marginal consumption, for example, describes what it would take, in terms of lower prices, to get a consumer to buy just one more.

Marginal Tax Rate. In theory, those in the top income brackets should pay a higher tax rate. Those earning more than $1 million, for example, would pay a higher marginal tax rate, say, 50 percent on the extra income instead of the lower tax rate paid on income at the lower thresholds. But in many countries, this is not the case.

Market Capitalization / Market Value. A publicly traded company's market capitalization is derived by multiplying the number of shares outstanding by the share price. The market cap figure gives us an idea of the company's relative size, allowing us to compare companies across borders and across market segments.

Market Economy. See Free-Market Economy.

Market Maker. "I bid twenty-five and offer twenty-six. What do you wanna do? You wanna buy or you wanna sell?" A market maker is a professional trader who makes a two-way price for an item of value. The price that a market maker is willing to

pay, the bid price, is always lower than the offer price. By buying low and selling high all day long, the market maker usually
ends up making a lot of money.

Marx, Karl. The father of communism. The German economic
philosopher and sociologist Karl Marx wrote *Das Kapital,* the
first major work outlining the principles of the communist
economic model. In it, he predicted the demise of capitalism and called for the creation of a socialist economic system
based on the following principle: "From each according to his
abilities, to each according to his needs" (see Communism).

Master of Business Administration (MBA). The main way to break
into the world of business and management. Most universities
around the world now offer MBAs to allow their students to
learn the skills to manage organizations.

Mean / Median. Both words describe the average, but they use a
different calculation. The mean is the simple average, which
consists of simply adding up a list of numbers and dividing
the total by the number of items in the list. This is used in
most economic calculations, such as average per capita income
or average unemployment rate. Sometimes, it is useful to be
aware of the manner in which economic figures are distributed. Median income, for example, tells us the point at which
half the members of a population are above and half below.
Like a median highway strip, the median is the point at which
50 percent of the numbers in a list are higher and 50 percent
are lower.

Mercantilism. The economic policy of using a consistent trade
surplus to accumulate wealth and power. A mercantilist econ-

omy emphasizes exports over imports. Consumers in the home country suffer, but businesses and government amass enormous wealth from foreign exchange receipts that can be used for saving and investment.

Merchandise Trade Balance. The narrowest measure of a country's trade, the merchandise trade balance counts only such "visible" goods as wine and laptops, not services. This measure is often referred to in the press as the *trade balance, trade deficit,* or *trade surplus,* even though a country's total trade figure should include all trade, such as financial services and income from foreign investments (see Current Account).

Merchant Banking. The term *merchant banking* refers to the practice of a bank or securities house investing in its clients' businesses. In some countries, an investment bank is also referred to as a *merchant bank* (see Investment Bank/Investment Banking).

Merger / Mergers and Acquisitions (M&A). Buying or selling companies, or working to bring them together, is referred to in international banking circles as *mergers and acquisitions,* or M&A. Many mergers are fueled by the desire of companies to reap the benefits of increased synergy, taking advantage of each party's strengths and reducing redundant costs.

Metadata. See Data.

Metcalfe's Law. The more, the merrier. Metcalfe's law postulates that the more organizations or people participating in a network, the more effective it becomes. This is particularly relevant in the new economy, where websites and online exchanges tend to work better when more participants are involved. Metcalfe's law is based on the postulation that the value of a network increases in a square; when the number of participants increases by two, for example, the value of the network will increase by four.

Microcredit/Microloan. *Microcredit financing* refers to the practice of providing small loans or microloans to developing-country entrepreneurs who are not able to get money from traditional banks. Because they lack collateral, steady employment, or verifiable credit history, many people in developing countries cannot meet even the most minimal qualifications to gain access to traditional credit. When it became apparent that the repayment rate from microcredit loans was exceptionally high, even by commercial bank standards, many NGOs and charities began setting up microfinancing operations of their own. Grameen, Positive Planet, and Kiva are just a few of the most successful microcredit operations that provide small loans to artisans, farmers, and small-business owners in developing countries around the world.

Microeconomics. The study of an economy's individuals and firms is called *microeconomics*. It is the opposite of macroeconomics, which looks at the big picture like unemployment and GDP growth. Microeconomics, like a microscope, looks at the economic behavior of individuals and how firms make decisions under various economic conditions.

Minimum Wage. The lowest hourly wage permitted in an economy. Minimum-wage laws exist in most but not all modern industrial economies. Many credit minimum wage as an effective tool for reducing poverty and income inequality. Some politicians and many economists criticize minimum-wage laws as counterproductive—by setting minimum wages too high, the laws hurt small businesses and discourage them from hiring new employees.

Modern Monetary Theory (MMT). Instead of using the central banks' authority to raise or lower interest rates, referred to as "monetary policy," some economists and politicians have begun to look at another powerful tool, referred to as Modern Monetary Theory, that allows governments to circumvent central banks by printing massive amounts of money to increase the money supply, thus stimulating economic growth. The problem is that inflation can come roaring back at a moment's notice, and many governments lack the prudence provided by the world's central banks to make the correct economic decision. The fear is that many politicians will issue money to pay for increased government spending without considering the possibility of provoking new inflationary spirals.

Monetarism. The economic theory based on the belief that changes in the money supply control economic growth (see Money Supply). Monetarists believe that inflation can best be controlled by limiting the money supply.

Monetary Policy. In contrast to fiscal policy, which is determined by government decisions related to taxes and spending, monetary policy is decided by central banks, such as the U.S. Federal Reserve and the European Central Bank. By regulating the money supply and interest rates, monetary authorities can pretty much control economic growth and, hopefully, the rate of inflation.

Money Laundering. The purpose of money laundering is to take illegally earned money and pass it through a legitimate business operation, such as an offshore company with little financial oversight. In the end, the money looks like it's been earned legally and can then be spent without arousing suspicion.

Money Market. The market that brings together short-term borrowers and lenders is referred to as the *money market*. Most short-term investments (such as Treasury bills or fiduciary deposits and CDs) are traded on electronic exchanges and special floors set up in banks and securities houses scattered around the world.

Money Supply. A country's money supply has several different components, ranging from coins and bank notes to deposits in savings and checking accounts. The money supply most often referred to in the news is M1, which consists of all currency in circulation as well as money in easy-to-access bank accounts, not long-term deposits (see Monetarism).

Monopoly. Complete control of one sector of production within an economy is referred to as a *monopoly*. A sole producer of a good can, in theory, raise prices without limit. Monopolistic behavior is illegal in most advanced industrial economies.

Moody's. One of the biggest credit rating agencies in the world. Moody's, like Standard & Poor's, provides up-to-date analyses of the financial health of countries, companies, and other borrowers in the world economy. Moody's stamp of top quality, AAA, is awarded only to the world's most creditworthy borrowers.

Mortgage-Backed Security. A mortgage-backed security is backed by payments from mortgages. Instead of keeping the money that is expected to flow in over the future, the banks and finance companies that issued the mortgages hand over this money flow to be repackaged into securities that can be sold to other investors. The advantage for banks and mortgage companies is that they get their money up front and don't have to worry about the borrowers going bankrupt. The problem for the investors is that they may end up owning worthless pieces of paper if enough of the borrowers stop making their mortgage payments.

Most-Favored Nation (MFN). A preferred status for trading partners. The United States used to give this status to selected nations, implying special access to the domestic market in goods and services, but in an age of burgeoning trade, trading partners are now given the more anodyne title: permanent normal trade relations.

Multilateral Trade Agreements. An agreement between three or more trading partners to liberate trade in goods and/or services. Regional and global trade agreements are by far the best way to make sure that countries reap the rewards of comparative advantage, letting each produce what it does best. By the beginning of the twenty-first century, most multilateral trade agreements had stalled, mainly because of the reluctance of governments to dismantle semipermanent barriers to trade, such as agricultural subsidies and protective tariffs on imports of manufactured goods. Most countries found it easier to establish trade agreements on an ad hoc basis (see Bilateral Trade Agreements) and settled for a one-step-at-a-time approach to liberalizing trade.

Mutual Fund. A mutual fund is a collection of bonds or stocks sold as a single investment. The advantage of a mutual fund is that investors are able to diversify risk over a wide range of securities within a single investment vehicle. Mutual funds are especially appropriate for people wishing to invest internationally; investing in mutual funds makes it easy to avoid mistakes in markets where information on individual companies is not easily accessible.

NAFTA. See United States–Mexico–Canada Agreement.

NASDAQ. The National Association of Securities Dealers Automated Quotation System was the world's first major electronic stock exchange. NASDAQ trades many new economy stocks, such as Intel and Amazon. Its goal is to become a global trading powerhouse by merging with or acquiring electronic trading exchanges in many other countries around the world. In addition to providing domestic market indices like the NASDAQ Composite Index, NASDAQ provides several global market summaries, including the NASDAQ Global Select Market and NASDAQ Global Market indices.

Nationalization. The government taking ownership of previously privately owned enterprises is called *nationalization*. Nationalizations are common under socialist or communist regimes that prefer to have all means of production in the hands of the government. Expropriation is nationalization that doesn't pay the previous owners for their assets.

Negative Interest Rates. When central banks try to stimulate an economy, one of their most effective tools is to lower interest rates, providing an incentive for consumers and businesses to borrow and spend more. But when interest rates are lowered to zero and the economy still needs a stimulus, a new tool— pioneered by countries with strong currencies and low growth rates, such as Switzerland, Denmark, and Japan—is to lower interest rates below zero. These negative interest rates have the effect of charging depositors to store their money in the bank, theoretically providing an even greater incentive to spend the money instead of saving it. But why would anyone put their money in a bank account that charges them money to store it there? It only makes sense if a depositor has so much money it wouldn't fit under the mattress or if the depositor thinks that the currency will continue to climb in value—making the negative-interest investment a source of eventual profit.

Negative Yield Curve. See Negative Interest Rates, Inverted Yield Curve.

Net Asset Value (NAV). To calculate the true value of shares in mutual funds or open-end funds, it is necessary to add up all the fund's assets—such as securities and cash—and subtract all the liabilities. This figure is then divided by the total number of shares outstanding to give investors an idea of what each share in the fund is worth.

Net Assets. What a company really owns. A company's net assets, or net profit, is what's left after deducting all the costs or liabilities of doing business. Basically, net assets are what is left over when a company's debts are subtracted from its assets. Stockholders consider this to be the part of the company that belongs to them. Net assets are also referred to as *stockholders' equity* or *shareholders' equity*.

Net Income. Another way of saying *profit*. Net income is determined by subtracting all expenses from a company's total revenue. It tells us what a company has earned over a given period of time (see Earnings).

Net Profit. See Net Assets.

Net Worth. An individual's net worth is calculated by adding up the monetary value of all assets, including house, car, and bank accounts, and subtracting all the liabilities, such as mortgages and credit card bills. The net worth of a company is called *net assets.*

Nongovernmental Organization (NGO). When the United Nations was established in 1945, the founders coined the term *nongovernmental organization* to designate the activities of non-profit organizations working in the public sphere without direct control by national governments or intergovernmental entities. The number of NGOs in the world has been estimated to be more than ten million, and their activities range from health-care and human rights advocacy to environmental activism and education. Doctors Without Borders, the World Wildlife Fund, the Sierra Club, and the Red Cross are all examples of international NGOs.

North American Free Trade Agreement (NAFTA). See United States–Mexico–Canada Agreement (USMCA).

Offshore / Offshore Companies. A company that does little or no business in its home country is referred to as a *nonresident* or *offshore company.* Many countries treat offshore companies' profits differently from the profits of normal companies; they tax them, usually, at a lower rate.

Oligarchy. Based on the Greek word meaning *few to rule,* an oligarchy is a type of government where the power rests with a small number of people. Oligarchic leaders often enrich themselves and their families at the expense of the workers they are ostensibly there to protect. In many countries with oligarchic leaders, those with close ties to the ruling party control vast segments of the economy. This economic system is sometimes referred to as *crony capitalism.*

OPEC (Organization of the Petroleum Exporting Countries). OPEC was set up in the 1960s to coordinate the production of oil, thus allowing the member countries to better control the market. The fourteen OPEC members consist of Iran, Venezuela, and the major Arab oil producers of the Middle East.

Open Market Operation. Central banks use open market operations to control economic growth. By buying and selling securities on the open market, the U.S. Federal Reserve and other central banks are able to inject money into the financial system—or remove it, if that's what they desire. Since money held at central banks is not considered to be part of the money supply, any purchase of securities by the Fed increases the U.S. money supply by the amount paid. Alternatively, when the Fed sells securities on the open market, the U.S. money supply is reduced by the amount paid by the purchaser and placed in the central bank's vaults. Most of the securities bought or sold in open market operations are government bonds.

Option. An option gives the holder the right to buy or sell something at a certain price in the future. A stock option, for example, is a call option that gives the holder the right to buy a certain number of shares, called *underlying shares,* at a certain price in the future. The opposite, the right to sell the underlying share or other asset, is called a *put* (see Stock Option).

Organisation for Economic Co-operation and Development (OECD). The OECD, based in Paris, France, groups together the world's major economies. In addition to providing statistics and documenting all aspects of the member countries' economies, the OECD serves as a forum for discussion and coordination of economic policy.

Output. Another word for *gross domestic product* (see Gross Domestic Product). Output is the total number of goods and services sold in an economy during a given period of time.

Outsourcing. Taking advantage of advances in telecommunication and computer capabilities, many companies in rich countries have decided to send many low-skill operations abroad. By the beginning of the twenty-first century, such operations ranged from call centers in India to back-office bookkeeping operations in Eastern Europe. The idea is to take advantage of lower salaries abroad. Even online tutoring allows students with broadband access to interact with low-cost tutors (usually based in developing countries) to get online help in subjects ranging from languages to mathematics.

Over-the-Counter (OTC). Over-the-counter shares are not traded on established stock exchanges but are traded electronically, reducing overhead and oversight. Most OTC stock sales are for small companies that don't meet the strict financial requirements necessary for listing the shares on major exchanges, such as the NYSE or NASDAQ.

Par. When a bond sells at 100 percent of its face value (nominal value), it's said to trade *at par*. For most bonds in the dollar-denominated sector, the face value of bonds is $1,000. The price of most bonds does not stay at par for long. Once the bond is issued, whenever interest rates rise or fall in the market, the bond's price is adjusted, rising above or falling below par, to make the bond's return competitive with other securities in the marketplace.

Paradigm. The rules of the game. In economics, you shift the paradigm by changing the rules governing how the economy is perceived and consequently how it works. The Internet, for example, has changed the paradigm of how economies produce and sell goods and services. Based on the concept of weltanschauung, or worldview, a paradigm consists of the sum total of beliefs and values that make up a society or economic system.

Paris Agreement / Paris Climate Accord. Adopted in 2015, the Paris Agreement brought together 196 countries in an effort to reduce climate change. The measures included everything from curbing carbon emissions to investing in renewable energy. The goal was to keep the increase in average global temperatures below 2 degrees Celsius, or roughly 3.6 degrees Fahrenheit.

Patent. The exclusive right to market a specific product or service in a given market. Patents are usually issued by government authorities, such as the U.S. Patent Office. Without patent protection, companies would never invest as much as they do into research and development. In some developing countries, patents—on life-saving drugs, for example—are often ignored because the patented product is often too expensive for people on low incomes to afford.

Peg/Pegging. See Currency Peg.

Per Capita. Often translated as *per person.* Putting a per capita value on an economic statistic is often the best way to understand the number's true effect on the economy's inhabitants. Per capita spending, for example, helps us understand the "real" effect of something like health care or education. It allows us to put the numbers on a more human scale.

Perestroika. Russian for *economic restructuring, perestroika* was the buzzword for Mikhail Gorbachev's daring plan to reform the Soviet Union in the 1980s. Along with the move for more political openness, referred to as *glasnost,* perestroika's goal was to make the economy more efficient by decentralizing decision-making (see Centrally Planned Economy).

Permanent Normal Trade Relations (PNTR). The latest word in accommodating trade. The United States used to give most-favored-nation status to selected nations it wanted to encourage trade with, allowing special access to the domestic market in goods and services. Now it's referred to as *PNTR,* even though, in a perfectly functioning world economy, *all* nations should have permanent normal trade relations.

Phillips Curve. The economic principle that inflation is linked to unemployment is shown by a curve, usually referred to as the Phillips curve in honor of the economist who popularized it, that shows that low inflation is usually accompanied by high unemployment and, conversely, that high inflation is accompanied by low unemployment. The idea is that during times of low unemployment, there aren't enough people around to take all the available jobs, and employees will ask for—and probably get—higher salaries. This leads to inflation, a rise in prices. In the new economy, however, some economies are able to take advantage of advances in technology to keep from having to hire more employees, reducing the demand for higher wages and thus reducing the need to raise wages and prices.

Plaza Accord. On September 22, 1985, an agreement was reached at the Plaza Hotel in New York City to devalue the dollar—particularly against the German mark and Japanese yen—through coordinated intervention in the international currency markets. The goal was to make U.S. industries and farmers more competitive on the international markets. The agreement was signed by five nations: France, West Germany, Japan, the United States, and the United Kingdom.

Poison Pill. When a company wants to defend itself against a hostile takeover, it may attempt to render itself unattractive through certain "unhealthy" financial maneuvers. A poison pill defense may involve a drastic increase in debt or selling off valuable pieces of the company to ward off evil takeover artists. Unfortunately, even if a poison pill defense succeeds in keeping the company in the hands of the original owners, it often ends up irreparably harming the company and managers it was meant to protect.

Pollution Rights. See Emissions Trading.

Preferred Stock. Stocks that pay a fixed dividend are called *preferred stock*. In some ways, a preferred stock is like a bond in that its fixed dividend resembles an interest payment. Preferred stock is usually considered to be "senior" to common stock, which means that in the event of a bankruptcy, holders of the preferred stock are paid before those holding common stock. However, owners of preferred stock—like bond owners—usually have no voting rights.

Primary Market. When new stocks and bonds are issued, they are often traded in a primary market before they are allowed to join the ranks of seasoned securities on the world's markets. A primary market for bonds, for example, usually exists until the payment date, when interest payments start being calculated and the life of the bond really begins. Primary market trading normally takes place among banks and securities dealers, not on established exchanges.

Prime Rate. The prime rate is the interest rate that U.S. banks charge their best corporate customers. Like LIBOR (London Interbank Offered Rate), the prime rate is often used as a guideline for determining other interest rates that banks charge on loans to riskier customers. Following the guideline of "low risk, low reward," a bank's prime corporate customers are usually able to pay the lowest interest rates in the market.

Principal. Anyone making a loan wants to get paid back at some time and earn a little interest along the way. The amount of a loan that has to be returned to the lender is called its *principal*. A bond's principal is often called its *face value*.

Private Equity. Private equity ventures in the twenty-first century encompass a wide range of activities, but can generally be divided into three main areas: venture capital, growth capital, and leveraged buyouts. The words *private* and *equity* refer to the main goal of private equity activity, which is to purchase privately owned companies or publicly listed companies that are then delisted from exchanges. Once in the hands of private equity managers, the companies are made more efficient and eventually are sold—often for a hefty profit.

Private Placement. A new issue of stocks or bonds that is too small to be treated as a full public placement, such as a large IPO or a full-fledged bond issue, is referred to as a *private placement*. The securities issued in a private placement are often sold only to a small group of institutional investors (see Institutional Investor). Usually, there are fewer reporting requirements on private placements, and the securities are usually not traded on the open market once they have been placed in the hands of the investors.

Privatization. Privatization is the selling off of state-owned companies to improve efficiency and bring more money into the government's coffers. Countries burdened by the debt and losses of poorly run public companies often turn to privatization to solve their economic problems. The opposite of privatization is nationalization (see Nationalization).

Producer Prices / Producer Price Index. Measured "at the factory gate," producer price indexes track the price of goods before they enter the retail chain. These figures provide early warning signals of inflation, allowing central bankers to adjust the economy before the price rises show up in the more commonly watched CPI (see Consumer Price Index).

Productivity. Productivity is defined as the number of goods or services produced by a given unit of labor, capital, land, and so on. One of the hallmarks of the twenty-first-century economy has been a marked increase in productivity as new technologies have allowed people to produce much more than before for a given amount of time spent.

Profit. The proverbial carrot that balances the stick of bankruptcy. A company's profit is what's left to give to the stockholders, the company's owners, after paying all the bills in a given period. Profit is the driving force behind most economic activity in free-market economies. In accounting, a company's profit is often referred to as *net income,* or *earnings* (see Earnings).

Profit and Loss Statement (P&L). The financial overview of a company's activities over a given period of time is called an *income statement* or, more commonly, a *profit and loss statement.* A typical P&L starts with income, called *revenue,* then deducts all the cost and expenses of doing business to arrive at the bottom line: net income, which is what's left after deducting taxes and other fees from the profit.

Program Trading. Instead of buying stocks as an investment to hold and cherish for years, program traders try to take advantage of discrepancies in the markets, buying large numbers of stocks—or options, or bonds, or futures—in a market where prices are slightly out of line with prices in other markets in other parts of the world. Program traders use computers to track the prices of a wide variety of securities in markets around the world, using that information to buy where it's cheap and sell where prices are slightly higher (see Arbitrage).

Purchasing Power Parity (PPP). Unlike currency exchange rates, which are determined by the market, PPP looks at what your money actually buys in each country—calculating, in a sense, its purchasing power. PPP looks at the prices of a basket of goods and services—which can include everything from housing to haircuts, from bread to movie tickets—to arrive at a "real world" exchange rate. Purchasing power parity is often used to compare the size of economies around the world when traditional exchange rates don't tell the whole picture. China, for example, where prices are much lower than in Europe or the United States (if you use official exchange rates to make the comparison), would be ranked much higher if you used equivalent prices for the goods and services produced there.

Put Option. A put option gives the holder the right to sell something at a certain price over a certain period of time. Like other options (see Call Option), it is a right, but not an obligation. So you would only exercise a put, selling a stock or bond for the put's fixed price, if the real price is lower. The price at which a put allows you to sell the underlying security is called its *striking price*. An investor who thinks the price of something will go down in the future will buy a put option, hoping to profit if the market moves in the expected direction. As the price of the underlying asset goes down, the price of the option will go up.

Quantitative Easing. Faced with the economic meltdown following the 2008 crash, some central banks opted to stimulate their moribund economies via quantitative easing, using the unlimited purchasing power of central banks to buy large quantities of bonds in the open market to pump cash into the economy. Central banks use quantitative easing to create money where previously none existed. Basically, a central bank "creates" money every time it dips into its "vaults"—essentially a black hole of unlimited financial resources—to buy existing bonds from banks or other investors. These purchases, often referred to as *open market operations,* inject new money into the economy because the bank, instead of holding bonds, is now holding the "cash" it got from the central bank. This money can now be made available for loans to consumers and individuals, thereby stimulating economic growth.

Quota. In international trade, a *quota* is a limit on the quantity of a good that may be imported into a country over a certain period of time. Contrary to tariffs, quotas are particularly effective in disrupting international trade. With tariffs, you can just lower the price of the good to make it competitive in the country that has erected the trade barrier. But with quotas, once the limit has been reached, no more goods—at any price—may be brought in. Fortunately, quotas are usually the first trade barriers to go when countries sign free-trade agreements.

Rating. Bonds and stocks often are given a rating by specialized agencies to allow investors to compare them without going into all the financial details. AAA is usually the best rating. Having a triple A means a company or government can get the best terms for loans and other debt. Other investment grade ratings include AA, A, and BBB (or Baa). Anything below that is said to be speculative, or, in the case of C ratings, very risky.

Rational Expectations. Much of modern economic theory is based on the concept of rational expectations: that people, when armed with all available information, will make rational decisions. Lower prices, for example, will always get people to buy an equivalent product. Unfortunately, consumers and businesspeople don't always act rationally; they often buy the product they like even though it may not be in their best economic interest. *Errare humanum est*—"To err is human"—even in the world of economics.

Real. It's usually much more important, especially in high-inflation times, to look at real figures—those that take into account the effect of inflation. Real income, for example, may go down, even if the nominal amount goes up—as long as inflation is high enough to offset any gains made from the higher salary. Any value that has been adjusted for inflation is referred to as *real*.

Real Estate Investment Trust (REIT). Instead of buying a piece of property and holding on to it for years before selling it through a real estate broker, a REIT investor buys a security, a piece of paper that represents ownership in a "basket" of real estate investments, such as shopping centers and apartment houses. The advantage of real estate investment trusts, besides certain tax benefits, is that the investor can buy and sell their share like any stock or bond—on a quoted market—and not have to worry about mowing the lawn or repairing the roof.

Receivables. "Counting your chickens before they're hatched." On a balance sheet, something that's owed to the company can be treated as an asset even before it's actually been received. These receivable assets can actually be sold or packaged into securities to trade on the open market. Receivables become current assets once they've been paid in.

Recession. A recession is a prolonged economic slowdown. Normally, a recession is "official" if an economy stops growing for two consecutive quarters. When an economy is seen to be heading into a recession, central banks usually lower interest rates to stimulate the purchase of goods and services and business investment. The effect is usually salubrious: economic growth returns and unemployment is reduced. Unfortunately, this isn't always the case. Japan, during the first years of the twenty-first century, reduced interest rates to zero, and still the economy languished.

Repurchase Agreements / Repos. The purchase of securities with the agreement to sell them back at a certain price and at a certain time in the future is called a *repurchase agreement*. Repos are essentially a loan, or a form of short-term investment. Central banks, such as the Federal Reserve or the Bank of Japan, often use repurchase agreements to inject money into, or remove it from, the economy at large. When traders hear that the Fed is doing repos, they often act accordingly, buying or selling on their own, expecting the Fed's action to lead to a rise or decline in interest rates.

Rescheduling. It is said that when a customer owes a bank a small amount of money and can't pay, the customer is in trouble, but when the customer owes the bank a large amount of money and can't pay, the bank is in trouble. Confronted with problem borrowers who can't repay their loans, creditor banks—or creditor nations—often reschedule the loans, essentially giving the debtors more time to come up with the money. If a country has no hope of growth without additional funds—such as many African countries during the first years of the twenty-first century—the loans are forgiven, removed from the creditors' books.

Retained Earnings. When a company makes a profit, it can choose to distribute its net income to the company's shareholders in the form of dividends or keep it for future use. What doesn't get distributed remains on the company's books as retained earnings.

Return on Equity (ROE). Return on equity is the relationship between net income and the price of the company's stock. It is calculated by taking a company's profits over the course of a year and dividing it by the net assets the company uses to create those profits. The ROE shows how efficiently the investors' money is being used to generate income.

Road Pricing. To reduce pollution and overcrowding of public roads, cities sometimes set up a system of electronic devices to monitor and charge for the roads' use. From San Diego to London, road pricing has helped to drastically reduce the number of cars coming into the city center. By charging more for cars to use roads at certain times of the day, road pricing can be a powerful economic incentive to reduce traffic jams. It gets commuters to make more efficient use of roads or even switch to less polluting ways to get to work, such as carpools or the use of public transportation.

Robot. See Artificial Intelligence.

S Corporation. See Limited Liability.

Sarbanes-Oxley. The U.S. Congress passed the Sarbanes-Oxley Act in 2002 in response to corporate abuses, particularly the bankruptcy of Enron and WorldCom. Officially called the Public Company Accounting Reform and Investor Protection Act of 2002, Sarbox, as it is commonly called, established new standards for the way publicly traded companies conduct business, particularly how company boards, management, and accounting firms are allowed to function.

Savings. In any economy, income that is not spent is referred to as *savings*. A high savings rate means that the economy has more money for businesses to invest, because most savings are kept in banks where they can be lent out for other uses.

Savings and Loan (S&L). Savings and loans are financial institutions that take depositors' money and make loans, primarily to finance clients' real estate purchases. In England, savings-and-loans-style banks are usually called *building societies*.

Securities and Exchange Commission (SEC). The SEC is a federal agency that oversees and regulates financial markets and securities trading in the United States. The primary goal of the SEC is to protect the public from malpractice and fraudulent behavior in the securities industry. The closest thing the world economy has to an SEC is the BIS (see Bank for International Settlements), based in Basel, Switzerland.

Security/Securitization. A security is a financial instrument that represents something of value. A security can be anything from a stock to a pollution right to a savings bond. Even an IOU is a security because it is a promise to give to the holder something of value, usually money. Banks sometimes securitize their assets—mortgages or credit card debt, for example—by grouping them in blocks and selling them, as bonds or other securities, to investors.

Series A Series B. Venture capital funding usually takes place in several stages. The first major investment coming from venture capitalists gives them the right to series A shares to compensate them for the money provided, usually in the range of $2 million–$10 million. A typical series A round would give investors approximately 10–30 percent of the company's shares, with the rest being held by the company's founders and initial investors, such as angels (see Venture Capital) or friends and family who provided early money to get the company started. The capital raised during a series A round usually lasts for one to two years and allows the company to begin the process of establishing the company's brand and hire the first employees. The next round, called series B, simply continues the process of issuing new shares (reducing the owners' stake) to reward investors for the money they provide.

Share. See Stock.

Sharing Economy. The sharing economy gives us access to others' unused or idle assets. From cars to designer clothes to vacation homes, the sharing economy allows virtually everyone to avoid ownership and still have permanent access to needed goods and services.

Sharp Power. Nonmilitary efforts to "win friends and influence enemies" abroad can be divided into two types of power: soft power and sharp power. Surpassing benign soft-power initiatives such as sending orchestras on world tours or setting up cultural centers in foreign lands, sharp-power efforts can include everything from using social media to manipulating elections to providing economic aid in order to garner political or economic influence.

Short Sale. In most of the world's stock markets, investors are allowed to sell stock they don't own as long as they agree to provide the securities at some time in the future. The reason for selling short is that the investor believes that the stock's price will go down and they want to benefit from the future fall in prices. By selling in advance, the investor gets to take advantage of the higher price. When they cover their short position by buying the securities at a later date, they pocket the difference in prices. The opposite of going short is the more traditional investment strategy of going long, buying securities to keep in the hope that the price will rise at some point in the future.

Sierra Club. One of the world's largest environmental groups, the Sierra Club has taken a leading role in finding economic in-

centives, such as road pricing, to reduce pollution and environmental destruction. The Sierra Club was founded in 1892 by
the outdoorsman and preservationist John Muir.

Single Market. In addition to providing common external tariffs
(see Customs Union), the European Union has created a single market, ensuring totally free movement of goods, services,
capital, and people. Any country hoping for full access to the
European Union economy—including EU holdouts Switzerland, Iceland, and Norway—has had to allow EU passport
holders to live and work in their countries as a condition for
free access to the world's largest trading bloc.

Smith, Adam. The father of modern economics. Adam Smith was
an enlightened eighteenth-century Scotsman who believed
that the markets worked best when left to take care of themselves. He introduced the world to such terms as *invisible hand
of the marketplace* and *division of labor.* His book *The Wealth of
Nations* provided the foundation for the modern capitalist economic system.

Smoot-Hawley. The Smoot-Hawley Tariff Act of 1930 raised
tariffs on thousands of imports to the United States. The idea
was to stimulate the economy by encouraging local production. The result was somewhat different. When other countries retaliated by raising tariffs of their own, U.S. exports
plummeted, resulting in job losses and a significantly wors-
ened depression.

Socialism. The basic idea of socialism is that an economy should
ensure an equitable distribution of wealth. Sometimes confused with communism, the socialist model allows for some
private control of the means of production. There are many

free-market socialist economies. Paris, for example, didn't stop being a thriving, elegant capital when the French elected a socialist government. Sweden and other Nordic countries are often cited as models of how capitalism and socialism can co-exist to everyone's benefit.

Socially Conscious Investing / Socially Responsible Investing / Corporate Social Responsibility (CSR). Socially conscious investors make an effort to invest their money in companies or funds that correspond to a specific view of how the world should be run. Many socially conscious equity funds, for example, invest only in companies that have proven corporate social responsibility by treating their workers well, for example, or using sustainable resources, such as planting a tree for every one they cut down. Many investors have also begun insisting that the money they put into the world economy support businesses that have a favorable social or environmental impact. Pension funds, college endowments, even big banks have begun including impact investments as an increasingly large part of the trillions they invest annually, in an effort to support businesses that have a favorable social or environmental impact. Individual investors can choose from a variety of exchange-traded funds—the MSCI World Index offers more than ten ETFs—and other investment vehicles that concentrate on companies and projects with particular emphasis on sustainability, social benefit, and governance.

Soft Power. See Sharp Power.

Sovereign Debt Rating. Sovereign debt consists mainly of bonds or other securities issued by central governments. As opposed to companies, sovereign debt is backed by the full faith and security of the government and is, therefore, considered to be the most unlikely to default. If sovereign debt is issued in the country's own currency, it is virtually impossible to default: all the government would have to do is issue currency to back the debt. The most highly rated sovereign debt is from the wealthy countries of Europe, North America, and Asia. U.S. Treasury bonds, British gilts, and Swiss government bonds, for example, have all been rated AAA, the highest rating available.

Sovereign Fund. Instead of investing excess reserves in bonds or overnight deposits, many countries and states have set up sovereign funds to make equity investments, buying companies or shares of companies from around the world.

Special Drawing Right (SDR). A type of money that was created by the International Monetary Fund (see International Monetary Fund) to provide an alternative to gold or other currencies. SDRs are used to keep accounts and make payments within the IMF system. Many countries also use SDRs as a reserve currency. The value of an SDR is based on the value of a basket of currencies, including the U.S. dollar, the Japanese yen, and the euro.

Special Economic Zone. When a government wants to attract foreign investment and trade to a specific region, it sometimes sets up a special economic zone that provides incentives like low taxes or reduced import and export barriers. The idea is to stimulate economic activity to create jobs and improve the standard of living within the zone. One of the most successful special economic zones has been Shenzhen, in China. Other special economic zones include Manaus in Brazil, Subic Bay in the Philippines, and the Aqaba Special Economic Zone in Jordan.

Speculation. A speculator buys or sells something for one reason only: to profit from the investment's subsequent rise in price. In contrast to hedgers and arbitrageurs, who take advantage of market discrepancies to make money, speculators think they know something that the other investors in the market haven't figured out, and they act on it by buying or selling in the marketplace (see Arbitrage and Hedge).

Spot Market. A trade executed for immediate delivery and payment is called a *spot trade*. The alternative to spot trading is buying or selling on the forward or futures markets, where trades are executed at fixed prices for delivery or payment at some future date.

Spread. The difference between the purchase price and the sale price. When you buy or sell foreign currency, for example, the price changes, depending on whether you're selling or buying. If the difference between the bid price and offer price is big enough, the exchange can make a lot of money on the spread. Theoretically, if the spread were big enough and if you bought and sold long enough, you'd end up with virtually nothing.

Stagflation. Where economic stagnation meets inflation. Stagflation occurs in an economy with high inflation and low growth. This phenomenon rarely occurs because inflation is usually the product of an overheated economy, not a stagnating one. Stagflation is a worst-case scenario for central bankers, where inflationary pressures are so strong that even an economic downturn isn't enough to quell the pressure toward rising prices.

Standard & Poor's (S&P). One of the world's biggest ratings agencies, Standard & Poor's looks through a company's books—or another entity, such as a country or a securitized loan—and makes a judgment about how creditworthy the country, company, or entity is. This judgment is usually given in the form of letters. AAA, for example, is used to describe the most creditworthy debtors.

Stock. Stock is ownership in a company. This ownership is usually represented by pieces of paper, or electronic bookkeeping entries, called *stock* or *shares.* Stockholders (also called *shareholders* or *shareowners*) have a claim to the earnings and assets of the company. If the company makes a profit, anyone holding the company's stock can share in the benefits, usually paid out as dividends. If earnings are retained within the company, stockholders can still benefit; positive news and increased cash usually lead to a rise in the price of a company's shares.

Stock Index. A stock index tracks the prices of a group of representative stocks to give investors an idea how the market as a whole is doing. Most indexes are weighted, giving more importance to shares of big companies, but the Dow Jones Industrial Average is technically just an average because each share, whatever its price and value of shares traded, is given equal weight in estimating the market's movement on any given day.

Stock Index Future. A stock index future allows investors to benefit from the rise (or fall) of a stock index like the Hang Seng Index in Hong Kong or the S&P 500 in New York. Buying or selling a stock index future is equivalent to buying or selling all the shares in the index. If the index goes up in value, the buyer of the stock index future profits handsomely. If it goes down, anyone who sold the stock index future short also profits (see Short Sale).

Stock Option. A stock option gives the holder the right to buy a certain number of shares, called *underlying shares,* at a certain price in the future. The opposite, the right to sell the underlying share or other asset, is called a *put.* Many companies provide employees with call options that allow them to profit when the share's price goes up. The holder of a stock option, like any other option (see Option), bears no risk in the sense that if the market doesn't move enough to make it worthwhile to exercise the option, the option is simply allowed to expire.

Stock Split. A stock split increases the number of shares in publicly traded companies. It does nothing to change the company's total market capitalization. The only thing that changes is the price of the individual shares. A hundred-dollar share, for example, would usually be split into two fifty-dollar shares to facilitate trading.

Stock Swap. See Swap.

Stockholders' Equity. Sometimes referred to as *net worth,* stockholders' equity is determined by subtracting a company's liabilities from its assets. It is also sometimes called *shareholders' equity.* Theoretically, if a company were to use all its assets to pay off all its liabilities, whatever is left belongs to the shareholders.

Structural Change. An economy is said to undergo structural change when factors of production, such as labor markets or investment policy, are radically altered. In the twenty-first-century economy, technological advances and the use of the Internet have allowed economies to grow and produce well beyond normal levels.

Structured Investment Vehicle (SIV). A sort of virtual bank, a structured investment vehicle allows investors to use short-term funding, usually commercial paper (see Commercial Paper), to finance purchases of long-term securities. Since short-term interest rates are usually lower than long-term rates, most SIVs make money on the spread, or difference in interest rates between the two types of securities.

Subprime Debt / Subprime Mortgage Securities. Loans issued to borrowers with a less than perfect, or prime, credit rating. Subprime debt usually requires a higher interest rate to compensate for the higher risk of the borrowers. This debt is sometimes repackaged into securities that, in theory, have a lower risk of failure (see Collateralized Debt Obligation).

Subsidiary. A company that is controlled by another is referred to as a *subsidiary*. The controlling company or corporation is referred to as the subsidiary's *parent* and acquires control by owning enough shares to determine the composition of the subsidiary company's board of directors. For accounting purposes, a subsidiary is treated as a separate entity, paying its own taxes and subject to separate regulation by authorities. A company that is totally integrated into the parent company is referred to as a *division*. A wholly owned subsidiary, where all the shares are owned by the parent company, is also referred to as a *branch*.

Subsidy. Subsidies are government payments to businesses, ostensibly to help them through economic hard times. Most subsidies are criticized as being a waste of taxpayers' money because they often end up rewarding inefficiency; in many economies, badly managed and inefficient industries would not survive if they didn't receive generous government subsidies. Examples include shipbuilding, steelmaking, and some areas of agribusiness, such as sugar and cotton producers.

Supply and Demand. All free-market economies work on the principle that the supply of any good or service is limited. The less there is of it—gasoline or wheat, for example—the more expensive it will be. Application of the law of supply and demand allows consumers and businesses to decide how to allocate their resources—hopefully in the most economically rational way possible.

Supply-Side Economics. Based on the view that producers and consumers can stimulate economic growth better than governments. The idea of supply-side economics is to reduce taxes, taking the money from the government and putting it in the more productive hands of companies and individuals. By reducing taxes, money is freed up for saving and investing by consumers and businesses, stimulating the economy more efficiently than if the money were pumped into the economy through increased government spending (see Laffer Curve).

Surplus. A surplus occurs whenever there is more coming in than going out. A trade surplus, for example, occurs when a country sells more abroad than it imports, increasing the inflow of foreign exchange. A government budget surplus occurs when tax receipts exceed expenditures.

Swap. A swap is a trade agreement between two or more counterparties, such as banks, to exchange different assets or liabilities. A swap allows both parties to obtain the right mix of assets and cash flows. A bank, for example, might swap yen assets for dollar assets, or floating-rate loans for fixed-rate loans to reduce risk and increase profitability.

Synergy. Synergy occurs when two or more parties combine their particular skills or assets for mutual gain. In foreign trade, *synergy* refers to the comparative advantage of letting each country produce and export those goods and services that it produces more efficiently. In the end, the theory goes, when each country is allowed to do what it does best, everyone is better off.

Takeover. Anyone can take over a company if they own or control enough shares. In a hostile takeover, for example, outside investors usually borrow large amounts of money to buy enough shares to acquire the company. This allows them to restructure the company as they see fit, often selling off assets to pay off the acquired debt. Management, in many cases, tries to avoid hostile takeovers by restructuring the company in a way that makes it difficult for the new investors to make a profit (see Poison Pill).

Tangible Net Worth. The "real world" view of a company. Tangible net worth is an accounting tool that evaluates a company by looking only at its tangible assets and liabilities, which include everything from cars and cash to bank deposits and loans. What gets left out is intangible assets like brand names and goodwill, which have no quantifiable value. Many twenty-first-century companies like Netflix or Facebook have almost no tangible assets; the power to generate profits via online services constitutes the bulk of their net worth.

Tariff. A tariff is a tax on imports. In most cases, tariffs are a percentage "penalty" to the importer and can range from a few percent to more than a hundred percent of the declared value. The money is pocketed by the government in an effort to discourage the import of goods that could compete with those in the local market. As far as trade barriers are concerned (see Subsidy and Quota), tariffs are, in fact, the least difficult to get around as long as you have enough money to pay the extra cost of importing the product. The goal of most free-trade agreements is to eliminate quotas and reduce tariffs and subsidies.

Tax Haven. A country that offers extremely low tax rates to individuals or companies is referred to as a *tax haven*. By reducing or eliminating taxes on profit or income, tax havens, such as small islands in the Caribbean or Pacific, are able to attract business and large amounts of private wealth. Some countries, such as Monaco and Switzerland, are considered to be tax havens, even though their tax rates aren't as low as those of many offshore islands; they're just lower than their neighbors'.

Third World. During the decades following World War II, the world was divided into three distinct economic areas: the first world of developed capitalist countries, the second world of communist or Soviet nations, and the emerging economies of the third part of the world. By the beginning of the twenty-first century, however, the term had lost a lot of its original meaning. The Soviet second world had collapsed, and many emerging economies, such as Chile, Singapore, and Korea, had reached a level of development that surpassed many of the economically advanced countries of the first world.

Trade Balance. A country's trade balance sums up all international purchases and sales of goods and services, plus all international financial transfers, such as interest payments on foreign debt. This balance gives us an idea of who's running a trade deficit and who's running a trade surplus. Many people erro-neously call the current account the *trade balance*, but they're not exactly the same thing. The current account, in addition to adding up all trade in goods and services, also includes in-come from investments abroad, such as interest or dividend payments (see Current Account).

Transparency International (TI). A Berlin-based international or-ganization, Transparency International aims to fight graft and bribery in the world economy by working with such other in-ternational organizations as the OECD to expose, investigate, and unmask corruption throughout the world. One of its most effective tools is to publish lists of countries and companies that encourage and condone corrupt business practices.

Twin Deficit. See Double Deficit.

Underemployment. Economists define the underemployed as people who are working only part-time or are working at a level that is significantly below their training and qualifica-tions. Normal unemployment rates don't usually include the underemployed because they only count those who are ac-tively looking for a job—registering, for example, with an of-ficial entity such as a government-run employment office.

Unemployment. One of the most watched economic statistics is unemployment. It tells politicians and economists how well an economy is working and how it should be regulated. When unemployment gets too high, the economy needs to be stimu-lated; when it gets too low, the economy needs to be slowed down or inflation may rear its ugly head (see Phillips Curve). A certain amount of unemployment is considered good for an economy; there have to be some people looking for work to keep the economy running smoothly.

Unicorns. Start-up companies that achieve a value of more than $1 billion are referred to as *unicorns*, reflecting their rare, mythical status among venture capital investors (see Venture Capital). Examples of unicorns include Airbnb, Pinterest, and Didi Chuxing. The term was coined by venture capitalist Aileen Lee in 2018. Companies that reach a value of more than $10 billion are referred to as *decacorns*.

Unilateral Trade Barrier. Like one hand clapping in the dark, unilateral trade barriers are imposed by one country acting on its own to limit imports. These barriers are usually set up to protect local producers from foreign competition—in theory, giving them time to improve their productivity and efficiency. The problem is that local producers, once given the comfort of a protected market, rarely make the sacrifices to improve their products or lower their prices. In addition, unilateral trade barriers often cause other countries to erect barriers of their own.

United Nations Conference on Trade and Development (UNCTAD). UNCTAD, the principal organ of the UN General Assembly dealing with trade, investment, and development issues, brings rich and poor countries together in periodic forums to solve problems related to international trade and development.

United Nations Development Programme (UNDP). The UNDP was set up to promote sustainable development around the world. Its goal is to help developing countries create jobs, protect the environment, and, in the end, hopefully, eliminate poverty. Based in New York City, the UNDP is the third-highest-ranking entity in the UN system and is funded through voluntary contributions from UN member countries.

United States–Mexico–Canada Agreement (USMCA). Announced in 2018, the United States–Mexico–Canada Agreement was intended to replace the North American Free Trade Agreement (NAFTA) with an accord only slightly different from the previous version. The new agreement included updates on protecting intellectual property rights, digital rights, environmental policies, and labor practices. The only major alteration to the original NAFTA had to do with automotive manufacturing. To qualify for tariff-free imports, 75 percent of an automobile's parts had to be made in North America, and at least 40 percent of the automobile had to be built by workers earning at least sixteen dollars per hour. Canada and Mexico rejected U.S. attempts to alter the dispute-settlement system as well as an attempt to insert a sunset clause automatically ending the new agreement every five years in the absence of new approvals from all three governments.

Universal Basic Income (UBI). To reduce income inequality, some have proposed establishing a minimum income, sometimes referred to as *universal basic income*, which would provide every member of the economy with a sort of living wage that is not dependent on the person's needs. Unlike food stamps in the United States or the dole in the United Kingdom, universal basic income would be provided to everyone regardless of their income level. The source of the funds for universal basic income is, under most scenarios, expected to be government-based. In the absence of an independent source of revenue, such as oil or gas royalties, funding for UBI would in all probability have to come from increased tax revenues from companies or those with jobs.

Value-Added Tax (VAT). A tax applied at each stage of production is called a *value-added tax* because every time a product's value is increased, the person or company adding the value has to pay additional tax. The idea is to make taxation progressive and to distribute the tax burden more evenly between producers and consumers. In contrast to a sales tax, which is paid only at the moment of the final sale, a value-added tax is paid by each party in the production process. VAT is used in almost every modern industrial economy except the United States.

Velocity. Economists use the word *velocity* to describe how quickly an economy grows in relation to available money. The "speed" of money tells us what an economy can do with the money supply at its disposal. When a country produces a large GDP (see Gross Domestic Product) with a relatively small money supply, it is said to have a high velocity of circulation.

Venture Capital (VC). Money that is invested in new companies, usually not showing a profit but having a lot of potential for growth, is called *venture capital.* The idea of venture capitalists is to get in early. When the company finally takes off and begins showing a profit—leading to skyrocketing stock prices—the venture capitalists and others who invested early can reap huge rewards. Venture capital investors who invest their own money are sometimes referred to as *angels,* reflecting the fact that without the investors' intervention, the fledgling company wouldn't be able to survive.

Volatility. The movement of a price over time is referred to as *volatility*. A stock, for example, is said to be highly volatile if its price changes a lot and changes often. Essentially, volatility measures both the frequency of movement and the magnitude. Most investors don't like volatility, so it becomes a big factor in determining the price of a stock or bond or any other security with fluctuating prices.

Wage-Price Spiral. The inflationary wage-price spiral involves rapid price rises followed by equally rapid demands for higher wages, which result in more price rises. Like the proverbial chicken-or-egg scenario, no one knows which comes first, the rise in wages or the rise in prices, but the end result is summed up in two words: *uncontrolled inflation*.

Wall Street / the City / Bahnhofstrasse / Kabuto-cho / Pudong. The part of a financial capital where trading is done is often referred to by a major street or district. The city of London is where most of the banks and trading houses are located. The New York financial center is called *Wall Street*. In Zurich, it's the *Bahnhofstrasse*. In Tokyo, it's the *Kabuto-cho*. When Venice was the center of the world economy back in the Middle Ages, the banks and money traders were clustered around the Rialto Bridge. Hence, Shylock's famous line in Shakespeare's *The Merchant of Venice:* "What news on the Rialto?"

Warrant. A warrant gives its holder a right, but not the obligation, to buy a stock or other security at a certain price during a certain amount of time. It's like an option (see Call Option), but a warrant usually isn't traded on open exchanges. Warrants are often attached to bonds to make the bond more attractive and to allow the issuer to pay less interest.

Welfare State. A country where the government takes primary responsibility for the health and well-being of its citizens is referred to as a *welfare state*, as opposed to a state where the individual is expected to take care of everything. Many modern economies are built on the welfare state model, where cradle-to-grave education, health care, and even job creation is taken care of by the central government.

White Collar. See Blue Collar.

White Knight. In business, a white knight is a company or person who steps in to help another. In the takeover game, a white knight can be someone who helps management thwart an unwanted buyout by agreeing to purchase enough shares to block the takeover bid.

Withholding Tax. A tax deducted at the time a dividend or other form of income is received is called a *withholding tax*. In most countries, interest payments on bonds and stock dividends are subject to a withholding tax, thus allowing the tax authorities to be paid first—the withholding tax is automatically deducted up front from what is owed to the stock- or bondholder.

World Bank. Founded at the same time as the International Monetary Fund, the World Bank loans billions of dollars every year to developing countries, mainly for long-term projects to fight poverty and encourage economic growth. Unlike the IMF (see International Monetary Fund), which provides short-term lending and assistance, the World Bank looks for long-term solutions to the problems in the world's poor countries. The World Bank gets most of its money from the contributions of developed countries and by borrowing on the international capital markets.

World Economic Forum. The World Economic Forum is held every year in the Swiss ski resort of Davos. These meetings bring together business leaders and politicians in an informal setting to discuss and direct the world's major social and economic problems.

World Intellectual Property Organization (WIPO). Based in Geneva, Switzerland, the World Intellectual Property Organization, as its name implies, promotes the protection of intellectual property in the world economy. This United Nations organization provides an international forum to solve difficult intellectual property issues, such as the validity of pharmaceutical patents and music copyrights.

World Social Forum. Held every year, the World Social Forum brings together socially conscious leaders to discuss world issues in a less "capitalist" setting than that of the World Economic Forum in Davos. The two meetings usually coincide (see World Economic Forum).

World Trade Organization (WTO). Based in Geneva, Switzerland, the WTO provides a forum where disputing countries can meet to remove or rectify barriers to trade. When the WTO makes a ruling, the guilty country is supposed to remove the illegal trade barrier. If it doesn't, the country that has suffered from the trade barrier is allowed to erect trade barriers of its own, usually in the form of tariffs.

World Wide Fund for Nature / World Wildlife Fund (WWF). Based in Gland, Switzerland, the World Wide Fund for Nature is the world's premier organization for protecting endangered species. In the United States and Canada, it is still referred to by its original name, *World Wildlife Fund.*

WTO. See World Trade Organization.

WWF. See World Wide Fund for Nature.

Yield. "Many happy returns." Yield, the return on an investment, is usually calculated in terms of a percentage. When a bond, for example, is said to be yielding 8 percent, the purchaser can count on receiving an average of 8 percent per year until the bond is redeemed. Yields can be applied to almost any investment in the world economy, from real estate to stocks and mutual funds.

Zero-Coupon Bond. A bond that pays no interest obviously has to provide something extra to make it attractive to investors. Zero-coupon bonds are almost always sold at a discount. The buyer pays less than the bond's face value, knowing that, at a determined point in the future, the bond will be repaid in full. The difference between purchase price and redemption price gives a kicker to the investor to forgo the interest payments normally provided on most bonds.

Zero-Sum Game. A zero-sum game is based on the concept that one side's loss is equal to the other side's gain. This concept was developed in the context of game theory, where economic and political decisions are made rationally, producing clear winners and losers. In the real world, however, there are few true zero-sum games. Inventing a better mousetrap doesn't hurt anyone except a few inefficient mousetrap makers—and, of course, the mice.